Happy Singlehood

Happy Singlehood

*The Rising Acceptance and Celebration
of Solo Living*

Elyakim Kislev

UNIVERSITY OF CALIFORNIA PRESS

University of California Press, one of the most
distinguished university presses in the United States,
enriches lives around the world by advancing scholarship
in the humanities, social sciences, and natural sciences. Its
activities are supported by the UC Press Foundation and
by philanthropic contributions from individuals and
institutions. For more information, visit www.ucpress.edu.

University of California Press
Oakland, California

Library of Congress Cataloging-in-Publication Data

Names: Kislev, Elyakim, author.
Title: Happy singlehood : the rising acceptance and
    celebration of solo living / Elyakim Kislev.
Description: Oakland, California : University of
    California Press, [2019] | Includes bibliographical
    references and index. |
Identifiers: LCCN 2018038419 (print) | LCCN 2018042483
    (ebook) | ISBN 9780520971004 (Epub) |
    ISBN 9780520299139 (cloth : alk. paper) |
    ISBN 9780520299146 (pbk. : alk. paper)
Subjects: LCSH: Single people.
Classification: LCC HQ800 (ebook) | LCC HQ800 .K53 2019
    (print) | DDC 306.81/5—dc23
LC record available at https://lccn.loc.gov/2018038419

Manufactured in the United States of America

28 27 26 25 24 23 22 21 20 19
10 9 8 7 6 5 4 3 2 1

CONTENTS

ILLUSTRATIONS

ACKNOWLEDGMENTS

I express my gratitude to the many people who saw me through this book: to all those who provided support, talked things over, read, wrote, offered comments, allowed me to quote their remarks, and assisted in the editing, proofreading, and design.

First and foremost, I owe much gratitude to all those surrounding me. I thank my dear family, whose love and appreciation are irreplaceable; my colleagues at the Federmann School of Public Policy and Government at the Hebrew University, whose professionalism is a true inspiration; and all my wonderful friends, whose support and encouragement are at the very core of this book.

This book is certainly not mine alone. I worked on this book with the most brilliant and diligent team of people I have ever known, and I owe them my deep gratitude. Above all, I thank my outstanding research assistant, Aurel Diamond, whose help was truly invaluable. I also thank all the interviewers who helped me collect the qualitative data presented here. A special thank you to Mark Moore and Kiera Schuller. Without their help, the interviews, data gathering, and analysis would have never been completed on time. I also thank Eviatar Zlotnick for punctiliously helping me in collecting and analyzing a major part of the blog posts about singlehood.

Last, but certainly not least, I thank Naomi Schneider, the chief editor of this book, and her entire team at University of California Press for believing in this work and pushing me high and above. Thank you all.

Introduction

It is Friday night in conservative Jerusalem. I am a little kid. The public siren, the same one that calls out attacks, begins its two-minute wail, announcing to the city that it is Shabbat time. My family is ready: the table is beautifully set; the house overflows with succulent aromas of the delicious Friday night meal my mom has prepared; and we are all dressed in clean, white-collared shirts. My mom lights five candles: one for each of my parents and three others for her children, my two brothers and me. Standing on tiptoe, looking out the window, I see lights dotting the neighborhood. Every apartment shelters a seemingly happy family enjoying delicious food in a clean dwelling; men, women, and children poised to spend this night and the next day together. No phones. No television. Just family time.

I walk with my father to the synagogue, where every family has its own reserved spot. Everyone around me seems content, even holy. But over in a corner, I always see one man—the same man—standing with his only child, himself an unmarried guy in his thirties. The father's wife has been dead for years, and everyone knows the son. Everyone knows he is unmarried, too. I watch them every time, curious to know what they feel, how they spend their evenings. They never seem happy, at least not to me.

I see them to this very day, more than twenty years later, when I visit my parents and return with my father to my boyhood place of worship. The father, now hunchbacked, and his son still live together; both are unmarried and shy, and they keep to themselves.

When I grew up and moved to New York City for my doctoral studies, I discovered a totally different world, full of singles who seemed like "the bold and the beautiful." It was the fast-paced, competitive New York that everyone hears about, but which in real life is even faster. Everyone rushed from one thing to the next, from one sexual encounter to another, trying to engage in "big-city life." They did not need marriage to fit in. In fact, meeting someone in Manhattan with a family was more the exception than the rule. When someone said, "Hey, guys, I'm getting married" (and moving to Queens, of course), the underlying message came in loud and clear: "I'm done—game over."

Looking back now, I realize how naive I was in my assessment of these two contrasting worlds—married and single. Not everyone lived happily ever after in the tightly knit community of my childhood neighborhood. Some members endured divorce, including my own two brothers, while others continued life in miserable, unhappy marriages. It seems to me, upon reflection, that the latter probably suffered more than anyone. In fact, I often reflect on the old man and his unmarried son living in their own world. Should I have felt pity for them, or was I blinded by my own ingrained family-normative prejudice?

I also think back to my fellow New Yorkers rushing from date to date, jumping into relationships only to quickly realize they wanted out as soon as possible, feeling suffocated and urgently needing to breathe the air of freedom. Still unmarried myself, I understand now that we were neither bold nor beautiful. We shuttled back and forth; we ran hard, but without purpose. In a way, we mirrored the rats we saw every day in the subway tunnels driven by hunger and distress.

Apparently, marital status is last on the list of things we believe we should accept. We are open to various sexual identities, we celebrate different ethnicities, and we tolerate a wide array of political views, yet we still live in a society where singles, especially in advanced adulthood, are urged to couple up or otherwise face prejudice. In one study, for example, one thousand undergraduate students were asked to list characteristics they associated with married and single individuals. Married individuals were referred to as mature, happy, kind, honest, and loving. Conversely, singles were perceived as immature, insecure, self-centered, unhappy, lonely, and even ugly.[1]

These stereotypes hurt both singles and couples. Singles—whether they are divorced, widowed, or never-married—clearly suffer in the most overt way. But this does not mean married people fare much better. The same stereotypes often pressure individuals to marry despite uncertainty over being ready for such a big commitment or doubts about being with the right person. Couples may marry only to realize later they made a bad or premature decision. Of course, divorce looms in such cases, after which 70–80 percent of divorced people remarry and face an even greater likelihood of a second divorce.[2]

Therefore, in this book I investigate the many aspects of modern singlehood, analyzing the cases in which singles accept, even celebrate, their marital status. Indeed, negative societal perceptions of singles are so internalized that singles often blame themselves for not being married. "I'm not sure what's wrong with me," I heard time and again in the interviews I conducted for this book. As I will explain in detail, the choice to internalize the negative stereotypes or shrug them off is critical in distinguishing between happy and unhappy singles.

In other cases, it is not stereotypes against singles that prompt low-quality, rushed marriages but rather loneliness.[3] Here again, a decision based on the wrong reasons often ends badly. In fact, research shows that married individuals can be just as lonely as their single counterparts even though they partnered up.[4] Instead of facing loneliness at its roots, many people chase partnership only to discover that loneliness is a stand-alone problem, the cure for which lies mainly within oneself, as researchers have repeatedly argued.[5]

And yet, despite the prevalent social and psychological forces that push people into marriage, reality is inevitably changing and doing so rapidly. Today, unmarried individuals are the fastest-growing demographic group in many countries.[6] According to predictions, approximately one-quarter of newborns in the United States will never marry.[7] Official statistics in China indicate that the percentage of one-person households rose from just 4.9 percent in 1990 to 14.5 percent in 2010.[8] The percentage of one-person households in several major European cities has already exceeded 50 percent, and singles account for around 40 percent of all households in countries such as Sweden, Norway, Denmark, and Germany.[9] Adults are marrying late, divorce is more prevalent, and public attitudes toward the social status of marriage reflect a decline.[10] Across the world, despite all prejudices and beliefs against it, singlehood is the growing trend.

We are feeling something, wanting something, and doing something that we have yet to agree upon. The world is going single, but cultural disapproval still lingers. The result is that many people who are part of a rising trend of living alone and going solo are still pressured into marriage. The pressure itself makes them unhappy, often more than their marital status, but distinguishing between the two can be difficult, even impossible.

This situation creates a cognitive dissonance among the unmarried population. Many singles stated in interviews that they are looking to marry someone; but from what they told me, they don't behave that way. Existing cultural and social values pressure people to say they would be happy to marry, but their everyday dating and relationship decisions indicate otherwise. They raise the threshold for a potential partner to almost impossible standards, as if to say they need an exceptional argument to stop going solo. It seems society is still in denial about the fact that times are changing, and that there is a rumble under the age-old institution of marriage.

Married people are not different in this sense. Of course, some live happily ever after with their partners, but others envy the rise in singlehood and want out of wedlock. My findings show that the difference between unhappy singles and unhappily married individuals is often simply the fact that the latter group succumbed to the social and psychological pressures to marry. Both groups are unhappy and trapped in unbearable situations thanks to the stigma of being unmarried, on one side, and witnessing the trend toward singlehood, on the other.

This gap between social and psychological pressure to marry and the reality of rising singlehood itself, in which people all over the world are abandoning the institution of marriage in growing numbers, is central to this book. We often find ourselves behaving in ways of which we are not fully aware: we think one thing and do another; we believe in "couplehood" but live in "singlehood." We have not yet fully made the link between our true feelings and the attitudes enforced by social norms.

The reason for this disconnect, I argue, is that many are still afraid of accepting singlehood. They see singlehood negatively; or rather, they are blind to the full potential inherent in this way of living. The role of this book is thus to put a spotlight on the mechanisms behind the rising trend of accepting and celebrating solo living.

Having a clear and more benign image of singlehood will allow individuals to freely choose whatever lifestyle fits them best. Some, of course, will continue to choose marriage. However, even this choice can arise from a more relaxed environment that allows for entering marriage at the right time and under the right circumstances. Such a well-thought-out decision will certainly lead to better marriages for those who choose marriage, while others will feel more comfortable going solo. Becoming more aware of the myriad possibilities for singlehood to foster happiness and well-being should liberate those who, until now, have been challenged with deviating from the norm.

Indeed, the phenomenon of rising singlehood is not new. Many researchers have documented the decline in marriage rates, and policy makers closely follow changes in the modern family.[11] The Danish government, for example, has even started ad campaigns encouraging citizens to marry and to have more sex.[12] In the United States, the media has also addressed these changes, with television shows such as *Seinfeld* (1989–1998), *Sex and the City* (1998–2004), and *Girls* (2012–2017) and films such as *How to Be Single* (2016).

The conversation has already begun, but this book takes it one step further. It is not about the social phenomenon of rising singlehood in and of itself. The actual social transformation goes far beyond discussing the phenomenon, and this book concerns the next stage of singlehood: the mechanisms that allow a better quality of life for those taking part in this rising trend.

Happy Singlehood: The Rising Acceptance and Celebration of Solo Living discusses questions such as: How do singles effectively deal with the fear of aging alone? How do singles face discrimination? How do social activities play out for singles' happiness compared to that of couples? How do values rooted in individualism and postmaterialism help singles embrace their lifestyle? What are the differences among singles by choice, singles by circumstance, divorced individuals, widows, cohabiters, and married people in how they increase their life satisfaction? Finally, how can policy makers cater to the growing singles population and increase singles' well-being?

This inquiry is mostly new to academic research on singles, which until now has frequently shied away from asking these critical questions, focusing instead on measuring and observing the phenomenon of singlehood itself alongside declining marriage and birth rates and rising divorce levels. At the same time, popular media and the self-help industry have generally fixated on how to alleviate loneliness but without basing their work on comprehensive research. Hence, this book expands the current literature beyond asking descriptive questions, by inquiring how singles can achieve happiness in everyday life despite social headwinds. Such an investigation leads to evidence that supports or rejects the common discourse about singles that is prevalent in popular media and the self-help industry.

An even more ambitious goal of this book is to propel individuals to think about a new reality: the evolving ways in which human beings around the world are organizing their social and family lives. I analyze the specific needs of the growing singles population and outline several pioneering proposals—including innovative living arrangements, communities, and social interactions—to set the stage for an era of happy singlehood. In this sense, you should feel free to start with the chapter that ignites you the most.

The silent minority of singles may soon grow into a vocal majority. Public demonstrations about rising rents for singles' housing, cohabiters' unclear legal status, impoverishment of single parents, and tax rights of divorced people have already taken place in several metropolitan centers around the world. In Tokyo, for example, a demonstration organized by the group Call for Housing Democracy demanded that the government reduce rents. The organizers told the reporters of the *Japan Times,* "The chances of getting into a public housing unit in the capital is now 1 in 20 for families and 1 in 57 for singles, and by singles the government means retired people. If you're young and unmarried, you have no chance of getting into public housing, regardless of how poor you are."[13] Such protests signify the increasingly important, and urgent, need to discuss the factors contributing to singles' happiness and well-being. Policy makers should address these needs and begin finding ways to cater to this population.

This book is, therefore, also a call to action. It calls for researchers and policy makers, who are not used to thinking of singles as a disadvantaged minority, to focus more on their growing numbers and the numerous obstacles they tackle.[14] The time to rise—for the continually overlooked population of singles—has come. Its unique needs, lifestyle, and living arrangements deserve more attention, and I detail them in this book. I sincerely hope it serves as a modest contribution to the singles population, a roaring giant who has just awakened.

THE RESEARCH APPROACH USED IN THIS BOOK

The findings and ideas presented in this book are based on a thorough assessment of the existing literature as well as new quantitative and qualitative findings. On the quantitative side, using advanced statistical models, I analyzed large, highly representative databases from over thirty countries, which allowed me to employ solid empirical data to address the question "What makes today's singles happy?" (see below for a discussion of the term *happiness*). I used multilevel models based on integrative databases from several sources that surveyed hundreds of thousands of individuals. These sources include the European Social Survey, American Community Survey, the US Census Bureau, the World Bank, the United Nations, and the Organization for Economic Cooperation and Development. The statistical investigation provides an accurate picture of current trends in singlehood and is presented in an accessible way for both academic and general readers, in the form of maps, charts, and examples.

On the qualitative side, I conducted 142 personal interviews of single people in the United States and various European countries. For this purpose, I was assisted by a highly qualified research team. Together, we interviewed people from different locales, men and women, young and old, straight and gay, city dwellers and residents of small towns, all with differing socioeconomic and ethnic background. The average age among interviewees is 43.9, with the oldest aged 78 and the youngest aged 30 (see below for the reason for the lower age limit of 30). In addition, women are 56 percent of interviewees, and the average self-reported income level, on a scale of 1 to 10, is 4.7. Of course, all the names of the interviewees have been changed to maintain anonymity. Interviews were transcribed, and central themes relating to the research questions have been identified and categorized systematically.[15] I designed the interviews to be as impartial as possible, with care taken to ensure that questions were emotionally neutral. I avoided questions indicating predetermined conclusions about motivations and incentives for being single and/or feeling positive or negative about single status.

Furthermore, I supplemented interviews with a systematic analysis of over four hundred blog posts, over three hundred newspaper and magazine articles, and thousands of comments and Facebook posts on singlehood. A purposive-snowball sampling approach was used to identify singles' blogs and posts. This sampling strategy is suitable in such cases, where a true random sample is not possible because of the absence of a known population. Rather, a sample with specific characteristics (e.g., blogs about singles) needs to be put together.

Writer profiles were examined to identify the authors' self-declared age, gender, and location, when possible. Most writers' characteristics were easily identifiable; some information, however, required a deeper exploration of content from multiple blogs or posts. The thematic content was then analyzed to identify the topics that singles wrote about. So that I could examine reliability, this content was coded independently by two trained assistants familiar with the codebook. In a later stage, I supplemented both this analysis and that from academic literature with newspaper and magazine articles relevant to the subject of singlehood. This supplementation informs the evidence supporting this book with contemporary and up-to-date information. The coding system for all qualitative data uses a bottom-up procedure similar to the grounded theory approach.[16]

DEFINITIONS USED IN THIS BOOK

For the purposes of this study, I define single people as those who identify as divorced, widowed, or never-married, and I distinguish among the three categories throughout. Demographically, only individuals more than thirty years old were selected from the databases, and this is also true for the interviews, blogs, and posts. I chose the age of thirty to represent a population that is generally above the average age at first marriage: singles who have already encountered assumed social pressure and thus face the consequences of not being married. In contrast, younger individuals are many times in a transition phase and do not think about marriage at all.[17]

In addition, I separately categorized those who currently cohabitate with a significant other, estimated at around 10 percent of the population.[18]

Thus, cohabitation is considered a midpoint category in this book and not part of singlehood per se. On one side, cohabitation is now closer to marriage both socially and legally, with common marriage laws providing rights similar to those granted to formal marriages in many places, such as the United States, Australia, Canada, and various European countries.[19] On the other side, cohabiting is still close to singlehood because it is also based, at least in part, on the increasing frustration and disillusionment with the institution of marriage.[20] Fear of marital commitment and aversion to the risk of divorce have contributed to the number of couples choosing to cohabitate for significant periods of time without getting married.[21] Moreover, in some contexts, cohabitation has an immediate impact on the share of singles in the population. Cohabiting relationships are less stable and more short-lived than marriages, and they are more likely to end in separation, independent of the couple's age, income, or number of children.[22] As a result, a higher proportion of people are expected to spend longer periods of time as singles, both before and after cohabitation. The reader should be aware of this complexity, and I analyze cohabiters separately from other categories of singles as much as possible.

Furthermore, while singles share many of the same challenges, they are affected differently according to more nuanced social and familial situations. Having children is one prominent issue in this sense. For example, a single person with nearby supportive children or grandchildren operates in a different reality than a single with no descendants. Therefore, in all the statistical analyses, I employ a special variable to account for those with children. In addition, I differentiate between those who cohabitated in the past and those who never lived with another person. In the interviews, these differentiations are much easier to make, since the interviewees usually revealed their marital status in detail; I state this information where relevant.

Of course, there are always more subgroups that should be treated carefully. One example is singles in a serious relationship who live alone. It was not an easy task to distinguish these groups from nonexclusive singles in some of the statistical analyses estimated for this book. For this reason, the qualitative data herein, in which these sub-groups are distinguishable, is highly important and complements our knowledge about singlehood.

It is important to note that there are significant overlaps, but subtle differences also exist between singles, the unmarried, and those living alone. Different branches of research on singles opt for different defini-tions according to research needs and the nature of available data. In many large demographic data sets, for example, attention is often paid to one-person households. Individuals who live in one-person house-holds are often single, but not exclusively. Particularly in rapidly devel-oping countries with high rates of internal migration, such as India, one member of the family (usually the husband) may live permanently or semipermanently in another part of the country for work purposes, sending money home whenever possible.[23] Therefore, I am careful to state explicitly when I use information about one-person households.

On a separate note, the notion of *happiness*, a subjective well-being, is at the center of this book and should be briefly discussed and defined. Happiness is viewed here as the degree to which people judge their lives more or less favorably.[24] This is a modest definition against the background of many cultures and philosophers that attribute ethical virtues, social devotion, and even transcendental Nirvana to the term *happiness*.[25] Nevertheless, I stick to this reductionist definition following many studies that found it to be widely agreed-upon and to unify many cultural interpretations.[26] For example, one study compared dictionary definitions of *happiness* across thirty countries spanning a period of 150 years, accounting for both time and culture. This study found that the most widely shared aspects of the definition were feeling lucky and experiencing favorable external conditions.[27]

Still, there is no denying that understandings of happiness vary, and one cannot know what exactly stands behind someone's answer in a survey to the scalable question "How happy are you?" Respondents coming from different cultures or different age-cohorts might vary in the meanings they assign to the term *happy*. For example, studies show that young people associate happiness with excitement, while older individuals link happiness to peacefulness.[28]

To address these difficulties, this book considers large samples ranging across age and locale while accounting for cultural, social, and personal differences as well as the average degree of happiness in each country. The power of large databases is that outliers usually cancel each other out; hence, answers can still be studied, broadly speaking.[29] Thus, although imperfectly, this study assumes that, on aggregate, the question in the European Social Survey, for example, is useful enough because such examination not only carries strong statistical power but also affords generalized conclusions based on various cultures while using multilevel analysis to account for differences. In my research articles on the subject, I delve deeper into these considerations with detailed and rigorous analyses, and those interested will find there much more information regarding the results presented here.

One must admit that by not asking what makes an individual happy, policy makers and researchers are missing out on a huge opportunity for increasing overall population welfare.[30] This holds true especially in light of nascent positive psychology that seeks to reframe classic approaches by focusing on improving happiness and avoiding the negative at the personal and populational levels.[31] Therefore, I urge the reader to use the proposed definitions as practical, applicable, and beneficial tools of analysis, and to cautiously determine if the findings of this book resonate with you.

CHAPTER ONE

The Age of Singlehood

On one special day of the year, you can find a bunch of single men jumping into a river wearing only underwear (or less), while single women run down the streets of major cities wearing wedding dresses. The Guanggun Jie, or Singles' Day, is a new, popular Chinese festival that celebrates being single with shopping, festivities, and socializing with friends. Originating in 1993 as a day for singles to party with single friends at universities in Nanjing, one of China's major cities, this festival has become the largest online shopping event in the world and a cultural marker for modern Chinese society.[1] Its date, November 11 (11/11), was chosen because the number 1 represents a single individual. Although this day is widely called Singles' Day, in China it is also known as the "bare sticks holiday" because the numerical date of the holiday resembles unaccompanied twigs or sticks, which, in Mandarin, is a metaphor for single individuals. Throughout the years, this holiday has developed as an anti–Valentine's Day, and branding it a singles celebration proved a tremendous success. The online retail giant Alibaba made more than twenty-five billion dollars in revenue on 2017's Singles' Day, four times more than on 2017's Cyber Monday, the biggest online shopping day on the American calendar.[2]

Given the higher percentage of singles in the United States, it is a little surprising that the Singles' Day movement began in China. But

America joined in the fun quickly. The American version of National Singles' Day was first observed in 2013 on January 11 (1/11). Here again, the number 1 is the almighty symbol of singlehood. In 2017, the date was changed to coincide with National Singles' Week in September, which the Buckeye Singles' Council in Ohio began celebrating in the 1980s. In an interview with *Singular Magazine*, Karen Reed, the founder of National Singles' Day, said:

> China's Singles' Day was actually the initial inspiration for starting a Singles' Day here.... I also felt it was necessary to create a fresh, new singles holiday because so much has changed in recent years. Twenty-first century singles are a new breed. Today's singles are a vibrant, diverse demographic and a force to be reckoned with....
>
> Definitions of singlehood are complex—single by choice or circumstance, legally or figuratively, solo forever or just for now. Reaching single people as a group is a daunting task. And sometimes the best way to approach a massive, virtually unsolvable problem is to bypass the details, jump high on top and shout with one voice—we're here! Then do it again. And again.[3]

It is striking that even a few decades ago such festivals of singlehood would not have been imaginable. But the institution of marriage has been undergoing profound changes that are altering the face of modern society. The Chinese celebration of Singles' Day did not come out of nowhere. China saw a precipitous fall in the mean size of households from 5.4 persons per household in 1947 to merely 3.1 in 2005 corresponding to the change from an agricultural society to a modern, urban one.[4] It is really hard to comprehend, for example, that a Chinese young man who grew up in a rural area surrounded by his uncles and aunts, all working in one field and growing rice, now lives in a fundamentally different landscape—probably in a tiny apartment in a multistory building in one of the smoggy megacities of China—and works at a mammoth factory until late evening. In fact, more than 60 million Chinese households were registered in 2014 as single occupancy, up from 17 million one-person households in 1982, all while the Chinese population grew concurrently by a mere 40 percent.[5]

In Europe, more than 50 percent of households in major cities such as Munich, Frankfurt, and Paris are occupied by singles.[6] In the United States, 22 percent of American adults were single in 1950, while today this number has jumped to more than 50 percent,[7] and one in four American newborns is predicted to never marry.[8] At the same time, getting married before having children has become less prevalent in developed nations. The proportion of American children living with two married parents decreased from 87 percent at the start of the 1960s to 69 percent in 2015.[9]

Japan is probably the global leader in the rise of singlehood. The latest survey from the Japanese National Institute of Population and Social Security Research shows that, in 2015, one-third of Japanese adults under the age of thirty had never dated and over 40 percent were virgins. Furthermore, among unmarried Japanese, almost 60 percent of women and 70 percent of men aged eighteen to thirty-four were not in a romantic relationship, an approximately 10 percent rise from the 2010 survey and a whopping 20 percent increase from the 2005 survey. In fact, 30 percent of men and 26 percent of women stated they were not even looking for a relationship.[10]

In 2006, Maki Fukasawa, a popular author in Japan, wrote an article in which he referred to the increasing number of men not interested in intimate relationships as *sôshoku danshi*, or "herbivore men." Since intimacy and physical relations in Japanese are referred to as "desire of flesh," labeling a man an herbivore indicates a fundamental withdrawal from relationships. Moreover, it connotes a fundamental deconstruction of Japanese masculinity in which the once vigorous, procreating man of miraculous, postwar Japan has become anemic and even lost.[11] Notably, *sôshoku danshi* was on the 2009 short list of a national "buzzwords of the year" competition and, by 2010, was accepted as a standard noun.[12] While buzzwords tend to have short lifespans, soon after this term gained prominence, one survey revealed that 75 percent of Japanese single men in their twenties and thirties considered themselves herbivores.[13]

These trends are spreading rapidly, especially in the developed world, where the main forces behind the rise in singlehood, discussed later in this chapter, appeared considerably earlier than in other regions. Processes such as individualism, mass urbanization, increased longevity, the communications revolution, and the women's rights movement all began taking hold within developed nations in the late nineteenth century and early twentieth century. A short-lived exception to this trend was observed in the United States, where World War II and the development of the suburbs brought about a short "golden age" in the 1950s, when people married early and the birthrate increased.[14] However, the single lifestyle gained steam again in the 1970s, after the social emphasis on individualism, rooted in consumerism and capitalism, spread in the United States, Europe, and other developed countries, again pushing people away from marriage and toward a postfamily culture.[15] The map in figure 1, which is based on the most recent data from the United Nations, illustrates the prevalence of singlehood across the globe.

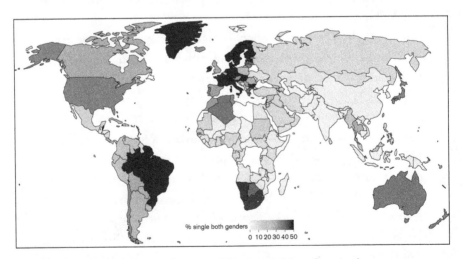

Percentage of singles between the ages of thirty and thirty-four, in the years 2010–2014. Source: United Nations, Department of Economic and Social Affairs, Population Division, *World Marriage Data 2015* (POP/DB/Marr/Rev2015).

Although, as the map shows, the trend of singlehood is most pronounced in the developed world, the phenomenon is spreading globally. South American, Middle Eastern, and even African countries have seen a rise in the number of singles over the past decades.[16] Evidence from many Asian countries, including India, South Korea, Vietnam, Pakistan, Bangladesh, and Malaysia, indicates that people are marrying later in life, getting divorced more frequently, and, most significantly, choosing to live alone in growing numbers.[17] In fact, singles today are the fastest-growing relationship demographic in many countries.[18] It is not surprising, then, that one report predicts that the proportion of singles in the world is expected to jump by an astonishing 20 percent by 2030.[19]

Even more tellingly, these trends also manifest in conservative and ultraconservative societies farther afield in the Middle East. Iran, for example, is going through unprecedented changes in singlehood patterns. Traditionally, relationship patterns in Iran have been strongly influenced by religious and cultural expectations, with legal and societal constructs that promote early, lifelong marital commitments and discourage divorce. Yet a look at population statistics reveals that Iran has undergone significant social change at both the macro and micro levels over the last three decades. The fertility rate underwent an unprecedented drop, decreasing from 7 children per woman in 1986 to just 2.1 in 2000.[20] While this is partly explained by a government program that encouraged the use of contraception, a statistical analysis reveals that contraception awareness and accessibility accounted for only 61 percent of the drop, while 31 percent is attributed to changes in marriage patterns.[21] Young Iranians, in particular women, get married later, get divorced more frequently, stop having children earlier, or simply choose not to marry at all.

Another case exhibiting the extraordinary emergence of singlehood in conservative societies is that of the United Arab Emirates. In 2014, more than 60 percent of Emirati women over the age of thirty were single, and the divorce rate was 40 percent, up from only 20 percent just two decades earlier.[22] The trend of getting married late or abstaining from marriage was already under way in the 1980s when Emirati men, in an attempt to avoid paying the lavish dowries typical of Emirati marriage arrangements, started seeking brides from abroad or decided not to wed at all.[23] The phenomena of delaying marriage and marrying nonnationals led the government to establish a fund to encourage inter-Emirati nuptials. Today, a male citizen who marries an Emirati woman is eligible for a monetary grant with additional benefits for each child born. The government also invested resources in matchmaking and weddings. Here is an excerpt from the UAE's official government website:

> The UAE Government aims to build and maintain a stable and consolidated Emirati family and to fortify the Emirati social and demographic structure, by encouraging Emirati men to marry Emirati women. In this regard, the UAE established [the] Marriage Fund under Federal Law No. 47 of 1992, complementing and integrating with the social policy set up by [the] late Sheikh Zayed Bin Sultan Al Nahyan, the Founding President of the UAE.... Besides the Marriage Fund, there are entities in each emirate that provide services such as: finding a match; providing community centers and majlis venues for wedding ceremonies; providing counselling before and after the marriage.[24]

While thirty-two thousand families benefited from this grant in the first ten years of the program, the marriage statistics seem to suggest that the legislation has been ineffective in staving off the rising number of singles. Indeed, these trends are replicated in Arab and Muslim states across the Middle East and North Africa, with projects and initiatives similar to the United Arab Emirates' Marriage Fund failing to prevent the move toward singlehood in Bahrain, Saudi Arabia, and Qatar.[25]

Almost everywhere, it seems, the number of people delaying marriage, living alone, or choosing to be single is on the rise. Understanding the mechanisms and context-specific factors behind the demographic changes in marriage is key to deciphering happy singlehood, and they are explained in detail in the following sections. However, the reader should feel free to skip this introductory part and skip straight to the second chapter onwards, where I discuss happy singlehood itself.

WHY DID WE STOP FALLING IN LOVE WITH MARRIAGE?

We live on the tip of an iceberg. Throughout most of human history, life and livelihood involved three basic frameworks, layer within layer: the nuclear family, the extended family, and the local community made up of groups of families. As the basic building block of society, the family had unchallenged status, and thus marriage—the starting point of a new family—took center stage. Families assumed the responsibilities that local authorities and governments take today for one's welfare, health, education, and housing at all ages. Undistinguished from the family, a person's profession was most often linked to family history and the family's role in the community; any deviation from this role would likely have shifted or upset the balance therein.[26]

This, however, changed drastically following the Industrial Revolution and the emergence of the modern welfare state. The family's traditional role in an individual's welfare, once indispensable, was gradually reassigned to the rising powers of the state and the market. Given that the family was no longer essential to survival, a series of changes affecting families and marriages began taking shape.

In the following sections, I discuss eight major mechanisms underlying the changing status of marriage: (1) demographic changes, (2) changes in women's roles, (3) risk aversion in an age of divorce, (4) economics, consumerism, and capitalism, (5) shifts in religiosity, (6) popular culture and the media, (7) urbanization, and (8) immigration. These eight categories are neither exhaustive nor independent and are liable to interact with and affect each other. The main point, however, is that such forces act simultaneously, making the rise in singlehood a real and sustainable trend, perhaps even unstoppable. The combination of these forces is so powerful that it seems time for us to face reality, embrace the trend, and start paving a way to an age of *happy singlehood.*

Demographic Changes

Recent changes in the demographic makeup of various populations have significantly spurred the rise in singlehood. One major shift involves plummeting birthrates all over the world. Some notable examples of decreasing fertility rates, according to the Organization for Economic Cooperation and Development database, are Mexico, which went from 6.6 births per woman in 1970 to 2.2 in 2016; Indonesia, from 5.4 to 2.4 in the same period; and Turkey, where the rate declined from 5 to 2.1.[27]

In the Western world, these changes happened even earlier. The fertility rate began to drop significantly below the replacement rate in most western European countries during the 1970s and 1980s.[28] Today's numbers are unprecedentedly low. For example, the fertility rate in Spain is 1.3; 1.4 in Italy, Germany, and Austria; 1.6 in Canada; 1.7 in the Netherlands and Denmark; and 1.8 in the United States, the United Kingdom, and Australia.[29]

By proxy, a lower fertility rate prompts the start of several processes that produce more singles. First, giving birth to fewer children allows marriage to be delayed—that is, the biological clock must tick only until delivering the first or second child, not until the sixth or seventh, allowing childbirth to start later.[30] Second, the burden of divorce is less severe with fewer children, if any, to care for during the fallout.[31] Third, a lower fertility rate means some people have no need to marry or partner at all: rearing one or two children as a single parent is less daunting than parenting half a dozen.[32] Fourth, the consequences pass to newer generations, because growing up in a smaller household is associated with a future smaller household size. Thus, the process is perpetuated.[33]

Another demographic change affecting singlehood is increased life expectancy, which results in many older adults living longer on their own.[34] The miracle of modern medicine has significantly extended the average lifespan, especially in the developed world. In 1940, approximately 11 percent of American society was sixty-five or older. By the 1970s, this rate had risen to about 17 percent, while a 2010 estimate stands at 21 percent.[35] The latest Organization for Economic Cooperation and Development statistics indicate that life expectancy at birth in member countries is now almost eighty years.[36] As the number of years we live increases, so does the potential amount of years an individual lives alone after divorce or widowhood.[37] For instance, data from the Survey of Health, Ageing and Retirement in Europe indicate that among Europeans aged seventy-five and older in 2015, 57 percent were widowed.[38] Additionally, the number of older Americans (in this case, age fifty and over) who divorced in 2010 was more than twice the number in 1990.[39]

In developing countries, the rapid increase in life expectancy is projected to increase the older population, thereby drastically inflating the number of singles. In China, for example, the average lifespan increased from 68.5 years in 1990 to 74.8 years in 2010. Hence, single occupancy among older adults has increased considerably.[40] Moreover, this phenomenon initiates a chain reaction whereby the physical, economic, and social challenges of living alone in old age often place a social and financial burden on the younger generation.[41] This burden, in turn, may prompt younger people to delay marriage and avoid additional commitments. This is especially true in Chinese society, where the ratio between the old and young generations is alarmingly disproportionate because of the one-child policy.[42]

In some regions, the sex ratio also markedly affects the number of singles. An imbalanced sex ratio reduces the pool of local potential partners and, as a result, leaves many people single. In some parts of India, for example, the sex ratio is as low as sixty-two women per hundred men.[43] Even Haryana, a North Indian state, home to one of India's richest and most developed regions, suffers from a highly distorted sex ratio: eighty-eight women of all ages for every hundred men. In such imbalanced conditions, some young men simply cannot find a bride. In fact, the situation has grown severe enough that one local council decided, in 2015, to relax the ban on intercaste marriage, making it easier for villagers to marry among their neighbors, an unprecedented move in traditional India.[44]

Today, sex imbalances occur mainly under three scenarios. First, a strong preference for male children has led to unbalanced ratios in China, Korea, parts of India, and in some smaller communities across the world.[45] Second, certain internal and international migration waves are sex imbalanced. For instance, the 2016 report from Eurostat (the statistical office of the European Union) shows that, among the applicants for asylum in Europe, 75 percent of fourteen-to-thirty-four-year-olds, and 60 percent of thirty-five-to-sixty-four-year-olds, were men.[46] This imbalance limits their choices, at least within their own communities, until they overcome language and cultural barriers. Third, internal migration to big cities also causes a sex imbalance. For instance, the Williams Institute reports that college-educated women and homosexual men concentrate more highly in American cities.[47] In Manhattan, there are approximately 32 percent more single, college-educated women than single, college-educated men. Moreover, 9 to 12 percent of men in Manhattan identify as gay (versus approximately 1–2 percent of women in Manhattan who identify as lesbians). Naturally, this narrows the pool of potential partners for women.

These recent demographic developments are changing the foundations on which the institution of marriage is based. Some are viewed as irreversible, such as birthrate decline and increased life expectancy, which many researchers predict will continue.[48] Others, such as sex imbalance, may be temporary because they involve ongoing social processes such as the integration of migrants and already-reversed governmental measures such as the one-child policy in China. All of them, however, combine to deconstruct the ways families are formed.

The Role of Women in Society

Another significant contributor to the rise of singlehood is the fundamental shift in women's social roles during the twentieth century.[49] Particularly in the West, a more gender-equal society places less pressure on women to get married and have children and, at the same time, provides them with opportunities to advance professionally and academically. In the past, women had limited choices regarding marriage because they depended financially on men. Women who were unable to provide for themselves or their children were forced to live within family units to ensure financial survival.[50] Today, however, increased gender equality, especially in Western labor markets, has allowed more women to flourish outside of traditional relationship arrangements, leading to a decline in relationship formation and sometimes even to prioritizing career over family.[51]

A parallel factor reducing marriage rates is women's advancement in the education system. Research finds a strong relationship between women's higher level of education and older age at first marriage.[52] Studies also found an association between increased career resources and women postponing or avoiding child-rearing.[53] Underlying these trends is the belief that young women in college or in their early career stages are not ready for marriage and motherhood.[54]

Furthermore, public opinion of single women has become less critical. The creation of social groups and activities for single women counters the stigma of being a "spinster," providing the opportunity to be identified as a single woman without necessarily feeling like an outsider.[55] Thus, while single women remain a focus of negative social judgment, a new discourse is enabling more women to choose singlehood while associating a feeling of empowerment with the decision.

Even in more traditional societies, where the law still discriminates heavily against women and prohibits them from divorcing their husbands,[56] feminist developments have influenced family structure and relationship formation.[57] For example, Arab women have become increasingly empowered, especially during and following the Arab Spring, which took place between 2010 and 2012 and involved women in unprecedented numbers.[58] Although parts of the Arab world are undergoing a retrograde process in which the younger generation skews more conservative,[59] women's status remains on the rise, and women exert more independence in deciding when and whom to marry. This has resulted in a sharp decline in fertility rates and a steady increase in the average age at first marriage.[60] Even women who want to marry do not always find a suitable partner. The advancements in women's status and independence have turned out to be unappealing to some men, who sometimes seek women with more traditional values.[61] Indeed, these expectations are gradually changing, but they are still common in many societies and are negatively affecting marriage patterns.[62]

Additionally, women's decisions to enter relationships, get married, and start families have recently been shaped by medical and technological advancements. At a time when fertility treatments have become more effective and readily available, women are less pressured to marry and start families at a young age, when they would likely be more fertile.[63] Some governments even subsidize fertility treatments for single women, providing more options for having children. Therefore, women wishing to delay marriage can afford to do so even if they want children. Indeed, investigations of insurance coverage for assisted reproductive technologies have found correlations between increased access to fertility treatments and older age at first marriage.[64] This is particularly true for affluent demographics that enjoy more comprehensive insurance coverage.

Likewise, women who want children but prefer to raise them alone can use sperm banks. The sperm bank industry not only has allowed single women to become pregnant but also, in some contexts, has decommodified sperm. By personifying donations and romanticizing the donor-recipient bond, sperm banks often add significant emotional tenor to a sperm donation. This change eases and facilitates the choice of many single women to start families, by providing at least the idea of a second parent, which is frequently desired and idealized.[65]

Risk Aversion in an Age of Divorce

A less considered but highly important factor is averting the risk of divorce, a life event that carries dire emotional, societal, and fiscal consequences. When divorce rates rise sharply, so do attempts to avoid marriage altogether.[66] Without even being aware of it, people calculate the benefits and losses from different life events, especially in individualistic societies, where personal well-being is at the center. Making the calculation shows that divorce imperils one's happiness, while marriage promises very little gain.

In an award-winning and groundbreaking longitudinal study covering fifteen years, Richard Lucas and his team found that marriage has a temporary positive effect on happiness, but that after two years one's level of happiness typically reverts to the baseline level that existed before saying "I do."[67] It is striking to find a biological basis for this in the brain chemical phenethylamine, which is associated with feelings of well-being.[68] Researchers argue that the decline in happiness (and the frequency of sexual activity) may occur either because neurons become habituated to the effects of phenethylamine or because levels of phenethylamine decline over time.[69] Even researchers whose studies show a slight, lasting happiness advantage conferred by marriage[70] admit that this uptick is partly due to the selection effect, whereby happier people tend to marry, rather than marriage bringing happiness to the perennially grumpy.[71]

In contrast, the negative consequences of divorce are more permanent. Lucas, who did not find a lasting effect of marriage, found that in cases of divorce, happiness drops before legal action, bottoms out during divorce, then gradually rebounds but does *not* return to baseline.[72] Later studies confirm these results time and again.[73] Even among those who argue that marriage evidences a lasting—albeit small—advantage, they nonetheless concur that divorce significantly reduces happiness, to a greater extent than marriage raises it.[74]

These remarkable findings are not merely an academic exercise. They reflect a reality in which marriage contributes less to happiness than is often assumed. First, two years into a marriage, satisfaction spirals down toward baseline levels. Second, divorced people are less happy than ever before. They sink below baseline—and stay there.

Younger men and women can do the math, so they treat marriage with caution. In an age less bound by tradition, when people are more connected to their own well-being, men and women peel the imagined benefits of marriage away from the real ones and conclude that marriage may not be worth the risk. And the risk is high: recent data show that about 40 to 60 percent of Western couples divorce, and that developing countries are catching up with these numbers quite fast.[75]

Averting the risk of divorce has direct and indirect long-term effects on the number of singles in society. A direct result is that marriage rates decrease as divorce-averse behavior becomes more prevalent.[76] An indirect result is that the increasing rates of divorce-averse behavior cause more children to be born out of wedlock or to grow up in single-parent families after divorce. In turn, children of the unmarried are less interested in marriage for themselves and feel free to choose otherwise.[77] In this sense, divorce-avoidance tactics indirectly, but inevitably, perpetuate the process and change societal attitudes to favor single life.

In addition, risk avoidance causes many people to simply delay marriage rather than avoid it completely. But ironically, those who marry at a late age are significantly more likely to divorce. The evidence indicates that the likelihood of divorce increases by approximately 5 percent each year after the age of thirty-two.[78] Therefore, if a young person employs marriage-averse behavior to dodge divorce and, in doing so, waits until his or her thirties to marry, the possibility of divorce looms larger. In turn, once divorce grows more prevalent, it, again, creates deterrents against marriage for others. Given that the average age at first marriage is approaching, or above, thirty in most industrialized nations, this phenomenon can be expected to fuel divorce rates further.

Avoiding marriage as a risk-aversion tactic may manifest differently depending on the type of society. In conservative nations, which are often less industrialized and more collective, the taboo of divorce and resulting stigma can act as a deterrent to marriage. Thus, it can inadvertently encourage prolonged adolescence or deferring marriage as a risk-management tactic in order to avoid highly negative social consequences.[79] This, combined with the fact that premarital cohabitation is frowned upon in conservative societies, means that individuals delay relationship formation of all kinds in these societies, at least overtly, as a risk-evasion tactic.

In more individualistic and industrialized societies, risk-avoidance takes the form of cohabitation in place of marriage.[80] Since the dissolution of cohabitation is easier and more common than marriage dissolution, it alleviates relationship deterrents and the associated risks. Cohabitation provides freedom to move in and out of sequential relationships while staying unattached between them. Thus, the acceptance of cohabitation in liberal countries increases the number of cohabiters and uncoupled individuals alike.

In 1998, the House of Representatives in the Netherlands was one of the first parliaments to formally recognize registered cohabitation through legislation. At the time, it was considered a policy breakthrough. Yet some researchers questioned whether this legislation sparked a fundamental shift in relationship formation. An evaluation study was commissioned to illuminate the consequences of this move. In seven focus-group interviews with forty participants, the study found that the participants agreed with the risk-reduction strategy whereby cohabitation is less binding and permanent than marriage and allows more flexibility and independence. In other words, cohabitation, as a risk-reduction relationship strategy, has displaced marriage, particularly in the context of the Netherlands' high divorce rate.[81]

The link between fear of divorce and a propensity for singlehood differs among demographic groups within populations. In the United States, studies reveal that faith in the institution of marriage and fear of divorce vary with minority status, education level, gender, and socioeconomic status. For example, one study looked at how gender and social-class distinctions shape views of divorce.[82] While over two-thirds of the participants were concerned about divorce, working-class women were the most skeptical about marriage because divorce would burden them both socially and financially. It is therefore unsurprising that in some societies the rates of risk aversion and single living are increasing most sharply among the lowest earners. This influence of socioeconomic factors, though not entirely uniform, has been noted and confirmed in a variety of contexts, showing the compounded effect of singlehood and economics.[83]

Economics

In his 1999 book *The Age of Parasite Singles,* Masahiro Yamada broke a taboo in drawing public attention in Japan to the growing number of thirtysomething singles still living with their parents.[84] Yamada coined the term *parasaito shinguru,* "parasite singles," for these young Japanese and argued that by living with their parents into their thirties, singles not only save money on rent but also manage to avoid responsibility for household chores. Indeed, approximately ten million young Japanese men and women had met the definition of parasite single in 1995. This number has increased by 30 percent, to thirteen million, today, despite the shrinking Japanese population, accounting for 10 percent of the Japanese people. Among Japanese singles, 60 percent of men and 80 percent of women fit this category, according to the most recent survey.[85]

Young Japanese singles are certainly not the only ones adopting this lifestyle. In English-speaking nations, the term *basement dwellers* carries similar connotations. In Italy, they are called *bamboccioni* (grown-up babies). Although these terms carry an unacceptable, derogative connotation by belittling a conscious decision made by young singles and their families, they say something about the interaction of economics and singlehood. This growing phenomenon means that the incomes of many of these singles are disposable, which allows for an enjoyable and economically secure lifestyle. In contrast, moving out or getting married would mean giving up this type of casual affluence.[86]

But economics affects singlehood in multiple ways, and it seems that all roads lead to the rise of singlehood in today's world. Whether the condition is economic hardship, security, or development, all three situations provide good reason for people to remain single.

Economic hardship and recent financial crises have shaped the way singles approach relationship formation. Many singles delay marriage, fearing the inability to support a family.[87] Even if disadvantaged men and women value marriage highly, they are less likely to believe in their ability to remain financially stable and therefore sustain marriage and avoid divorce. In many societies, financial stability is regarded as a prerequisite to marriage.[88] Thus, in times of economic crisis or lack of employment opportunities, young people spend a larger portion of their lives single.[89] The time and resources required to be financially stable compete with the commitments required for a romantic relationship.

Following the 2008 financial crisis, young people in certain European countries, such as Spain and Italy, suffered from both the crisis itself and increased housing prices. Because housing costs can absorb a major share of disposable income in Europe, many young people simply decide to delay marriage and spend their prime dating years advancing economically.[90] In fact, it is not uncommon to spot adult singles in today's Barcelona or Milan having sex in a car after a night of partying. They do it there simply because they have nowhere else to go. When the night ends, they go home—to their parents' houses.

Even when governments try to alleviate young people's economic insecurity, singles do not hurry into wedlock. Here, the logic works differently: young singles choose not to marry because the financial incentive for living with another person decreases. In Sweden, for instance, the large welfare state allows many people to move into their own apartments after high school and live independently, at least financially. Young Swedes have seized on this as an incentive to stay single. No wonder the share of one-person households in Stockholm is among the highest in the world, standing at 60 percent.[91]

Conditions of economic development, too, promote rising singlehood, a great example of which is India. Although India is still widely traditional, economic development in the country has given more young people economic independence, and as a result new family forms are becoming more common.[92] Increasing purchase power has allowed young Indians to consider living independently, which would not have been possible before.[93] Many Indian singles leave their families and move to big cities where jobs are available.

Moreover, living alone is not only possible now but also more accepted. Modern India is becoming open to Western values because of exposure via telecommunications and films. Thus, the shifts toward independent living and economic development coincide with the emergence of individualism, which has been associated with delayed relationship formation, discussed in the next section.[94]

It is a riddle how almost all economic conditions lead to the dissolution of marriage. All over the world, it seems singles are basically looking for an excuse to forgo wedlock. Whether to save money, earn more, or spend more, young singles simply think of marriage as a commodity and conclude that the "juice is not worth the squeeze." Nonetheless, economics carries a deeper meaning than simple income/expense calculations. The values and cultural foundations behind economics, and its influence on the rise of singlehood are reviewed in the following section.

Capitalism and Consumerism

Earlier, I discussed a popular book about young Japanese who maximize their disposable income by living with their parents and remaining single.[95] But the term *parasite singles* is derogatory and does not capture their true preferences. Young singles in today's Japan simply changed their tastes and reordered their priorities. They prefer going out with friends, pursuing career goals, and developing a fashion palate before entering relationships.[96] Surveys show that this choice is based not solely on economic considerations but on a change in values as well. In fact, 45 percent of women and 25 percent of men ages sixteen to twenty-four reported they are not interested in, or may even despise, sexual contact, even if noncommittal.[97] Moreover, almost half of all respondents had not engaged in sexual activity in the month before the survey. Instead, traditional cultural and familial values have been mostly replaced by consumerist ones. Thus, today's Japan is an example of a value shift: away from tradition and religion, toward a market-oriented, career-driven, consumerist culture.[98]

Japan is an extreme example, but all over the world capitalist and consumerist trends give rise to singlehood. Several factors are at play here.[99] First, the ascendance of consumerism extols the individual who buys and sells on the free market with fewer obligations to his or her larger society, culture, or family. In turn, consumerism frees people to pursue their own interests rather than those of others, thereby causing them to eschew traditional values. As the ideals of individualism and self-actualization spread, people reconsider whether marriage will serve them well. Careers become more important and are tied to women's independence and self-actualization. While there is some evidence to suggest that married people are better off financially,[100] the preference for being an independent consumer with individualistic tastes has displaced the financial incentive to form relationships.[101]

Second, capitalism makes people think about the value of different lifestyles and encourages comparison. Privacy becomes a desired good alongside rising incomes that give people the ability to live alone.[102] In this sense, capitalism does two things at once. For one, traditional values are replaced by more rational thinking with which people prioritize their preferences and assign values to them. For another, increased wealth allowed by the capitalist system affords people the opportunity to live by their values, often choosing independence over marriage, and privacy over family life.[103]

Finally, changes in the division of labor and the labor market create new flexibility and opportunities. People start working outside their families' professions, and work detaches itself from close familial circles. Moreover, the need to have children to continue the family business (e.g., by working on the family farm) and provide for parents becomes less common. Furthermore, in today's globalized world some professions require mobility and geographic flexibility. Thus, for many young professionals, tying the knot presents an obstacle to career advancement.[104]

One could even argue that markets prefer the single lifestyle because singles consume significantly more resources than do family units. Singles boost real estate markets because of the increased demand for apartments that allow people to live alone. An American report also indicates that singles use 38 percent more produce, 42 percent more packaging, 55 percent more electricity, and 61 percent more gasoline per capita than individuals living in a four-person family unit.[105] Divorced people, in particular, are seen as a potential growth market, because a couple that splits up results in two new singles who, out of necessity, consume products at a higher rate and seek new living arrangements, usually without roommates.[106] From a purely economic standpoint, singles' voluminous material consumption causes markets to adapt by catering to their needs and even encouraging them, hence promoting singlehood, as cynical as that may sound.

Responses to these phenomena are evident throughout various media. Despite persistent discrimination against singles in society at large, the media is now adjusting its approach and increasingly targeting singles through advertising,[107] especially with regard to housing, dating, and travel.[108] As a result, a consumer culture for singles has developed, which provides the means, legitimacy, and visibility for being single.[109]

Education

It is often the more educated who abandon relationship formation for individual and professional goals. One study found that the highest percentage of people living alone were individuals who had earned at least a bachelor's degree (15 percent), with the majority having received at least some college education.[110] My own analysis of the European Social Survey also confirms that the unmarried group is the most educated. In the above-thirty group, married individuals average 12.2 years of education, divorced people come in second with 12.5 years, the never-married group have 13 years, and cohabiters are the most educated, at 13.8 years on average (widowed individuals have the lowest average, but they are also older and thus excluded from this analysis).

The forces behind these numbers are complex. Higher levels of education have several direct and indirect effects on marriage rates: they are direct in that individuals still pursuing education are less likely to marry (thus, higher levels of education result in a shorter period on the marriage market); indirect in that higher levels of education imply more emphasis on career.[111] Consequently, one study shows that enrollment in higher education significantly reduces marriage and birth rates, even in countries that encourage individuals to start families during their studies.[112]

Another possible reason for these findings is that higher levels of education indicate values associated with independence and individualism, which, in turn, ease the pressure to marry and form a family.[113] One study, for example, found that education and cognitive sophistication encourage tolerant views and raise willingness to extend civil liberties to nonconformist groups.[114] Another cross-national study argues that education increases liberal attitudes across cultures and national contexts.[115] Similar trends have been observed outside of Europe and the United States, which are highly individualistic, suggesting that education can affect relationship status even in societies that do not value privacy and independence as much as in the West.[116]

In addition, higher education increases the potential for career-marriage conflict, especially when both partners work.[117] This conflict involves juggling the demands of progressing in the labor market, establishing a long-term relationship, and maintaining the balance between one's professional and personal life.[118] In exploring the causes and repercussions of the career-marriage conflict, several studies found that the balance between relationship formation and career is overburdened during the final years of formal education.[119] This situation leads many young people who once focused on finding a partner to now choose career over marriage and advanced degrees over committed relationships.

Furthermore, advanced levels of education correlate with higher levels of income,[120] which moderate relationship patterns insofar as higher socioeconomic status allows people to live alone. As mentioned, privacy is a common good, and people can afford it when they enjoy higher incomes.[121] Higher levels of education usually reflect socioeconomic advantages and, as a result, have been found to increase the likelihood of living alone in both East Asia[122] and North America.[123]

Shifts in Religiosity

Many religious societies highly value modesty and traditional values, which form the basis of familism. They prefer late marriage over single or unmarried parenthood and view extramarital sex negatively.[124] Collectivism, which often characterizes religious communities, has also been found to be particularly important to relationships and family values.[125] In contrast, nonreligious individuals are more open to singlehood, and the growing prominence of individualism among nonreligious persons explains the number of never-married and unmarried people. Studies show that the diminishing role of religion relates to the record number of individuals choosing not to get married and to reduced fertility rates in the United States and western Europe.[126] My analysis of the European Social Survey shows that 12 percent of married individuals are not religious (score 0 on a 0–10 scale), compared to 23 percent of cohabiters, 18 percent of the never-married, and 17 percent of divorced people.

Even religious institutions opposed to singlehood cannot stop the flood of singles. In Catholic Mexico, for example, evidence shows that despite religious sentiments, marriage rates have overwhelmingly dropped while cohabitation rates have increased.[127] In Italy, studies show that despite a society rooted in Catholicism, religion plays a limited role in relationship choices: singlehood is widely prevalent, and Italy has one of the lowest fertility rates in the world.[128]

One explanation is that while religion generally relates positively to marriage, religious environments can also push people to forsake marriage because of tight restrictions relating to starting a family, giving birth, and divorce. In Mexico, studies show, people are refusing Catholic wedding vows to ease potential separation later on.[129] Instead, they prefer to cohabitate and move in and out of partnerships, allowing for periods of singlehood in between. Alternatively, those who already married in church and later separated simply choose to stay single or are forced to live with their next partner without officially marrying, because of church law. Mexico is not alone, as similar patterns have been observed in Spain,[130] Quebec,[131] and several countries in Latin America.[132]

Even among the devoutly religious, recent societal and generational processes of liberalization influence the decision to marry. For example, today's young evangelicals in the United States are more likely to adopt liberal attitudes toward premarital sex and single living.[133] Findings point to a shift in moral authority whereby young evangelicals believe that their own conscience, rather than God, is the true arbiter of right and wrong. Similarly, religious Muslims[134] and Jews[135] are demanding changes to the role of women in their communities, allowing women to delay marriage or choose divorce if unsatisfied with their partners. Even in highly conservative Hindu[136] and ultra-Orthodox Jewish communities,[137] in which marriage is traditionally arranged by the family and takes place at a young age, the hegemony is being challenged, allowing a more liberal approach for premarital introduction between young men and women.

Most fascinating, perhaps, is that the liberalization of attitudes toward marriage in religious environments occurs not just at the community and personal levels but within the leadership as well. Notably, and in part as a response to the rising number of young people leaving the Catholic Church, the Vatican has in more recent years shown leniency with regard to relationship-related matters.[138] For example, there has been a significant shift in the rhetorical stance of the Roman Catholic Church toward gays since the Second Vatican Council, differentiating between the act (i.e., homosexual behavior), which is still considered a sin, and the actor (i.e., the homosexual), who should be embraced.[139] Such liberalization undermines traditional familial values in general. In turn, across many religious communities, the increasing acceptance of people who live independently, who delay marriage, or who divorce facilitates the rise of singles inside the religious world along with the general trend.

Popular Culture, the Media, and Social Networking

On September 21, 1995, the popular American television show *Seinfeld* pretty much summed up its message about marriage in the opening episode of season 7, called "The Engagement":

KRAMER: You started wondering, "Isn't there something more to life?"

JERRY: Yes!

KRAMER: Well, let me fill you in on something: there isn't.

JERRY: There isn't?

KRAMER: Absolutely not. I mean, what were you thinking, Jerry? Marriage? Family?

JERRY: Well ...

KRAMER: They're prisons! Man-made prisons! You're doing time! You get up in the morning: she's there. You go to sleep at night: she's there. It's like you have to ask permission to use the bathroom!

As early as the 1980s, representations of twenty- and thirtysomething singles who do not need relationships to be happy began appearing in the media, affecting public opinion on the matter.[140] While the previous generation was raised on films, books, and tales depicting immaculate romances where couples ended up happily ever after, the American television industry in the 1990s and the first decade of the twenty-first century began promoting shows such as *Seinfeld*, *Sex and the City*, and *Will and Grace,* exposing entire populations to people who remained single into and beyond their thirties. The single woman began to be celebrated in popular media, and her image was reconfigured from "spinster" to "singleton."[141] For example, television critics see *Sex and the City* as an innovation in women's representation on television in that it validated single women's friendships and culture.[142] The show promotes, even encourages, women's right to sexual pleasure with no strings attached. Shows such as *Will and Grace, Ally McBeal,* and *Girls* portray single women as fashionable and sophisticated.[143] In other shows, such as *Seinfeld, Friends,* and *The Big Bang Theory,* singles are characterized by being social, full of laughter, and surrounded by friends who generate a sense of community.[144]

It is precisely because singlehood and single living have come so far that singles now see their lives reflected in film, television, and print media. In this sense, popular culture mirrors, even celebrates, singles' rise to sociocultural prominence. This process feeds itself as young viewers grow more comfortable with the idea of choosing the single lifestyle.[145]

These shows are so popular that their influence has spread beyond the Western world.[146] But similar portrayals are also produced in non-Western studios. An obvious example is the Indian entertainment industry, one of the largest in the world.[147] One study investigated the effects of Indian cable TV on Indian women over a three-year period. The study found that increased exposure to Indian media, in addition to foreign entertainment, was associated with higher autonomy and reduced fertility rates.[148] Another study, conducted in Brazil, found that the share of women who became separated or divorced increased significantly after Globo, the monopoly network of telenovelas, became available.[149] The effect was even stronger in small municipalities, where there is less exposure to liberal values. In an increasingly globalized world, very few countries are immune to the shift toward individualism,[150] and many societies are exposed to lifestyles that conflict with the deeply ingrained traditional family unit.[151]

Nowadays, the exposure to different family forms and relationship possibilities happens via the Internet as well. One study of Facebook users found that high Facebook usage correlates with negative relationship outcomes, such as conflict, divorce, and separation.[152] Another study found that active Twitter usage leads to more conflict among romantic partners, which, in turn, can lead to infidelity, breakup, and divorce.[153]

These contemporary means of communication challenge traditionalism and the institution of marriage by exposing users to alternative lifestyles. Once individuals see other ways of interaction and of satisfying their emotional needs, they rethink intimacy and reconsider their family situation. It is not necessarily human nature that is being changed so dramatically. Rather, these technological developments are revealing preexisting human needs. Technology has provided humans with more (perhaps even better) ways to express themselves and to follow their very basic desires, thereby leading to the rise of singlehood.

Urbanization

The growth of the city, too, links strongly to the rise of singlehood. This trend is especially salient in North America and many countries in Europe, where the number of households in cities has increased at a faster rate than the city population. More and more singles live in metropolitan areas, disproportionately to other regions.[154] My analysis of the US Census and the American Community Survey indicates a large concentration of singles in populated areas. The diagram in figure 2 shows that American singles—whether never-married, divorced, or widowed—tend to live in larger cities.

Yet the link between the growth of metropolitan areas and the corresponding proportion of singles extends beyond the West: there is ample evidence that singles in South Asia, East Asia, South America, and other regions are flocking to cities to join the postfamily environment.[155] Particularly striking are the changes measured in the Arab and

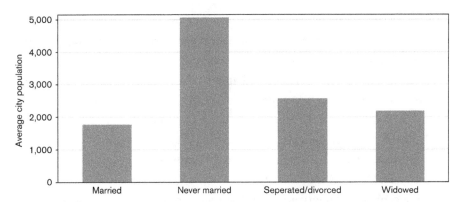

Average US city population by marital status. Sources: 2000 US Census and 2001–2013 American Community Surveys.

Muslim world, even in ultraconservative Iran, where urbanization has been shown to be associated with family liberalization.[156]

Urbanization has a marked effect on family structure and the post-family culture for several reasons. First, urban areas have sprawled in recent decades following economic development, and the percentage of people living in cities has risen globally. As a result, city housing prices have skyrocketed, and the cityscape has become even less conducive to the family lifestyle, which requires larger apartments.[157] Cities, in turn, have started to accommodate the increasing number of people living alone by providing greater numbers of smaller apartments, and the process continues to feed itself.[158]

Moreover, the diversity wrought by the growing number of people living in cities and urban settings has legitimized the forsaking of conformist, traditional values. The urban identity has become too heterogenic to feed into one collective format and has led to diverse societal beliefs, individualism, and a tendency to abandon family values.[159] Thus, urbanization increases the variety of living arrangements with a general shift away from traditional family units to more modern family households while also multiplying single-occupancy homes.[160]

The rise of singlehood in big cities also comes on the heels of domestic migration from the countryside. In many parts of the world, economic development and unprecedented geographic mobility have driven large-scale exoduses to urban areas. The new internal migrants are more likely than nonmigrants to live without family, because they are unfamiliar with the local community of potential partners, are far from the marriage obligations enforced by their extended families, and are flooded with the social, sexual, and leisure possibilities that the big city offers.[161] This is especially true for young individuals who tend to seek economic opportunity, professional development, and personal exploration rather than a secure family life.[162]

Indeed, as early as the 1980s, a study found a positive correlation in every US state between rates of internal migration and the proportion of single, unmarried, and widowed individuals.[163] In China, one study found that 41 percent of internal migrants in Beijing live alone, and that this proportion has rapidly increased over the last two decades.[164] One of the most interesting places to watch this process in its early stages is sub-Saharan Africa. Here, rural and village dwellers, who until recently worked in agriculture and depended on the family unit for support, are finding new opportunities within growing cities and moving there to work in industrialized professions. Although most of the offered jobs in these developing metropolises are still low skilled, the new, unmarried, internal migrants gain the economic ability to live alone, and they do so in growing numbers.[165]

Similarly, members of rural families who relocate to work in urban areas and send money back home find themselves living apart from their extended, and sometimes even nuclear, families. For these individuals, who are often married, the move to the city makes relationship maintenance more difficult but also allows them to explore other relationship possibilities, thus promoting singlehood.[166]

Finally, urbanization and internal migration increase educational opportunity and wealth, both of which promote singlehood, as explained earlier. These effects are especially strong in areas of high gender inequality like the city, because women advance significantly more in such places and feel more at ease living on their own. An example of this process can be found in Yemen, where development and urbanization have been associated with a sharp rise in education for girls. This has reduced the number of arranged marriages, increased the divorce rate, and raised the average age at first marriage.[167]

International Immigration

In several ways, international immigration also contributes to the rising number of singles. First, immigrants, especially refugees or economic immigrants, often arrive alone to find new opportunities for work and to send money home to relatives.[168] This may delay marriage, because the new immigrants must adjust to an unfamiliar environment, overcome difficulties in assimilation, and navigate a new culture while finding a match.

Second, international immigrants are more likely to move into cities than rural areas because cities have more economic opportunities.[169] As mentioned, cities expose new immigrants to more liberal and career-oriented societies less concerned with traditional values and family formation. As a result, communities of immigrants are expanding rapidly in many large cities; in fact, a few major European cities can claim that their populations of first- and second-generation immigrants have already passed the 50 percent mark.[170] These communities provide social opportunities and entertainment for newcomers, who feel they have many plausible alternatives for family life.

Third, as in the case of refugees, international immigration waves are often gender imbalanced. Construction workers, for example, who are in high demand in many destination countries, are usually men, while nursing-service workers are usually women. The problem is that professions usually vary by nationality. China, for example, sends large numbers of construction workers, while countries such as the Philippines send nurses.[171] As mentioned in the section on demographics, heterosexual individuals who wish to form relationships within their own ethnic communities find gender imbalance to be an obstacle in meeting a suitable partner.[172] These immigrants must either overcome social and cultural barriers and look beyond their communities in the host country or marry someone of their own group across borders.[173]

Fourth, some international immigrants reveal that they are totally fine living alone, as I discovered in the interviews I conducted with immigrant singles. Thus, international immigration, whose original purpose was to advance people economically, has morphed into a social transformation that allows immigrants to live as they wish. These immigrants feel freer to choose singlehood over marriage because they do not suffer the constraints of traditionalism arising from close proximity to their family and hometown community.[174]

TOWARD AN AGE OF HAPPY SINGLEHOOD

In his 1964 State of the Union address, President Lyndon Johnson declared a war on poverty. As the poverty rate in the United States approached 20 percent, a legislative program was laid out to eliminate poverty and create economic opportunities by expanding the federal government's role in health care, education, and welfare.[175] In the years after the program commenced, policies were enacted to provide food stamps, improve Social Security, fund elementary and secondary schooling, and create jobs for Americans. However, many policy experts and researchers consider these efforts as having failed, at least in a cost-benefit analysis.[176] Poverty rates in the United States have remained stubbornly high despite occasional downticks.[177]

In part, singles were to blame for these failures. In the debates that followed the War on Poverty, it was assumed, and still is, that married couples are better off financially than singles, more economically capable of supporting children, and less likely to be poor.[178] Some concluded, therefore, that one way of combating rising poverty rates was to encourage relationship formation and marriage. In analyzing Johnson's policies, a 2013 op-ed published by the Brookings Institution delivers exactly this message: "Unless young people ... stop having babies outside marriage, government spending will be minimally effective in fighting poverty. On the other hand ... redesigning the nation's welfare programs to encourage marriage hold[s] great promise for at last achieving the poverty reduction envisioned by President Johnson."[179]

Ron Haskins, the writer of the column, makes a simple argument: if we return to structuring our society on family units, the economic benefits will be high, and poverty will be reduced. Indeed, even fifty years after Johnson's original declaration, some still blame the singles population and want to inhibit the rise of singlehood.

The problem with this thinking, however, is that singlehood is becoming a common good in and of itself. It might well be economically smart for people to couple, but pushing citizens into marriage is not necessarily ethically justified. People choose singlehood for the many aforementioned reasons and are willing to pay for it. In fact, as already shown, many people choose singlehood over partnership whether they feel economically secure or not. Independence and individualism, together with education and liberalization, all lead to the single lifestyle.

Instead of fighting singlehood, policy makers and society at large may need to start accepting and making the most of it. The age of singlehood is not based only on one driving force; many incentives exist for being single nowadays. It is therefore not surprising that this trend is gaining traction despite discrimination and governmental policies that try to push people away from singlehood and toward forming nuclear family units.

The singlehood trend is taking hold in tandem with demographic changes, women's shifting role in society, rising divorce rates, economic development and changes, increasing consumerism, shifts in religiosity, cultural changes, urbanization, and immigration. Together, these forces seem unstoppable. They are creating societies based on a majority of singles and, consequently, are shattering the institution of marriage around the world. These forces may seem somewhat trivial, but our public institutions, most of which still promote deeply ingrained familial norms, are ignoring them, showing that these dynamics are too foreign—or rather too novel—to policy makers and the still-indifferent public. Understanding these various forces sheds light on this new social condition, helping to decipher what might make single people happy.

Given all the mechanisms described here, it seems there is no way back. Rather, we need to understand better how single living can produce joy and happiness and become an advantage instead of a source of agony. My mission in this book is to delve into the lives and statistics of happy singles, paving the way for those who either choose to be single or come by it via other circumstances. By no means does this book present an opposition to marriage or couplehood—if chosen freely and consciously. Rather, this book acknowledges the powerful trends that lead to an age of singlehood, while trying to answer the question: What makes singles happy?

CHAPTER TWO

Happy Singlehood in Old Age

The Inuit mythology tells the story of an old woman left behind in her village by her family. They provided her with a few insects to eat during the cold winter, but the old woman felt compassion for the insects. "They are living creatures and I should not do any harm to them," she said. "I'd rather die first."

While the old woman was gazing tenderly at the insects, a fox entered her hut and immediately began biting her, ripping open her skin. But to her surprise, the fox's assault had no effect on her. Instead, her old skin was simply taken from her body and a new, young skin appeared beneath it. The insects, apparently, were the ones who called the fox. And when her family returned to the village in the summer, the old woman was not there anymore. She had started a new life elsewhere with the insects.[1]

This story is seemingly about the power of giving and the virtue of compassion. However, if this is the lesson of the Inuit folklore tale, why is the hero of the story an old woman? And why was she left behind by her family? For example, the story equally could have been about a hungry young boy who saw some insects he could eat, but who, instead of killing them to satisfy his appetite, showed compassion and was thus rewarded. Indeed, it seems there is more to this story, and that through hearing about an old woman, we are exposed to one of the greatest fears of all: aging alone and being left behind. The old woman not only discovers a way to survive the cold winter despite her old age and ostensible fragility but also makes new allies and friends. Being alone puts her in touch with her surroundings, outside of her own family. Even after her family returns, she does not really need them anymore. She moves elsewhere and finds a whole new life in her senior years, filled with the new ties she forged and the compassion she treasures inside her. No wonder, then, that this story has passed through generations of Inuit.

I push this chapter forward in investigating singles' happiness because one of the most common and deeply ingrained reasons for marriage is not a positive one. Studies show that it is actually the fear of aging alone and dying without anyone at our bedside that drives us into marriage.[2] It is this image of getting old, dragging our way through the streets, alone, perhaps even sick, without anyone to talk to; the image of sitting on a bench in the park throwing pieces of bread to the pigeons and waiting for another day to be over; the image of returning at the end of the day to an old, cramped apartment, full of antique stuff that even charity shops are not interested in; the image of going to sleep alone in a single bed, thinking of what will happen if we get sick or die without anyone noticing. Those images haunt many of us, and we look for ways to escape this fate. Marrying someone and starting a family seems like a perfect solution: having someone beside us all the time, especially in the last part of life, feels comforting and reassuring.

As cynical as it may seem to use another person to assuage our fears, for many people it is a major reason to marry. A research team from the university of Toronto conducted seven comprehensive and complementary studies to examine how loneliness affects the incentive to marry.[3] Their findings show that 40 percent of respondents feared not having a long-term companion, and another 11 percent feared growing old alone. These fears, their studies show, led respondents to marry and settle for partners who were lower quality on one or more levels (e.g., emotional support, intellectual comparability, or physical appearance).

The main question, then, is whether marriage is really a good solution to the fear of loneliness and the desire for companionship. What would have happened to the elderly Inuit woman had she been married, or had she stayed with her family? Would she have been happier? To answer that, this chapter starts with a description of the challenges of loneliness in old age and a discussion of their finer dynamics. It then shows that these feelings of loneliness and the disadvantages they entail are actually not related to marriage. In fact, marriage may not be such a good way to escape loneliness in old age. Not only do married people feel lonely in surprisingly high numbers, but also long-term singles are often better equipped to deal with loneliness later in life. Following these findings, and based on the interviews I conducted, I discuss the ways in which older singles can be—and often are—happy and satisfied with their lives.

LONELINESS IN OLD AGE

Loneliness in old age is increasingly important nowadays. In fact, in early 2018, the British prime minister decided to nominate a minister for loneliness affairs, who would focus particularly on elders.[4] As shown in chapter 1, the increasing life expectancy around the world affects the proportion of people living alone. As life expectancy increases, so does the potential amount of time a person may live alone, either because of a longer widowhood or because of a longer lifespan as a never-married or divorced individual. This results in more adults being single for greater periods of time.[5]

Sofia describes in her blog a long process of learning to understand her loneliness after divorce. At the start of her writing, she felt very lonely without hope. Over time, however, these feelings transformed into empowerment and courage, and this chapter follows her transformation closely. Sofia began her blog at the age of sixty-six, after being divorced for nine years. She writes:

There are nights I lay in bed and wrap my own arms around myself just to feel touch.... Even just rubbing my hands down my arms or legs or touching my torso seems odd, but I'm starved—starved for touch. The only touch I do get is from my son, who I see once a month, if I am fortunate. He hugs me for a minute, and honestly the entire situation seems quite strange. I'm to the point now that I cannot imagine what it would be like to be kissed, caressed, or made love to by a man. The thought is foreign to me. Even the simple act of holding a person's hand would seem odd.[6]

Sofia longs for the touch of someone who loves her. She deeply feels emotionally isolated. Indeed, these feelings are more common among elders, and loneliness is the main problem identified in referrals of elderly people to social services. It also significantly correlates with entry into residential care, especially when compounded with deteriorated mental health and difficulties in mobility.[7]

But loneliness in old age may occur with or without marriage and mostly depends on self-perception.[8] Loneliness is defined as "a discrepancy between one's desired and achieved levels of social relations,"[9] and this discrepancy may concern the number of relationships or the level of intimacy in the relationship.[10] In either case, loneliness is a perception rather than reality. In this sense, one must also differentiate between loneliness and social isolation. While *social isolation* refers to the objective state of having minimal contact with other people, *loneliness* refers to the subjective feelings associated with perceived isolation.[11] The latter, the self-perception of being neglected, is the main factor associated with old age.[12]

The subjective nature of loneliness and, thus, the fact that it depends on self-perceptions, rather than on any objective situation such as being married or unmarried, is important. The perception of loneliness can vary significantly, independently of marital status. Married people can be socially isolated from their friends and relatives and even emotionally alienated from their spouses, while unmarried individuals can be extensively connected and receive support and love from a wide net of friends and family.[13] Even those who struggle with physical difficulties can choose to be embarrassed in front of others and isolate themselves at home or go out and interact with society.[14]

We will meet Sofia again in this chapter and see the process she went through and how she has evolved to become a proud single woman, full of confidence. She understood the subjective nature of feeling lonely and went through a process of addressing her needs outside of a relationship. But to understand her process, we must first delve deeper into the question of whether marriage helps with loneliness in old age and, if so, in what ways. Precisely because loneliness is subjective by nature, it is necessary to discuss the ways in which marriage affects loneliness. Such discussion may lead us to consider some alternatives to marriage that have a similar or even better effect.

MARRIAGE AND LONELINESS IN OLD AGE

Proponents of marriage argue that living as a couple or as a family helps prevent loneliness.[15] However, whether marriage actually reduces loneliness, taking into account all possible scenarios, is an empirical question to be tested. Of course, the benefits of a happy marriage with happy children, where everyone loves each other, are quite expected. The question, however, is whether marriage is a wise solution on average, for all people, across all age cohorts, and in various scenarios, including when it ends in divorce, separation, or widowhood.

Taking this into account, I have summed up the answers to the question of whether marriage is a good solution to loneliness in one simple chart (things will get more complex later on). In this chart, I analyze the loneliness indicator found in the European Social Survey across thirty countries and over several age cohorts. This analysis reveals a remarkable finding. See fig. 3.

This chart divides the population into two groups: the "ever married," those who chose the "marriage solution" at some point in life (some, of course, are still married), and the "never-married," those who did not pick the marriage solution. On the y-axis is the estimated degree

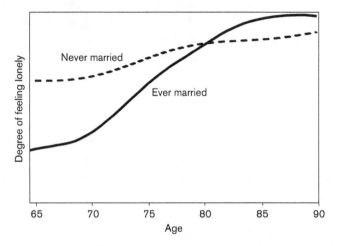

The incidence of loneliness, according to age and marital status. Source: Based on the European Social Survey.

of loneliness that respondents felt in the week preceding the survey. The graph shows that over time the effect of marriage on feeling lonely decreases; at the age of seventy-eight, it is even statistically better to have not married in the first place. On average, picking the marriage path has negative consequences from this age onward, not positive ones.

Furthermore, note that this graph does not account for the self-selection mechanism by which happier people are more likely to enter marriage than their counterparts, as explained in chapter 1. Therefore, in reality, the cutoff age should be lower, and being never-married should pay off at an even younger age. In other words, if one accounts for the fact that those who marry are happier before marriage and compares them to never-married individuals with a similar baseline of well-being, the effect of the marriage solution is expected to be even weaker (happiness highly and negatively correlates with loneliness, and the two are interchangeable in this sense).

It is clear what stands behind these remarkable findings: the population of divorced and widowed individuals. As will be discussed in detail later, divorced and widowed individuals feel lonelier and less happy than both those who have never been married and those who are still married. This is particularly important for elders, because the likelihood of being divorced or widowed rises with age.[16]

Of course, one can argue that mixing couples with divorced and widowed individuals is unfair, and the chart in figure 3 is therefore misleading. But, in fact, comparing only never-married individuals to couples is the true, logical sin.[17] The reason for this is simple, albeit bitter—no matter what you do, marriage ends in one of three (tragic) ways: widowhood, divorce, or death. Understanding this is tremendously important in deciphering the effect of marriage on our well-being, especially in old age. After all, no one really knows how their marriage will end. We tend to think that our situation is better than others, and that we have control over the fate of our choices. However, studies show no correlation between expectations and how marriage ends.[18] Thus, individuals hope to stay married and, moreover, to do so happily ever after. But being married, by definition, puts one in a "risk group" of divorce or widowhood, and we must always take this into account.

Still, I do not want to give the impression that I "cover up" anything in this chart. We all truly want to know what stands behind these remarkable findings. Therefore, I nonetheless distinguish between marital scenarios in the following section. It is important to see what each entails.

FOUR MARITAL SCENARIOS IN OLD AGE

To test the aforementioned results more accurately and with up-to-date data, I estimated four marital statuses separately—married, never-married, widowed, and divorced/separated—in relation to loneliness and happiness. I accounted for various intervening factors such as education, income, health, religion, sociability, and country of residence. I estimated these outcomes for ages sixty-five and above and, again, as a sensitive analysis, for ages seventy-five and above.

In analyzing the data, I discovered that widowed or divorced/separated people are the least happy and most lonely in comparison to both married and never-married people. These results hold true even when excluding singles currently cohabitating with another person. Widowed and divorced men feel 0.8 and 0.5 points lonelier, respectively, than married men on a 0–10 point scale, while never-married men feel 0.45 points lonelier. Among women, these numbers stand at 0.6 and 0.4 points for the widowed and divorced versus 0.35 for the never-married. Very similar differences exist in measuring happiness: those who are widowed or divorced are the least happy group, with a lag of 0.6–0.8 points (divorced women show the highest lag this time), while the never-married group shows a 0.4–0.5-point gap.

No doubt, married people are still the happiest and the least lonely of all groups, at least in subjective terms. But even this conclusion should carry two reservations. First, as explained above, couples experience elevated numbers in happiness, life satisfaction, and lack of loneliness because they showed elevated numbers in the first place, before marriage. Longitudinal studies show that those who eventually marry report being around 0.3 points happier (on a 0–10 scale) at their baseline.[19] Taking this into account, marriage raises elders' happiness level and reduces their loneliness (the two are highly correlated) only slightly, if at all.

Second, and perhaps more importantly, these results have been estimated for the generation born during and immediately after World War II. The expectation is that nowadays the value and sustainability of marriage is declining even more, and thus the effect of marriage on loneliness in old age will be much less benign for the succeeding generations. This is because marriage ends sooner among the younger generations, and people separate more often.[20] Moreover, people separate in higher numbers because they feel more comfortable, culturally speaking, have numerous support groups, and share the same situation with many more of their peers.[21] According to recent findings by the Pew Research Center, the so-called gray divorce is popping up in astonishing numbers. For example, among American adults age fifty and older, the divorce rate has roughly doubled since the 1990s.[22] These newly divorced individuals will soon become part of the larger group of the "ever married," making the marriage solution even less appealing because of fewer "happy ending" cases.

Whether one accepts or rejects these reservations, the gaps between married and unmarried individuals are surprisingly narrow. After all, how can married individuals ever feel lonely? But married couples, especially in old age, *do* feel lonely, and my findings show that the incidence of loneliness among couples only rises with age. In another estimate, I found that the share of married people feeling lonely is around 50 percent more at age sixty than at thirty, and that it doubles by the age of ninety. In a web post, Dan, forty-nine, exemplifies this quite plainly: "I am married. The thing is, though, my marriage is a passionate-less facade where I feel I'm just settling. But I am terrified of growing old alone. I feel trapped! What to do???"[23]

There are many reasons for being lonely within marriage besides sticking to a bad or simply boring relationship. These include feeling socially isolated after years of devoting oneself to the family, neglecting social networks, or feeling helpless in caring for an ill partner without anyone else to lend a hand. In fact, researchers prefer to divide feelings of loneliness into social and emotional dimensions.[24] *Social loneliness* refers to not having a wide circle of friends and acquaintances who provide a sense of belonging, companionship, and membership in a community. Correlates of social loneliness among older adults may include, for instance, reduced social activities and a lack of connection with one's own neighborhood.[25] *Emotional loneliness*, on the other hand, refers to feeling like there is no one close to whom one may turn.[26] This distinction is particularly relevant for older singles as it shows that the reasons for loneliness vary and that partnership is not necessarily the answer. Sometimes social loneliness is what matters, and this can actually stem from *having* a partner rather than *not* having one.[27] Indeed, studies show that turning inward, toward the family, for so many years might result in feeling socially isolated in older age.[28] In contrast, as I discuss in this chapter, many singles address loneliness with other forms of relationship, where friends, companionship, and a sense of belonging matter most.

These results are particularly important in addressing the argument that marriage is at least worth a try. After all, as the saying goes, what do you have to lose? If it does not work, just leave and uncouple yourself. The answer, apparently, is that you actually lose a lot. Several recent studies,[29] together with my own, show that marriage not only puts one at risk of divorce or widowhood, but also, and maybe more importantly, leaves one ill-prepared for being single. It seems that never-married older singles are intrinsically more suited to living alone in old age than widowed older singles who had fewer opportunities to learn how to do so. Singles who stay unmarried are better prepared when they are older because they know their way around, develop a support system, and do not depend on one person for better and for worse.[30] Long-term singles are also not burdened with the stigma of suddenly being alone, unlike the elderly widowed and divorced.[31]

It is interesting to think about. Part of the rationale for why married couples are happier immediately before and after their wedding is because marriage feels like a "magic solution," a means of securing oneself into old age. Using terms from the Inuit tale, the wedded couple feel they achieved the key to not being left behind in the village to eat insects like the old woman. However, how people feel at the time of their wedding, which, statistically, most commonly occurs around the age of thirty, is totally unrelated to feelings of loneliness forty years later, the time when people hoped to be secured by marriage. Almost paradoxically, exactly at the time during which marriage is meant to provide companionship, there is an increasing risk of widowhood or, alternatively, divorce, especially considering today's demographics and marriage statistics.

We might still ask: Why, then, do people marry without thinking of the long-term risk? There are two plausible answers. First, people do see the risk and indeed have begun to respond, thus the declining rates in marriage, especially within individualistic societies where people think of their personal needs and are free to choose their own way.

The second answer is that some people weigh the risk against the benefit, but it is difficult for them to feel and estimate the long-term risk, which the available evidence shows is simply hard to do.[32] In pension economics it is called the "myopia problem," which leads many governments to legally force citizens to save for retirement. The same might be true with marriage. The short-term benefit blinds many to the long-term risk. As stated in chapter 1, longitudinal studies show that marriage is mainly a short-term factor in increasing happiness, benefiting people only around the time of the wedding itself, with the effect declining after about two years,[33] while the risk lies far ahead in the future. This, of course, especially applies to older adults, since most of them are further removed from the transitory effect of the wedding.

All this means only that marriage should stop being the sole solution for loneliness in old age. There is something to learn about happily aging without a partner. Never-married individuals adapt to this way of living all their lives, but they are only an example for how people who are divorced or widowed may follow suit. All three groups can adopt certain strategies to live happily ever after, even without a partner.

THE SECRETS OF HAPPY OLDER SINGLES

Studies thus far have only scratched the surface of what it means to be prepared for living alone in older age. This is unsurprising, since the main perception, until now, has been that marriage is the solution to aging properly. But as noted previously, this is no longer necessarily the case, especially with the rise in life expectancy and changing demographics and marriage patterns. In the following sections, therefore, I delve into the interviews I conducted in order to identify the ways elderly divorced, widowed, and never-married people adapt to this new reality, accrue happiness, and overcome loneliness. Their ideas should speak not only to older adults but also, and perhaps primarily, to young people who marry out of the mostly false fear of being lonely and miserable in old age.

My interviews taught me that there is a whole different reality out there that might radically change our conception of marriage. Interestingly, although I knew that I was going to hear many happy versions of being an older single, I was still surprised by the magnitude and breadth of this phenomenon. I am not the only one. The researcher and writer Eric Klinenberg came to study singles after researching a seemingly different topic: disasters.[34] While investigating the sociological context of disasters, he tackled the issue of older singles who got caught in a natural disaster and the difficulties they faced. Thus, he started an investigation of the perils and challenges facing single people. However, he discovered that many elderly single people actually manage just fine.[35]

But not only researchers are surprised that many older singles live happily ever after. Some of the interviewees I talked with did not expect to be so content with singlehood when they were young. They were surprised themselves. After finding themselves alone, they simply felt happy with this situation and were not interested in altering it.

Therefore, it seems time to stop being so surprised and to start listening to what the happy older singles have to teach us all. In interviewing singles in old age and analyzing related blog posts, I tried to overcome their and my surprise by searching for answers more nuanced than the obvious fact that this population is happier than previously thought. I went on and asked what distinguishes happy older singles from unhappy ones. If we are to suggest that older singles hold the keys to raising the happiness of the entire population of singles and even that of couples, it is necessary to unpack how this demographic perceives their aging process as singles, and moreover, how they perceive their singleness as aging individuals.

It is apparent, and this is worth keeping in mind, that the answers to my questions varied greatly when I compared long-term singles to those who created traditional family lives and became singles later in life. For the first group, the prospect of being alone in old age represented, not a massive change, but an extension of their past and current lives. For the second group, and for those who were not single by choice, the process of being single forced them to adapt to their changing circumstances and to develop new habits and ways of living that would make their golden years go more smoothly. Thus, there is a need to hear both groups' voices to understand some of the mechanisms behind happy singlehood in old age. Both apply various strategies in adapting to single living.

Taking Ownership of Singlehood in Old Age

The first theme I found among happy older singles is the ability to look back and gain control over the circumstances that led to being single. In psychoanalysis, *life review* refers to the progressive process that people undergo in the last stages of life.[36] During this time, older adults normally reassess, reevaluate, and seek self-acceptance to consciously deal with unresolved past conflicts. For older singles, one very prominent unresolved issue is that of not having followed or fulfilled what is perceived to be the customary life stages into late age via a sustainable marriage. Happy older singles are those who can come to terms with not having followed the traditional family path, finding meaning in the life they chose to live or, for widowed individuals, in the loss they had experienced.

In one study, researchers set out to explore the aging experience of people over sixty who had never been married.[37] It turns out that those who were happy described their reasons for staying single in ways profoundly different from those of unhappy older singles. In short, happy older singles simply stated that they never wanted to marry whatsoever. They took responsibility for their lives and were satisfied with their social ties as a substitute for marriage.

Especially in the case of never-married individuals, involvement with friends, extended family, and community gave them the confidence to feel that they did not "miss out" despite all the prejudice against them. In contrast, unhappy older singles had a variety of reasons for not following typical life trajectories. While the reasons were not always dichotomous, it seems that the unhappy older always-single tended to attribute their relationship status to circumstances such as never finding the "right person," health reasons, or responsibilities that prevented them from dating.

More interesting in this study is that many of those who were single by circumstance and happy learned over time to accept their reality and even ended up enjoying the exclusive control that their single-by-choice counterparts sought from the beginning. It would seem, then, that the sooner long-term singles can be at peace with the question "Why am I single," the sooner they can feel whole with the "lost" opportunity to make a traditional family, and can break the stigma and enjoy independence.

Other scholars show that those who choose singlehood benefit from the same exclusive control over their lives and destiny, which transforms into a positive life review and higher self-esteem.[38] In particular, some studies have found that the sense of wholeness with never being married correlates with reduced levels of loneliness.[39]

This approach to singlehood was echoed in the interviews I conducted, as well as in the blog posts I analyzed, and it distinguishes happy older singles from unhappy ones. For example, an anonymous blogger, exact age unknown, writes: "So, you're getting old, you look in the mirror and wrinkles are sprouting everywhere and you're still single and never-married, so what!??? If you've remained unmarried for the right reasons; because you don't want to be in something you know God doesn't approve of, you've made mistakes and don't want to repeat, you don't want to be with someone just for the sake of not being alone, because you just won't settle for less, you're doing the right thing!"[40]

This blogger is happy with being single, and she makes it clear that this life course was intentional. In fact, it seems she feels elated and encouraged precisely because it is a choice. In contrast, Lisa, age fifty-seven, who lives in Brooklyn, testified that she is bitter and "jaded." In our interview, she said she does not want to marry anyone, and that she actually never believed in marriage. What makes her bitter now, however, is not that she is single but how she looks back on her past and feels helpless and staggered from being cheated upon. She said:

> I was in a long-term relationship, and the motherfucker left me for someone thirty years younger. They're married—he married her and they live in Sweden. [I feel] betrayed. I was happy; I was happy when I was alone. I'm done. I don't have another one in me—he killed my soul. This used to be my apartment, and now I sit on the outside of my home. I'm fifty-seven years old and I have three roommates—and I never thought I'd have a roommate in my life. I feel really bitter. I supported him for ten years and he fucked me, came home one night and said he wanted out.

Lisa looks back and sees cheating and betrayal. Earlier in the interview she stated that she had been suspicious of marriage all her life. "I never had a relationship more than two years," she said. "I never believed in that." But she thought the long-term relationship with this last guy would be different. Looking back, she is disappointed not only in her failed relationship but also in herself for trusting someone more than she thought appropriate. Someone else had talked her into a long-term relationship, and it was the same guy who ended it so abruptly. This narrative has led her to feel betrayed and helpless, without real control of her life course. The loss of control appears again when she ties her socioeconomic condition with her failed relationship. For her, having roommates stems from someone ruining her life, although she did not mention that her ex stole from her or caused loss of property, nor is there evidence of that.

Lisa and the anonymous blogger have thoroughly divergent views about why they stayed single. Their views are ingrained in a broader approach to life. While Lisa feels cursed, betrayed, and jaded, the anonymous blogger deems singlehood a conscious choice, the best choice of all possibilities and one of which she takes full ownership. These two different attitudes make these two people feel differently about being single. While Lisa is bitter, the anonymous blogger has no regrets and is happy with her marital status.

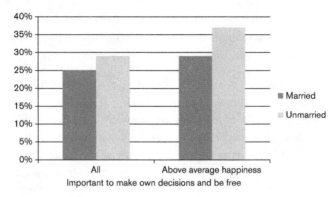

The degree of importance assigned to making independent decisions, among married versus unmarried individuals. Source: Based on the European Social Survey.

In my analysis of the European Social Survey, represented in figure 4, it is apparent that happy older singles highly value the ability to make their own decisions.

Among all singles (never-married, divorced, widowed), happy and unhappy, age sixty-five and above, 29 percent of respondents answered "very much like me" to the questionnaire item "It is important to make my own decisions and be free," compared to 25 percent of the married population. Furthermore, among those unmarried people who are above average in their degree of happiness, this number jumps to 37 percent, while among the married population it stands at 29 percent. This significant gap underscores the importance of autonomy in happy older singles' stance toward marriage.

The Silver Line between "A Lonely Old Man" and "Enjoying My Solitude"

The second theme arose when I compared answers from young singles to answers from older singles. In interviewing some of the younger singles, I heard time and again about the "fear of being lonely when I'm old." It seems that it is hard for some of the young people I interviewed to think of a happy single life; it takes time to make this shift. But in talking to older singles, I found that instead of feeling lonely and out of contact, the happy ones simply enjoy their solitude. These happy older singles dismiss the preconception that they must be lonely by drawing a clear distinction between solitude and loneliness. Ronnie, seventy-one and divorced, writes in her blog:

> Is it so bad to want to be alone, to enjoy silence and eschew so much social-izing? ... That word—solitude—makes the difference at any age because it is almost always a personal choice.... And, for me, there is one more plus on the side of solitude: being social exhausts me nowadays. After a meal or visit with friends, even those I love and adore, I not only want to be alone for a while, I *need* it to restore myself.... We should ... make the distinction between those who are unhappy or depressed about it and others who enjoy their solitude.[41]

Ronnie explains how being lonely is different from enjoying soli-tude, noting that loneliness and solitude are interrelated but conceptu-ally different.[42] Loneliness, or the negative feelings associated with not having a partner, family, or friends, mostly eludes happy older singles, who are extremely adept at engaging their extended families and vari-ous social networks for this need. Likewise, happy older singles tend to avoid social isolation—or the lack of contact with others—through various means of acquiring social capital, which I discuss extensively in chapter 4.

However, since many older singles live alone, they inevitably spend much of their time in solitude. While solitude is occasionally attended by a desire for company at home, happy older singles are capable of being at peace with solitary time; solitude does not mean loneliness or isolation for them but merely time spent alone. For some, solitude is a time to be relished, while others simply accept it as part of their routine.[43]

John Cacioppo, who headed the Center for Cognitive and Social Neuroscience at the University of Chicago, penned one of the fundamen-tal research books on loneliness.[44] In an interview he explained that "being

alone and being lonely are not the same thing, but they're both stigmatized in our society.... People who prefer solitude nevertheless look for
relationships out of guilt—but feel even guiltier once they're in one. A
happy single person is just as healthy as a happy married person."[45]

The older single person can thus achieve greater happiness by redefining what it means to be alone, lonely, and single. By taking practical
steps to circumvent being lonely, older singles can reduce death anxiety and improve well-being. Diane, a woman in her sixties, divorced
twice, lives in Seattle. She writes:

> Long ago, in a universe far away, I was married. And when that marriage
> ended, and I moved out on my own for the very first time.... thought I was
> going to die of loneliness. I had no one to talk to, no one to snuggle with,
> and no one who would rub my shoulders when I got home from a long day
> of typesetting.... Looking back on those times now, I laugh. I had only
> been on my own for six months—six months! Yet at the time it felt like an
> eternity. At this point, I've lived alone for nearly two decades.... I've
> become much more comfortable with my single self.... You can dance
> around your living room to bad '70s rock at 6 in the morning. You can turn
> your bathroom into a shrine to Carlos Silva. For better or for worse (to bor-
> row a phrase), it's your show.[46]

Diane describes a progression from loneliness to being comfortable
with her "single self," even reveling in her independence. There is a
hidden irony here, especially salient among elders: Married seniors
may spend almost no time alone, always having someone to do something with. However, they might be the most vulnerable to loneliness,
precisely because they never experience true solitude. If a married couple do not exercise their solitude "muscles," they may end up being
more vulnerable to loneliness and social isolation than their single com-
patriots. This is what happened to Diane after her first divorce. Here,
while being alone can become a neutral or even positive part of life for
never-married older singles, the inability to incorporate solitude into
a varied, active social and family life puts divorced and widowed
individuals at an especially high risk of emotional distress. Only after

Diane went through a process of rediscovering her "single self" was she able to find her solitude comforting and enjoyable.

Remember Sofia, sixty-six, whom we met at the beginning of this chapter, and who longed for the touch of another? Throughout her blog, she, too, documented a process of crossing this silver line between loneliness and enjoying her solitude. A year later, she wrote: "Right now, I feel pretty satisfied with life. I'm consumed doing something I love, which is writing. In addition, I'm busy with other things like hosting an Internet Radio Show, role-playing with friends, and taking a trip soon to Vegas. I had a funny thought the other day that if I met someone, and I ended up getting married, I might have to give up some of these time-consuming activities!"[47]

Obviously, both sides still exist within her. But after that process, she is capable of seeing the many advantages of being on her own. She occupies herself with so many activities that she actually rethinks this very deep desire that she had only a year earlier. Her desires will not disappear so easily, but the ability to see things differently and develop a sense of self-sufficiency is what matters for her happiness.

The fear of aging alone is largely based on both the stigma associated with being single and the preconception that being single means being helpless, sad, and lonely.[48] But for the happy elder, being single does not mean living in misery. While many feel the need to share their lives with another person and, in doing so, shape and adjust their lifestyles in tandem with those of their partner (as well as those of their own children), happy older singles follow a different path. As Henry David Thoreau once stated, "I find it wholesome to be alone the greater part of the time.... I never found the companion that was so companionable as solitude."

"I Am Able to Take Care of Myself in Old Age"

Adam is a young single, age thirty-two. He is tremendously successful at work and owns a nice apartment on the outskirts of Berlin. However, when I interviewed him, he listed physical vulnerability as the number one reason for getting married. He thinks about the day when he will experience difficulties moving around and have severe health issues. This possibility propels him to find someone to hold on to. Of course, he is aware that this thinking is not entirely rational: there is a good chance he will be divorced by then or married to an ill partner who cannot help him. Nevertheless, this fear pushes him toward marriage.

Adam is one example of a fascinating gap between young people and elders in their attitudes toward physical vulnerability in old age. It might seem counterintuitive, but young people fear being physically vulnerable in old age more than elders do. A special report by the Pew Research Center shows a sizable gap between eighteen-to-sixty-four-year-olds' expectations of old age and the actual experiences reported by elders. For example, 57 percent of the eighteen-to-sixty-four-year-old population anticipate memory loss in old age, while only 25 percent of those aged sixty-five and above actually experience it (the gap remains among all age cohorts: sixty-five to seventy-four, seventy-five to eighty-four, and even eighty-five and older). Furthermore, while 42 percent expect serious illness in old age, only 21 percent of those aged sixty-five and above experience the same. The final example is loneliness, which is a major concern and a central issue in this chapter. While an expectation of loneliness arises among 29 percent of young people, only 17 percent experience loneliness in old age.[49]

Even those who do experience age-related difficulties wield much more control over them than it might seem. What distinguishes happy older singles is the ability to foresee possible emergencies and to prepare accordingly. To that end, some older single interviewees described saving extra money, continuing to work, and even preparing last wills to *take control* of such unpredictable situations. In this third theme, happiness also relates to the practical adjustments that older singles make to manage physical and fiscal restrictions as well as responsibilities to themselves and others.

Fiscal means are particularly important in old age to ensure care in case of reduced mobility or health problems. Having an insurance plan or sufficient savings to fund such assistance necessitates precalculated investment. Yet in most countries, this requires sums of money that not every person possesses. For this reason, new solutions have recently started popping up across the globe. Co-residency, for example, reduces feelings of loneliness while saving costs.[50] In fact, the UN Population Bureau already suggested creating residences for unmarried seniors at the beginning of the century.[51] In Paris, an energetic, passionate group of feminists led by a woman named Theresa Clerc devised an exclusively female, self-governing cohousing collective for women who want to live independently into old age.[52] They care for one another, with no cooks, nurses, or other professional staff, although they leave one room for medical staff as needed. Other groups around the world have followed suit. Toronto, for example, has a coed intergenerational model, where young people live with older people and everyone benefits from taking different roles and responsibilities.

In an article about this rising phenomenon, the *New York Times* reports other such models.[53] One is the brainchild of Christine Perkins, an Ohio contractor in her early sixties who built for herself and three friends a house in rural Ohio that features senior-friendly perks such as electrical outlets that can be reached without bending over. She said she does not expect to care for her roommates who develop severe illnesses, such as late-stage Alzheimer's, but that she and her friends would be happy to take care of each other in many other, less-severe situations.

Alternatively, some older singles meet their needs through home-sharing with younger people, whereas the young people save money and often benefit socially from having roommates, older singles included. Although it is still not a conventional arrangement in most cultures, some are bucking the trend. Take Jonathan, for example. He is twenty-six years old, single, and a cashless full-time student living in

Jerusalem. Toward the end of his last rental contract, an unexpected computer problem forced him to overdraft his bank account. With no parental support, he was unable to pay rent and was eventually forced out of his home. Luckily, Jacob, a single man seventy years his senior, had placed an ad on the local noticeboards: "Student roommate wanted. Free rent and food in exchange for house chores and helping the retired landlord for a few hours every week."

Jacob lives alone and has mobility issues. His modest pension cannot cover the costs of daily help or let him vary his social life. But Jacob did have a small spare room. Following a short interview, Jonathan moved into Jacob's apartment; and in exchange for helping with basic tasks such as cleaning and grocery shopping, he was able to live rent-free. Jacob got live-in help at almost no cost to himself and benefited from the friendship they developed.

Perhaps without realizing it, Jacob and Jonathan are practicing inter-generational living and home-sharing. At the moment, home-sharing programs with students are gaining popularity around the world.[54] Although many home-sharing programs are run by nonprofit organizations, their potential benefits, efficiency, and ability to manage a wide variety of problems for different populations make this a very attractive governmental plan. The benefits for the older single are clear: affordable or free personal care and house help, companionship and friendship, and an increased sense of security. Furthermore, it is common for homeowners to accept rent at significantly reduced rates in exchange for assistance, which provides an additional source of income for the financially strained older single.

Another model gaining popularity is grandchildren moving in with their grandparents. They look after their grandparents while living comfortably without the need to pay rent.[55] In other cases, older singles rent their spare rooms to travelers and benefit from the companionship and security of having someone around. Indeed, a new website called the "Freebird Club" (thefreebirdclub.com) promotes this idea by combining the qualities of Airbnb with a community platform. The website made special adjustments, such as sending clear notifications via text messages so that elders who struggle with emails can communicate with guests more easily. The platform operates as a business and community for seniors all over the world, undoubtedly benefiting older singles the most. In fact, the founder started this enterprise because he saw how much his widowed father enjoyed hosting people at his beautiful house.[56]

Finally, older singles often find resources within their own communities and neighborhoods. An increasing number of charities and government-run programs offer to make daily calls to senior citizens living alone.[57] In California, for example, there are approximately 250 community-based adult service centers statewide.[58] Maybe more importantly, many voluntary and unofficial initiatives support seniors within the community, offering classes, physical activities, and social gatherings. Shannon, who is in her fifties, left a comment on a *New York Times* article in which she describes her relationship with her older neighbors:

> I plan to take care of my older friends as they age. Some of them have children, but the children live thousands of miles away in some cases. The best social security is the community you build before you get old: do things for other people, trade favors, listen to them, and build the kind of bonds that will last when they really need you. One thing that helps is living in a stable community. I have lived in the same neighborhood for 25 years. It's a small rural neighborhood on a dead-end street. Most of my neighbors are beloved friends in their late sixties and early seventies. I am in my early fifties. When I retire, they will be approaching the age of needing a lot of care. I look forward to it.[59]

Back to Adam, thirty-two, who fears being physically constrained in old age: Despite not needing potential help until well into the future; despite the high chance of divorce or widowhood; despite the considerable gap between expectation and actual need; and despite the many extramarital options for support, Adam is still afraid of aging unmarried. His feelings pose a challenge. Why does he hold on to these fears?

Indeed, certain evidence suggests this is not merely a simple physical fear but also an emotional one ingrained in childhood.[60] Growing up, children are accustomed to being around many kids their age. This forms the basis of the common educational system. In kindergarten, school, and even college, children are surrounded by peers and those who protect and care for them. Slowly, each child's individual path diverges, and adults enter environments that are less socially intensive and less protective. It is no coincidence that when people separate from peers and protective figures, motivation to find a partner peaks.

Interestingly, though, the need for someone to assuage one's fears does not last. In fact, one study shows that the desire to partner declines sharply with age, even after taking into account selection into marriage and other intervening mechanisms.[61] While around a quarter of those unmarried or outside of a stable relationship aged twenty-five to thirty-four have no desire to marry, this ratio jumps to around two-thirds of singles aged fifty-five to sixty-nine, even among those who never married. Thus, the psychosociological pressure is highest in early adulthood, forming a bell curve, where the twenty-five-to-thirty-four-year-old age group is at the peak of wishing to marry.

Instead, happy older singles are those who succeed in feeling safe in various social arrangements into their adulthood, without the need to be married. Some of them—like Theresa Clerc, whose project helps elder women live together in Paris; Christine Perkins from Ohio, who constructed a shared home for herself and three friends; and Jacob, who lives with a student—take the initiative to ensure someone will be there, despite being single, in an innovative yet responsible way.

The Self behind Prejudices and Stereotypes against Older Singles

Older singles face a double social challenge: dealing with the stigma of being both old and single.[62] Long-term singlehood draws considerable criticism that implies "something is wrong" with that person,[63] and older adults endure further prejudice that assumes they are less healthy, less funny, and needier.[64] Giovanni, fifty-four, who was born in Italy and has lived in northern Israel for the past three decades, said in an interview: "When you enter a restaurant and you're alone, they always look at you like you're a weirdo. That wasn't always like that. Up to not so many years ago, I would go up to Eilat on my own and sit on the beach, and people would come—you know, girls, doesn't matter, 'How are you doing?' Because we were more or less at the same age. Today I show up like that, you know, they take distance, who is this maniac by himself? It's an age problem."

Giovanni experiences the social prejudices twice: Being alone feels weird to him, and this feeling only strengthens with age. When he was younger, being alone was forgivable in certain circumstances, like at the beach; but at his present age, it is not forgivable anymore in any situation. However, the fourth theme I found in my interviews and analysis suggests that happy older singles adjust their self-identities in order to deal with these societal pressures and prejudices.

Among older singles, self-perception varies between the never-married and the divorced or widowed. The long-term never-married set a good example for healthy self-adjustment. Early studies show that the never-married enjoy an advantage in their old age over other marital statuses because they never used marriage as a form of self-validation, and because they often develop habits suitable to their social situation.[65] In other words, long-term singles become accustomed to seeking opportunities for socializing, hence they have strong social networks around which they typically construct their identities. Thus, even amid criticism, prejudices, or social isolation, a sudden life change is less likely to affect their self-perception and, in turn, their levels of happiness.[66] Indeed, it was found that the older never-married show fewer signs of stress, are more likely to enjoy living alone, and report needing less social support than the newly single.[67]

Accordingly, the happy older singles I met had downplayed the differences between themselves and their married friends and family.

While some admitted to having been embarrassed at times by being single, they also insisted on not being perceived as an "outsider" or inferior just because of their lifestyle and marital status. Insisting on being equal to others and undeserving of prejudice is a source of strength for older singles. Some even emphasize their good qualities and what brings meaning to their lives; and by doing so, they construct an alternative identity. For example, Marry, sixty, who never married and lives in Georgia, told me in an interview: "If you're being sensible about it, you're using your single time as a time to grow and develop and be your real self.... It's up to the individual to kind of balance that, or to be doing the kinds of things and hearing the kinds of things that make one feel that it's okay. And it should be okay, for people to choose to be single."

Marry emphasizes the strength in being single and focuses on self-growth and development. It is no coincidence that immediately after constructing this notion, she also concludes that singleness is perfectly fine. By doing this, Marry basically applies ideas from positive psychology theory. She seeks to minimize and prevent the effects of certain negative thoughts by fostering a positive attitude toward herself and her subjective experiences.[68]

This raises the question of how positive psychology can improve happiness among older singles. Indeed, practical applications of positive psychology include practices such as positive affirmations, writing exercises, and self-reward.[69] The question is whether such practices improve the well-being of older singles, as Marry argues.

Although there are not many studies focusing on older singles, there is still enough evidence to suggest that the positive-psychology approach might have a significant impact on them. For example, studies find a strong, positive correlation between greater elder happiness and higher levels of physical health, cognitive function, and social capital.[70] However, something interesting happens when positive self-rating is added: Many of those who are not aging successfully as a result of poor health, loss of cognitive function, or limited social capital still report positive feelings about the self and rate themselves as happy. Positive self-rating, then, is an important factor that can offset other, more objective factors.[71]

This is closely related to the issue of one's attitude toward death. For older people, death is ever-present. Unlike younger people, most older people saw their parents dying, while some have witnessed their friends and siblings suffer from severe health issues.[72] However, among the happy older singles I met, death is framed more as "just another" event in their lives, and this perception leads them to see it as less frightening. They talked about it openly in our interviews, and it was apparent from their discourse that although they continually think about it, as everyone else does, they do so with a positive attitude and readiness.

I Am Surrounded with Love

The fifth theme is the construction of alternatives to intimate relationships. Although social support can be helpful for individuals of all ages, as I will show in chapter 4, older singles benefit from social capital in particular, and from developing diverse social networks, given their unique set of characteristics, needs, resources, and challenges. One study, based on a survey of 1,003 elderly participants, asserts that social support predicts life satisfaction in old age, and the effect even increased for the oldest participants in the study.[73] Another study shows that social support helps older singles simultaneously decrease anxiety and increase motivation to lead active and healthy lifestyles.[74] The benefits of friendship for older singles are very clear: in the absence of a spouse and children with whom to socialize organically, friends play an important role in ensuring the well-being of older singles.

While most people think of friends as people in the same peer groups, older singles can enjoy a wide variety of friendships.[75] In particular, they may have friends who are both single and married, of both sexes, and from different generations.[76] Earlier research found that the older married individuals typically view cross-sex friendships as taboo or as a potential threat to their spouse.[77] In contrast, more recent research suggests that such normative barriers limit older singles much less often, and as a result they are more likely to have friends of the opposite sex.[78] This variety of friendships results in greater well-being among older singles. Barbara, for example, is sixty-eight and has been widowed for twenty-four years. She writes: "I find myself reaching out, calling everyone I know and maybe just one has the time to go somewhere and do something. It works all the time. The more I reach out the better I feel and so do they. Being alone too long will eventually lead to depression. I've retired at 65 but kept busy with everything I could, gardening, trips, and love to help volunteer at the nursing homes. I find days that I've stayed home—others call and check up on me, I do the same."[79]

Barbara builds her life around activities with friends. She energetically pursues social activities and reaches out to her friends frequently. She said that this strategy helps her in raising her well-being, and her friends warmly welcome this approach. Another example is Kendra, fifty-two, who writes: "Being lonely has no age limits. Being sick has no age limits. When one lives their life in a way that is giving and supportive of others, they will receive love and support in their time of need. Conversely, if they live a more selfish, self-absorbed life, they might find themselves devoid of such support when needed."[80] Kendra contemplates being unmarried in older age and wonders whether she misses things or risks being lonely more than her married counterparts. Her answer is very clear: investing in social networks is rewarding and reassuring in times of need. This strengthens her and gives her meaning in a society obsessed with marriage.

While social support can manifest from having people around you, such as friends and extended family, or from living in shared communities, today's elders—and particularly elderly singles—also stand to gain social capital from using technology that allows otherwise isolated individuals to communicate with people they know and love, as well as with complete strangers. In fact, the wide variety of online communities, specialized help services, and support networks available for older singles can be very effective in increasing their happiness.[81] The following exchange illustrates how two older singles communicated and arranged to meet through the comments section of an article at the website *Senior Planet*.[82]

> Gordon: I just lost my wife in January 2017. I miss having a person to live with and share with. At 87 I may sound old, but I have a dear friend aged 55 who finds me attractive but is married and not about to disrupt her family by leaving him. Any interest? [6/26/2017, 8:25 p.m.]

> Vivian: I also live alone and have children 33 and 26. I'm still working, but evenings and dinners really lonely. [6/29/2017, 11:54 a.m.]

> Gordon: Vivian: if you look me up on Facebook you will see who I am ... as well as a lot of photos of my precious recently departed Beautiful wife of 68 years.... Thanks for sending me your message. [6/29/2017, 1:14 p.m.]

> Vivian: Hi Gordon, thank you for the response. It would be nice to have someone to share dinners, movies and just talking. I'll try and find you on Facebook.... What are your interests? It would be nice to get to know you. Enjoy your day. Vivian :)) [7/5/2017, 1:54 p.m.]

Gordon and Vivian probably continued talking on Facebook and arranged to meet for companionship. While stereotypes suggest that elders such as these two struggle to use smartphones, the Internet, and social networking websites, recent evidence shows that this is becoming less and less of a boundary.[83] In fact, over the last decade Internet usage and access to digital technology have been key to improving life satisfaction among the elderly, with the effect increasing in magnitude for weaker and at-risk groups.[84] Therefore, single seniors, who are at increased risk of isolation and loneliness, stand to gain from improved communication with friends and loved ones, particularly from younger generations.

Older singles also relate to their family resources differently than their married counterparts, placing greater importance on kinship. While married elders rely more on their spouses, older singles—especially the childless—activate broad family support networks in times of need.[85] Many singles take their roles as family members very seriously, with recent studies suggesting they value these roles more than married people do.[86] Indeed, in my interviews I found that happy older singles actively prepared for singlehood in later life by investing in their wider families. In particular, the unmarried elders are more likely to maintain close relationships with siblings and, in some cases, to cohabitate with a brother or sister.[87]

Some research directs special attention to the roles played by nieces and nephews in an older single's life.[88] Children usually know aunts and uncles the longest, and the shared family history, long-term relationship, and often comparable values facilitate meaningful and reciprocal connections as the aunt or uncle ages, especially if they never marry. A female blogger, exact age unknown, writes: "I'm a proud Auntie of a niece that I'm overly protective about, and a dog I treat as if she were my child. I know it's not the same but it works for me."[89]

In addition to investment in the extended family, community-based services are critical and effective in abating the feelings of loneliness and reducing the negative effects of the unique challenges facing older singles. Services such as senior centers that organize activities and clubs are especially effective because they provide shelter and security in emergency situations. These centers also cater to elders' need to spend time with others who face challenges similar to their own. They share interests with like-minded peers and participate in events that are suitable to their age brackets. Indeed, studies show that older singles, and in particular women, most frequently participate in center activities and, as a result, most easily expand their social networks.[90] These services are crucial for older singles who are childless, who live far from their children, and/or who are members of a minority group.[91] For them, senior centers increase the utility of social support and services.

Finally, animal-assisted therapy, or even simply owning a pet at home, has been shown to reduce agitation, depression, and negative behavior patterns such as anger and self-harm, increase levels of activity, and promote physical and mental health.[92] In my interview with

Tatiana, sixty-five, in a coffee shop, she did not mention being in any special and meaningful relationship at the moment. But after the interview, I returned to the table and found her in a Skype talk with her dog and dog sitter. It was a pivotal moment for me when I realized that her relationship with the dog is a core function of her life. She did not think to mention this during the interview, but when asked, she said her dog is indeed very dear to her and fills her life with joy and empathy.

While much of the research into pet ownership and animal-assisted therapy focuses on the relationship with the animal as a form of treatment for mental health issues, evidence increasingly confirms the positive effect of pet ownership in reducing social isolation and boredom among the elderly and solitary,[93] particularly with animals such as dogs, which require leaving the house and exercising. Walking outside with pets can improve people's communal involvement and social responses, specifically by increasing the likelihood of engaging in social interactions and increasing the length of conversations.[94] This is especially important for older singles, who are often already outside the labor market and have fewer opportunities to interact with others.

AGING HAPPILY UNMARRIED

The question of singlehood in old age encapsulates, in a way, the core principles of happy singlehood. The idea of being single in the late stages of life makes us confront some of the greatest fears that lead many to wedlock.[95] The results of my study question whether marriage is the only solution that prevents loneliness and increases well-being in old age. My findings show that while people tend to marry from fear of being lonely in old age, those who remain unmarried possess a repertoire of frameworks that better prepare them for single living. By accepting their relationship status, learning to enjoy solitude, building a network to assist with physical issues, overcoming stereotypes and prejudices, and finding alternatives to romantic relationships, long-term singles adapt to living alone and are happier and less lonely.

The causality in these findings is not immediately clear. To what extent is the repertoire for improving singles' well-being developed from their having to adapt to their reality, as opposed to the repertoire predisposing them to singlehood? It might well be that those who enjoy solitude, for example, tend to become or stay single, while the opposite is not true. This supposition touches upon the bigger question of whether the strategies described in this book are applicable.

As presented in the results, and based on the many other interviews I conducted, the stories of singles adapting to their reality suggest this repertoire of strategies can also be acquired or learned. People's ability to adopt these strategies once they realize they will stay single for a long period of time was salient throughout the interviews I conducted and posts I analyzed. Sofia is an excellent example. It took her nine years to start a blog, become aware of her situation, and accept it, and another year to adopt certain strategies to flourish in her singlehood. These strategies were not part of her routine, but she annexed them by transforming her lifestyle from singlehood to happy singlehood.

The Inuit folk story teaches us that we cannot always choose when we are alone, but we can decide to not *feel* lonely. The elderly woman might not have expected to be abandoned, just as a newly married young couple does not anticipate loneliness following separation or a spouse's death. Yet she coped with the new reality and thrived by making friends with the insects. Similarly, even singles who feel forced into singlehood can adopt strategies that make the best use of the abundance of opportunities available to them.

What may be surprising here is exactly how much older singles can enjoy their lives. In the folk story, the fox that was supposed to maul the Inuit woman to death instead brought her to a young and vivacious future. In the same way, we treat singlehood as a sure condemnation to suffering and loneliness; but as it turns out, long-term singlehood nurtures our adaptability and gives us the tools for preventing loneliness in old age while also nurturing true happiness. The older singles I encountered who forged creative social, financial, and housing solutions to meet the challenges of later life alone, have much to teach us. By understanding how older singles cope and thrive, we can understand how to improve the well-being of both singles and couples alike and, perhaps more significantly, open up an important discussion about why we marry in the first place.

CHAPTER THREE

Defying Social Pressure

I entered the community center of a beautiful building in the heart of liberal Tel Aviv, not knowing what to expect. I had been forwarded an email promising an introduction to an exciting workshop: How to Feel Good in Being Single, a series of meetings that would debut that evening.

I was thrilled. Here stood a perfect opportunity to see how singles could benefit from professional help in constructing a happy single-hood. I was eager to learn more. The sign at the entrance read: Anonymous Singles—Floor 4. With every step I took in the stairwell, I grew more excited. I knew I would witness the beginning of a movement.

The impending workshop shimmered like an oasis in the desert, a place of welcome relief and acceptance in a nation where family values are so ingrained, and where the birthrate is the highest among all countries that belong to the Organization for Economic Cooperation and Development. This would be a chance for real refreshment.

The room was crowded when I entered: over thirty people, most of them thirty to forty-five years old. The meeting began. Excitement pulsed through the air. A breakthrough for Israeli singles?

"Please raise your hand if you are *happy* with your singlehood," the workshop leader asked. Only one woman raised her hand.

"Please raise your hand if you are *unhappy* with your singlehood." Two women raised their hands, including the same woman who raised her hand previously. She was apparently ambivalent about her situation.

What about the others? I thought. Hearing whispers around me, one after another, I immediately received an answer. "Well, I'm fine, I'm just sick of people telling me I should marry ASAP," said one woman from the back.

"Me too," said a guy sitting in the middle. "I'm tired of hearing I'm too picky."

Someone else said, "People assume I don't love myself or I don't have enough self-confidence."

The workshop leader resumed control. "Okay, thank you, everyone. In this workshop, I will teach you tips and tricks on how to find the perfect match. We will practice different strategies in dating and empowering one another. You will very soon find a partner." She continued her introduction: "We will also learn how to write a perfect dating profile and how to flirt properly."

Wait, I thought, *they just asked for something different from this proposition.* Some people in the room may be interested in hearing about tricks and tips on dating, flirting, and developing alluring profiles, but what about what *really* bothers them? What about those who want to be comfortable in single life, the very situation they are in now? Surely, many of the participants were not looking for magic, romance, or unicorns. They simply wanted to adapt to their situations and defy the social pressure they experience.

Well, I should have known better; I was too optimistic. "Anonymous Singles Meetings" already means everything. Replace *singles* with *addicts, gamblers,* or *alcoholics* and you sense the stigma transferred to the participants. That is, singlehood is to be avoided or overcome, or—even worse—it is a trap, something to be escaped. And if you cannot escape, seek professional help immediately. Whatever you do, do not tell anyone you "suffer from singleness." It is unattractive and more than a little embarrassing. Like an unsightly skin rash, hide it and maybe no one will notice.

Tel Aviv is not too different from most other places. Across the world, cultural and societal attitudes are instrumental in determining individuals' choices regarding relationships and marriage. Children are being socialized and educated to marry and build stable family units.[1] Singlehood is still frequently viewed negatively in the eyes of both society and the individual, particularly singleness among women.[2]

Social pressure to marry pushes against the rising number of global singles and thus poses a puzzle: How and why do singles increasingly choose to stay uncoupled despite such pressure? What new strategies do they employ to overcome social stigma and to defy the surrounding stress?

To answer these questions, it is helpful to begin by comprehending the problem of social pressure, stigma, and discrimination against singles. That will allow us to focus, afterward, on strategies that happy singles use to overcome social pressure: increased awareness, self-acceptance, positive self-perception, direct defiance of discriminatory practices, and empowerment.

SINGLES' STIGMA AND SOCIAL PRESSURE

The origins of the word *stigma*, which can be roughly translated as "blemish" or "mark," are set deep in ancient Greek culture. *Stigma* referred to an easily visible tattoo or burn on the skin of traitors, criminals, or slaves that readily identified them as morally inferior, as "polluted individuals" who should be publicly avoided and shunned. The meaning has evolved since those early days, with the idea of stigma existing today in many different forms, affecting individuals for various reasons, including mental and physical disability, race, ethnicity, health, and educational background.[3]

Once individuals are stigmatized, it negatively influences their emotions and beliefs. In particular, negative psychological impacts of stigma engender mental illness,[4] reduced self-esteem,[5] depression,[6] and a negative self-identity, especially in threatening situations.[7] In addition, stigma directly precipitates educational, economic, and legal consequences—for example, friends and coworkers may exclude the stigmatized individual from certain activities because they feel that this single individual is not mature or friendly enough to be part of their social circle.[8] This may even shape the affected person's behavior and can cause further deterioration of his or her socioeconomic status.

Although it might surprise some, singles are heavily stigmatized despite comprising a majority of the adult population in many Western countries. In one study I mentioned earlier, one thousand undergraduate students listed characteristics they associated with married and single individuals.[9] Compared to single people, married individuals were more likely to be described as mature, happy, loving, and honest. Conversely, singles were perceived negatively as immature, insecure, self-centered, sad, and lonely. A subsequent part of the study, which asked the same students to describe married and singles at two different ages (twenty-five and forty years old), found that the negative traits of singles are perceived as more pronounced with age. Forty-year-old singles were deemed to be particularly socially immature, not well adjusted, and more envious—with gaps of over 50 percent in some measures—compared to the scores married people received. Moreover, the living arrangements of unmarried people were considered less optimal. As a result, singles are often defined by what they are not (e.g., married) or what they lack (e.g., a nuclear family or partner), creating a reality wherein singleness is seen as a deviation from the norm.[10]

These social norms are manifested both in discrimination against singles, known as "singlism,"[11] and in the focus on marriage, known as "matrimania,"[12] which combine to isolate singles. The negative images of singles are further fed and maintained by a wide variety of media and literature that paint them as undesirable.[13] Singles internalize this discrimination, stigmatization, and stereotyping spreading throughout society, practices that create negative social, educational, economic, and legal connotations for those considering going solo after divorce or the death of a spouse or simply choosing singleness in the first place.[14]

To estimate the extent of discrimination against singles, I analyzed the European Social Survey. Unfortunately, when it comes to discrimination, there is no direct question in the survey about singlism. However, by eliminating other discrimination types—ethnicity, race, language, religion, age, gender, disability, and nationality—I could measure and infer the extent to which singlism exists. From there, I found that unmarried people experience 50 percent more discrimination than married people.

Most worrying is the fact that, unlike other disadvantaged groups, singles often go unprotected from prejudice, frequently because singlehood is not viewed as meriting protection. The pressure to marry fits the relationship-and-family-structure hegemony. Therefore, the expectation that others are either married or, if not, do not want to be single are two assumptions so heavily normalized that those guilty of singlism are unaware they are abusing singles.

Many times, this prejudice is most pronounced within the family. For instance, Marta, who is forty-two and living in Los Angeles, far away from her parents in Chicago, spoke to me about still feeling pressure, with which many can identify:

> My family doesn't make me feel good about not being married. My father tells me I am being stupid for not finding some guy to take care of me. My mother always tells me if she didn't have to worry about me, then her life would be good. I tell her being married is not really security, because men leave and abandon their wives all the time. But then her response is that it is harder for men to leave if you are married to them. And she tells me stuff like, "If your boyfriend doesn't marry you, then he is going to leave you just like my former boyfriend of fourteen years did."

Unfortunately, Marta receives the message that she is "stupid," insecure, worrying her mother, and prone to abandonment. Within her own family, Marta tackles many fears and prejudices that singles all over the world experience in various contexts, either among family and friends or at work. In particular, negative attitudes toward singles increase with age, and stigma is especially strong for older singles, who are more likely to be viewed as vulnerable or reliant on others.[15]

Sadly, Marta's status might be considered more acceptable were she not only younger but also a man. Evidence suggests that single women endure more stigma than single men.[16] In these studies, gender differences are attributed to the extra discrimination, prejudice, and societal expectations placed on and levied against women, who, compared to men, hold fewer positions of status and authority, typically work under inequitable terms, and more often become homemakers.

Stigma is also more prevalent among traditional, religious, and socially conservative individuals who place great importance on family formation.[17] Consequently, single mothers in traditional societies are particularly at risk of being stigmatized, since singleness combined with child-rearing deviates most extremely from the traditional family norm.[18]

SOME EXAMPLES OF DISCRIMINATION AGAINST SINGLES

There are many ways (overt and covert) that society excludes and discriminates against singles. The literature on this topic barely scrapes the surface. Consider just a few fields in which singlism is common.

One famous case involves Shaela Evenson, who was fired from Butte Central Catholic Schools in 2014 after the diocese received a letter saying she was unmarried and pregnant.[19] Several years of tedious legal proceedings passed before a confidential settlement was reached with the school district and the Roman Catholic Diocese of Helena. Despite certain exemptions, religious organizations and schools cannot discriminate against unmarried pregnant teachers by firing them; American courts strike down this practice time and again. But discriminatory practices persist nevertheless.[20]

In another case, Zelda de Groen, twenty-four, a British teacher who was fired from an Orthodox Jewish nursery school for "living in sin" with her boyfriend, won her case of religious and sexual discrimination.[21] Zelda was subjected to a humiliating interview by her bosses, who told her that at twenty-three she should be married. The employment tribunal ruled that such treatment was "humiliating, degrading, and offensive."[22]

We are accustomed to viewing race, ethnicity, and sexual orientation as reasons for discrimination, but being unmarried is perhaps just as common a reason for firing singles or not hiring them in the first place, even if they simply make their own choices in their private lives (sufficient statistics have not yet been compiled). As recently as 2010, former Republican senator Jim DeMint of South Carolina explicitly said that "an unmarried woman who's sleeping with her boyfriend... shouldn't be in the classroom."[23] Many singles even do not pass school selection committees in rural towns, while others are tacitly pressured or even told outright to stay away from the children.[24]

Given this belief that singles' nonprofessional lives are not as valid or important as those of married people, singles are also frequently discriminated against in everyday office life. They are called upon to cover for colleagues and work overtime, under the assumption that they have the time to do so. They are expected to travel more often and to take vacation shifts when their colleagues with partners go home to their families. As a result, singles can typically work extra hours for little or no reward. A subtle, yet very common, supposition is described in the following post by an anonymous, unmarried male:

I've noticed the most singlism issues in the work environment. Married couples, especially those with kids, seem to think their schedule is somehow superior to mine, because you know, I'm single therefore I don't have responsibilities like they do. A few weeks ago, my company was holding a training class, offered on 2 separate days. As soon as I received word about the class, I immediately signed up for the first date, as I had the other day off and was planning to go to my best friend's BBQ....

A few weeks went by and 2 days before the training class was held, a company meeting was held. The training dates were brought up, and ... complaints started coming in. "Well, you know, I have daycare arrangements for that day, so I really can't," or "My kid's playoffs are on that day, can't make it," or "My kids have doctors' appointments that day and it'll be [a] long time to get them in if I reschedule," blah blah. So then they asked if people from the first date would be willing to switch to the second, as there can only be so many per class due to equipment availability, to help meet the others' accommodations. Of course, many were looking to me because they knew I was single, which in their eyes meant, "He can switch because he's single and doesn't have responsibilities." I simply said, sorry, can't switch, I have plans for a BBQ that day. Then it basically turned into[:] my kids are more important that your "leisure" BBQ.[25]

This story is one of many where singles are pushed to abandon their priorities and work harder. But besides being required to surrender leisure activities, singles also find that singleness entails lower earnings. One study found that married individuals earn approximately 26 percent more than singles in equivalent jobs.[26] Furthermore, many employers subsidize the cost of health care and other benefits for employees' spouses and domestic partners but offer no such care to parents, siblings, or close friends of single employees.[27] These practices and prejudices also spill over into job promotions, where singles progress more slowly than coupled individuals.[28]

Another way singlism manifests is through legislation that systematically advantages married individuals without also offering assistance to singles. For example, some countries entitle couples and families to governmental insurance, Social Security, and other benefits that singles cannot access.[29] Married individuals may also be granted special leave to care for their spouses (for example, in the United States under the Family and Medical Leave Act), while singles usually do not enjoy the same freedom to care for someone equally close. While some countries, particularly in the West, legally forbid such marital-status discrimination, these laws are far from universal; and even where they do exist, they are not necessarily implemented effectively.[30] Karen, who posted in a Facebook group for singles, deems it a matter of social inequality: "[I] met with my financial adviser yesterday for our annual review.

I was not aware of how badly singles are discriminated against post-retirement.... I'm infuriated, particularly in the light of the tax breaks in the United States for the wealthy and large corporations who can actually AFFORD this kind of steep tax rate."[31]

Karen is only one witness to singlism through taxes and legislation. In a detailed article published by *The Atlantic*, the authors reveal that over a lifetime, an unmarried person can pay as much as a million dollars more than a married one for health care, taxes, IRAs, Social Security, and more. In fact, the authors found over a thousand laws providing overt legal or financial benefits to married couples that are unavailable to singles. This is despite US Federal Code, which, in title 5, part III, says: "The President may prescribe rules which shall prohibit ... discrimination because of marital status."[32]

Societal prejudice against singles, and a preference for married couples, often extends into other fields, such as housing. One study tested the reaction of fifty-four real estate agents regarding their preferences, among three options, for renting out a property: a married couple, a cohabiting couple in a romantic relationship, or a man and a woman presented as "just friends."[33] While the potential residents were described similarly in terms of education, job, age, and interests, the clear majority (61 percent) of agents preferred the married couple, 24 percent were willing to rent to the cohabiting couple, but only 15 percent said they would choose to rent to the two friends.

Moreover, when one of the real estate agents preferred married couples and did not want to rent to the singles, the investigators challenged the decision as discriminatory. The typical response from the agents was to use the two friends' singleness as an explanation in and of itself, denying prejudice and discrimination. Unlike racism, sexism, or other commonly acknowledged forms of discrimination, singlism went unrecognized in this instance as a discriminatory practice. Elusive as it might sound, such discrimination has far-reaching implications on singles' well-being, as discussed in the following section.

THE IMPLICATIONS OF DISCRIMINATION
AGAINST SINGLES

As studies on other minority groups show, discrimination against singles can be quite damaging to their mental health and well-being (unfortunately, no clinical or statistical studies have yet measured the consequences of singlism). For instance, one study investigated the potential role of perceived discrimination in reduced mental health among lesbian women and gay men.[34] In this study, analysis of data from the National Survey of Midlife Development in the United States revealed correlations between perceived discrimination and indicators of mental health such as psychological distress, psychiatric disorders, feeling life is harder, and sensing interference with life.

Other evidence reveals how perceived discrimination can impair the mental health of racial minorities. A study involving young African American adults indicates that poor mental health could be predicted based on the number of racist or discriminatory events reported by the participants.[35] Similar conclusions have also been reached by those studying the mental health of refugees and immigrants.[36]

Subsequent and more recent meta-analyses have concluded that perceived discrimination affects not only mental health but also physical health.[37] In fact, perceived discrimination strongly associates with weight gain, obesity, and higher blood pressure among minorities.[38] In other studies, discrimination correlates with elevated levels of smoking, alcohol consumption, and substance abuse.[39] Evidence linking discriminatory practices and physical health has also been found for women regardless of their minority status.[40]

While the mechanisms affecting mental and physical health vary for different types of discrimination, the overall trend suggests that singles are likely to suffer regardless, something that my own research confirms. In my study, many interviewees reported on the damaging effect of discrimination. Jon, for example, who is fifty-three and living in Manchester, England, said in our interview: "I felt a lot of pressure from other people, pressure on myself. Gosh! You know, 'Better hurry up and find somebody.' I think it did weigh on me. I think I felt dissatisfied for a while."

These kinds of feelings are particularly strong for the widowed and divorced, who, in some societies and contexts, are more heavily stigmatized than other singles.[41] In fact, my analysis shows that discrimination harms the well-being of divorced, separated, or widowed singles up to 25 percent more than married individuals, *ceteris paribus.*

This negative effect is increased in situations where the social environment is unsupportive. While it has been shown that one's in-group support reduces the negative effects of perceived discrimination on mental health,[42] the lack of a supportive community may make some single populations more vulnerable, particularly the older ones.

Discriminatory practices and social pressure may be defied, however. Happy singles are those who have learned to make their way around and even forcefully confront these phenomena. It is time, therefore, to delve into the "toolbox" that, at least partly, facilitates happy, discrimination-free singlehood.

DEFYING SOCIAL PRESSURE AND DISCRIMINATION

Despite apparent cultural aversions to singleness, and despite governmental policies that discriminate against unmarried individuals,[43] an increasing number of people are not only choosing to be single but also thriving as a result.[44] While singles have traditionally been inured to negative self-perception, recent demographic changes have facilitated the creation of a "new" single who is less susceptible, or even immune, to singlism and stigmatization.[45] In turn, more recent evidence suggests that emerging new singles are happier than traditional singles.[46] The strategies benefiting the new single, however, have yet to be fully explored. Therefore, in the interviews I conducted, I tried to identify those strategies and practices that help singles defy social pressure, stigma, and stereotyping.

Increased Awareness of Discrimination against Singles

The first strategy disclosed in the interviews is simple to understand but quite hard to implement: awareness of discrimination and social pressure surrounding singles. A study investigating the effects of stigma-awareness on singles' self-esteem discovered a profound unawareness of singlism even among singles themselves.[47] Only 4 percent of singles spontaneously listed "singles" as a stigmatized group. And when explicitly asked whether singles were stigmatized, only 30 percent of singles and 23 percent of coupled people answered affirmatively. By comparison, 100 percent of gay males, 90 percent of obese individuals, 86 percent of African Americans, and 72 percent of women acknowledged that their group was discriminated against. Considering these results, it is unsurprising that the practice of singlism is considered acceptable.

Maybe more importantly, this research indicates that participants who increased their awareness of singlism also increased their sense of self-worth and happiness, signaling that discrimination-awareness is one critical pathway to alleviating the consequences of singlism. My interviews and data analysis also concur with the idea that happy singles are those who are aware of the social pressure they experience. In fact, becoming aware was the first step they took to deal with their situation and to confront social pressure. Lauri posted the following in this regard: "Realizing that I wasn't nuts for recognizing singlism and matrimania in the world, I actually feel better about myself and paint a clearer picture of things. I'm glad I can notice it now. It does make me fume sometimes, but really, it always had, I just didn't realize there was a reason for my anger."[48]

Simply noticing and identifying discrimination makes Lauri feel better. Singles' awareness and its effect on their mental health might be hard to understand. But consider other marginalized groups who, through social movements, have raised their own acknowledgment of the situation they are in and put the issue of discrimination on the public agenda, thereby boosting their mental health. In fact, a social movement might prove particularly necessary today, given that singles are simply not aware of the negative social attitudes toward them. Lauri testified further in a later post: "I wonder how many people don't recognize it as discrimination. I think there was a time in my 20s when I first started working that I felt like it was actually 'correct' to treat me like that."[49]

Positive Self-Perception

The second strategy my study revealed is the construction of a positive self-perception, which, in turn, contributes to singles' well-being, a fact supported by other studies.[50] For example, a study of 664 young adults found that positive interpersonal and social self-perception resulted in a hopeful outlook and increased well-being.[51] Research has also shown that positive self-perception correlates with high levels of happiness, especially (but not only) in strongly individualistic cultures.[52]

What is not clear, however, is how positive self-perception affects singles' happiness, and how it succeeds in defying social pressure. Researchers have yet to ask whether self-perception plays the same role in happiness for singles as it does for married and coupled individuals. Self-perception, in this sense, might be key to understanding how singles manage social pressure and thus raise their well-being.

Indeed, according to my findings, positive self-image and self-confidence are crucial to increasing happiness.[53] They work better for singles precisely because their problem is mainly social: many people around them criticize them, inhibit their self-confidence, and increase their negative self-image, sometimes without even noticing.[54]

Patricia, who is sixty years old and divorced, lives in Milledgeville, Georgia. She said in our interview: "I think it ... depends on how confident you are in your personal self. Like, if you were going around saying, 'Ugh, I hate being single,' then of course people will comment on it. But because it's not an issue in my life, ... I made a choice, and I am absolutely good with it."

Patricia was in good spirits throughout the interview. She thinks of her situation positively and is full of confidence. She suggests that her assurance in her choice to be single connects to her overall positive self-perception and helps her feel good about herself and her reality as a single woman.

Lina, thirty-seven, who lives in Frankfurt, Germany, puts even more emphasis on a positive self-image and self-acceptance:

> I think a lot of that [one's self-image and self-acceptance] depends on the image that you put out. If you accept yourself, then it's more likely that other people will just accept you. Funny story is, when I got to Germany, the people in the church, even though I wasn't married, they kept asking me if I was planning on having more babies: "When you're going to have more kids?" I was like: "Calm down, I need to be married." After a while there, it was just okay. But when I first got there, it didn't kind of dawn on them. So, this is why I say, if you accept yourself in general, people around you will accept you the way you are, and it won't matter to them.

My statistical analysis shows a similar connection between positive self-perception and the happiness of divorced, widowed, and never-married individuals. This effect is stronger for these groups than for married people. The unmarried group gains more from every additional uptick in their own positive-self-perception scale. Looking at it differently, and accounting for all other variables such as age, education, income, gender, and having children, an unmarried person with positive self-perception gains close to a 30 percent increase in happiness over an unmarried person without positive self-perception. As Maya, thirty-one, who was born in New York and currently lives in London, summarizes it: "It's interesting to see, and [to] really put it out there to people, that they are all on their own journeys. Seeing that it's a process of becoming much more comfortable with who you are, gaining that better sense of self."

Optimism plays a similar role. Having an optimistic outlook was a central theme in my interviews, and my findings matched some evidence from other cases showing that optimism mediates between self-perception and subjective well-being.[55] Jorgen, forty-six, who lives in Sweden, said: "I don't feel like I'm single; what makes me happy is that I feel like I'm protected, and I'm not worried too much. [I] just live the good life and that's it." Like Jorgen, optimistic singles who feel secure and less worried tend to experience improved happiness as a result. In my statistical analysis I found that singles who hold optimistic views experience around 35 percent more happiness than those without.

That optimism helps one feel better is quite obvious. The question is whether optimism plays a more important role for singles as part of their positive, forward-looking self-perception when compared to the self-perceptions of married individuals. I found an answer to this question in another statistical analysis I conducted, in which optimism proved particularly significant for unmarried people. Here, too, never-married, divorced, and widowed individuals increase their subjective well-being over that of married people for every additional uptick on the optimism scale. For example, take two individuals who are similar in all major characteristics, where the only difference is that one is married and the other has never married. If they both hold the highest levels of optimism, the never-married person will shoot up and be equal to the married person in terms of happiness, despite an initial disadvantage of 0.7 points on 0–10 scale (and this is even without considering the selection mechanism found in marriage, through which happier people marry). Both divorced and widowed individuals will also narrow the gap significantly in such a case, trailing only 0.2 points behind. In other words, optimism plays a more powerful role in singles' happiness than it does for married and coupled individuals. A plausible explanation is that the *internal* tendency to be positive and forward-looking benefits singles who have no *external* "safety nets," such as children and spouses. This internal tendency develops one's self-assurance and a sense of self-reliance that counters possible adversity.[56]

An additional aspect of positive self-perception is feeling valuable and accomplished, often through work, hobbies, or friends. Singles have a propensity to be friendlier and less materially focused, and they receive more meaning from their work than others do, as I discuss later in this book. Research shows, for example, that singles seek interesting, challenging, and more fulfilling work, and that they immanently gain more from their occupations than married people do.[57]

My analysis supports this research and shows that feeling accomplished and valuable helps the never-married and widowed groups gain a happiness level measuring 0.4 points higher than the gain of married people (on a scale of 0–10), while divorced people gain 0.2 points more the gain of couples. This means that merely feeling accomplished and valuable closes a significant gap between singles and married people. The reason for this is simple: singles find meaning outside of the nuclear family, and it boosts their self-worth.

The three components comprising positive self-perception described in this section—self-confidence, optimism, and feeling valuable— demonstrate possible pathways for improving singles' self-perception. Indeed, positive self-perception is certainly not easy to develop, and the precise way that new singles perceive themselves in relation to others likely depends on several additional factors, such as income,[58] level of education,[59] family support,[60] and religiosity[61] (these same factors also moderate self-esteem for people in general). One study, for example, indicates that higher levels of education, increased family support, and reduced religiosity are associated with singles' higher self-acceptance.[62] Other studies have found that cultural factors, and in particular individualism, moderate the self-esteem of individuals.[63] Therefore, singles' development of positive self-perception should account for these various other life aspects, supporting them both inside out and outside in.

Avoiding Negativity, Choosing Single-Friendly Environments

The third strategy is to avoid the pressure and discrimination surrounding singlehood. Many single-friendly environments are developing in major urban areas such as Los Angeles, London, and Tokyo, where it is considered "cool" to live on your own, with no age limit. There, the creation of single-friendly settings is not limited to such setting for the younger generations: single-friendly networks are also prevalent among middle-aged and senior singles.[64] Justin, a fifty-two-year-old, lauded Los Angeles in our interview: "In places like LA, I notice that most of the people around my age are single.... In a big city, like LA especially, it's more of a playful city than a let's-commit-and-have-babies kind of city.... This is such a fun city to live in."

Metropolises like Los Angeles promote privacy and allow singles to avoid negativity while also providing myriad opportunities to connect with others and to enjoy numerous activities. No wonder singles have flocked to major cities in unprecedented numbers, as shown in chapter 1.

Yet big cities are not the only locations that cater to the needs of contemporary singles. Even in rural, more religious areas, single-friendly environments are emerging, and the single life is a pressing topic in various churches throughout the United States.[65] In 2013, a remarkable article encouraged the Catholic Church to acknowledge and even celebrate the single life, particularly considering the high number of singles in the Catholic tradition.[66] The article relayed the following:

> At the end of the 40-minute sermon, the pastor looked up from his notes and began to ad lib: "I know that over 40% of you are single, so I should probably say something about singleness as well." My ears perked up. Since this pastor was such a scholarly guy[,] and since he had just given an exceptionally thoughtful sermon on marriage, I just *knew* that his brief thoughts on singleness would be equally profound. I leaned forward. "Here's what I want to say to all you single people: Don't have sex before you get married. Then when you get married, make up for lost time [wink, wink]."
>
> ... In a Church that was founded by a single guy, singles are terribly marginalized. There's something wrong with this picture.... We might not be walking down the aisle or gestating a baby, but God is doing some amazing things in our lives—from the "monumental" (such as helping us obtain degrees, launch ministries/businesses, pay off college loans) to the "mundane" (such as helping us serve our neighborhoods, pray for each other).

We must celebrate what God's doing in people's lives, whether it's similar to what God's done in our own lives or not. So, find reasons to throw big parties for the single people in your community.

This article echoed throughout the Catholic community and received many hundreds of supportive responses, including those from priests who decided to take the mission seriously. In these single-friendly environments, the representation and social configuration of single communities create conditions that better promote positive self-perception. By normalizing single lifestyles, these environments help reduce the singlism and matrimania that lead to reduced self-esteem in the first place.[67] Thus, as the number of single-friendly environments grow, singles deliberately seek out these spaces to improve their self-esteem and, consequently, their overall level of well-being.

In addition, single-friendly microsettings are being developed in many places. Co-residency and communal living arrangements provide singles with a supportive environment.[68] Various such solutions have been developed in recent years, including the market-oriented, singles-targeted WeLive, the sister company to the office-by-the-day rental concept WeWork. Currently operating in Washington, DC, and Manhattan, WeLive promotes the following: "WeLive is a new way of living built upon community, flexibility, and a fundamental belief that we are only as good as the people we surround ourselves with. From mailrooms and laundry rooms that double as bars and event spaces to communal kitchens, roof decks, and hot tubs, WeLive challenges traditional apartment living through physical spaces that foster meaningful relationships."[69]

Community spaces such as these let singles adapt to the lingering social pressure to marry by providing a safe, nonjudgmental atmosphere. These places attract like-minded people not only via laundry services and shared meals, but also by providing access to a flexible social network in which they can develop a sense of belonging. We should pay careful attention to the highly sensitive tone inherent in WeLive's statement. The physical space creates meaningful relationships—*meaningful* rather than *long-term,* and *relationships* (plural) rather than a single, *committed relationship.*

It is interesting to look at the LGBTQ community in this context. The queer population in effect has to deal with the *double* stigma of being queer and single. However, against the background of this extra burden, research into the living arrangements and social habits of LGBTQ individuals indicates that LGBTQ members, especially elders, tend to live together in shared accommodation more than other populations, enjoying the benefits of living in a queer-friendly environment.[70] It could be that members of the LGBTQ community, who are more used to social stigma, are actually less affected by the pressure to marry that others face and, as a result, are more likely than heterosexual singles to cohabit with friends. They already feel like outsiders, so they simply choose to at least benefit from the many advantages of living together with like-minded people.

Moreover, being around others who share an identity, face the same challenges, and empathize more fully with one's social situation can both increase happiness and reduce the risk of depression. Indeed, studies show that queers who keep similar friends close to them enjoy more social resources and feel better.[71] In fact, ethnic-minority LGBTQ elders, who might face triple and quadruple social stigma, are particularly likely to benefit from being around those who identify with them.[72] Therefore, singles who can find single-friendly environments are expected to gain not only the benefits of increased social capital but also the added value of being able to share with others and experience empathy.

Direct Defiance of Discriminatory Practices

The fourth strategy that emerged in my findings is the outright defiance of discriminatory practices. Such an approach is certainly not new to the many groups of ethnic and sexual minorities who have fought for their rights and place in society, and who already receive recognition by many governments and institutions.[73] However, this is still not a common and accepted practice for singles. They must fight creatively and individually against discriminatory practices. Ross typifies such an approach, as illustrated by his remarks in the *Irish Times:* "I do get the head cocked to one side and the sympathetic voice saying, 'Oh, are you still single?' In return, I'd quite like to put on a sympathetic voice and say, 'Oh, still in a relationship? Can't hack it on your own?' It completely invalidates my life as a single person."[74] Ross has no intention to attack married life here. He emphasizes the self-defensive nature of his proposed reply that might change the other person's perspective by pointing out that there is more than one way to live. Such answers might help singles garner acceptance and further defy social pressure to marry.

Even more straightforward than Ross is Rachel, a divorced woman aged forty-nine. She posted in her blog a combative piece titled "A Call for Single Action":

> By accepting the current system that relies on marriage and family for our most basic support, we might be guilty of systemic evil. Maybe it is time for us to stand up to the forces that are moving us further and further away from a compassionate society and take a single action: As singles, we take our responsibility seriously to support each other by fighting for social supports that are embedded in the societal structure....
>
> As singles, we know more than anybody else that true independence is actually interdependence. We can use this knowledge to work for a more compassionate society—and ensure that the increasing number of singles are taken care of no matter what they do for a living or how old they are, even when they choose to remain single for their whole life.[75]

Rachel wants everyone to take personal responsibility. As she sees it, if everyone accepts the call to promote singles' rights, no one will denigrate those who express their freedom by remaining unmarried, as opposed to those who spend their lives in a coupled relationship. Her earnest desire lies in reducing stigma and building a society that no longer excludes, or opposes the interests of, single individuals.

Rachel is not alone. Such calls are growing louder every day, but real changes are still scarce.[76] Nevertheless, research shows that such a movement not only produces actual social change but also benefits and energizes those participating, as evidenced in other social movements.[77] Thus, actively defying discriminatory practices constructs a social identity and alleviates some of the challenges therein. In this sense, protesting is a first step toward empowering singles.

Empowerment

The fifth strategy is to empower oneself by adopting a positive view about one's singleness rather than feeling neglected or unattractive. This strategy is different from developing a positive self-perception, because instead of focusing on the individual, it involves perception of one's *situation* as a single person. In this case, happy singles view their relationship status positively and do not allow their singleness to unduly influence their happiness. An anonymous, never-married female, age thirty-four, writes in her blog: "Being single is an adventure, especially if you're someone who has never been single and suddenly find yourself there[,] or if you've lived a life where you've never felt comfortable with being single but suddenly realize that learning to be comfortable with being single is the most important thing you can do for yourself."[78]

Recently, researchers have argued that rather than looking at all singles as one homogeneous group when studying stereotypes of singles and single life, a basic distinction should be made between two types of singles. The first group, called "singles by choice," is composed of people who are happy with their relationship status and are not currently looking for a partner. The other group, "singles by circumstance," includes those who desire marriage and are currently looking to be married. Of course, individuals can switch groups, but the two groups are different in terms of how they feel about their singleness and to what extent they accept it.[79]

Empowering singles who are happy with their permanent or temporary singleness is especially important, because they often face the most severe social problem. Research has shown, perhaps counterintuitively, that these singles are perceived more negatively than those who would like to couple.[80] In particular, those who are single by choice are perceived as more miserable and lonely than those who are single by circumstance, and the latter are viewed as more mature and sociable. One explanation for these findings is that those who are single by choice may be seen as defying the social norms of matrimania and, thus, elicit others' anger, while singles by circumstance elicit empathy.[81]

Therefore, empowering singles concerns not only feeling good about singleness but also about recontextualizing both society and the attitudes of the surrounding people to be more benign. In the interviews I conducted, I found that the ways in which singles interpret others around them are crucial to overcoming criticism and to feeling good about their singleness and social standing.

There are many ways to adopt positive views. The emerging books and articles seeking to empower singles can be seen as part of a quick and simple way to bring about change. Despite skepticism, studies show that books promoting positive thinking have a lasting and positive effect on the well-being of readers.[82]

Furthermore, a meta-analysis of thirty-nine studies shows that positive psychological interventions have helpful effects on subjective well-being measured at three- and six-month intervals following the intervention.[83] In other words, there is substantial evidence indicating that empowering interventions, such as attending a course, participating in a workshop, or taking consulting sessions, can further improve singles' happiness, enabling them to face social tensions and discrimination.

In a way, this brings us back to the anonymous singles meeting I attended. Some single people want to find their match and try the marriage route. Others, however, urgently seek a way to feel at ease with their current situations. Workshops that train singles to be at peace with their marital status are few and far between. It is clear, then, that innovative and insightful workshops should be developed to address the urgent need of many singles.

What content might such workshops offer? Consider the myriad seminars designed to improve and prolong marriages. Psychologists and educators can develop workshops and courses catering to the single lifestyle in the same way. Indeed, many support groups already exist to help divorced and widowed individuals overcome loss and separation. Yet there is a need to do more than just overcome the past. Unmarried individuals are also capable of enjoying their new circumstances, and seminars for the newly divorced or widowed should be designed with this goal in mind. In the same vein, schools should make information about the single lifestyle part of their curriculum. While some children will never marry, almost all of them are sure to be single at some point in their adult lives. Understanding how to be single and how to deal with matrimania should be in everyone's social toolbox.

Many aspects of being a happy single are laid out in this book. But this chapter presents perhaps the most crucial step to entering happy singlehood. The five strategies described here—awareness, positive self-perception, avoiding negativity, defying discriminatory practices, and empowerment—are all essential to breaking the social chains that are not necessarily related to one's own needs and will. Once freed from social burdens, singles can find ways to thrive and can pave the way for a truly happy singlehood.

CHAPTER FOUR

Sleeping Alone, Bowling Together

In his first English-speaking film, *Repulsion*, Roman Polanski delved into the world of seclusion and being single. In this 1965 psychological horror movie, Polanski focuses on Carole Ledoux, a manicurist who lives with her older sister in London. Beautiful but introverted, the young woman repeatedly refuses the courtship of a handsome young man and avoids any relationship with him. When her sister and her boyfriend leave on vacation, the already-distracted Carole begins a downward spiral into insanity. Every darkened corner shields a potential predator in the delirious mind of this beautiful, self-isolated woman.

Polanski cleverly juxtaposes three worlds of singles and relationships. The first is the world of unrewarding relationships: Carole's sister's boyfriend is impatient and insensitive, while Carole's colleague at work, Bridget, complains about her boyfriend and cries, "Just bloody men! They promise you the Earth and then … [give you nothing]." Polanski emphasizes how Carole, working at a salon, is part of a world where women are enslaved in industries designed to satisfy the needs of men without truly addressing their own desires (Polanski himself has been highly criticized in this sense, and he previously pled guilty to unlawful sexual intercourse with a minor).

The second world involves those who refuse to enter relationships. Polanski brings to light a deep, common fear of human beings: the fear of social and emotional isolation. Carole epitomizes the stereotypes of an unmarried woman who has no one to care for her. She does not take advantage of her beauty but, rather, isolates herself until her tragic death.

The third world, mostly forgotten in critiques of the film, highlights social interactions and groups of singles. Time and again, Carole looks from her sister's apartment window and sees joyful nuns playing catch in a convent garden. This social alternative, where friendship replaces romanticism by providing support and happiness, is underdeveloped in the film—certainly fitting the 1960s, when such an option was alien outside of religious contexts. Still, it seems Polanski paints this alternative as the sanest and most alluring. The nuns support each other emotionally and socially and, in doing so, create a rigid structure that magnetizes both Polanski and his protagonist, Carole.

Carole's eschewing of partnering up is not considered insane anymore. While 72 percent of all adults aged eighteen and older were married when this film came out, today the number hovers around 50 percent.[1] Yet, it is still puzzling how society overcame Carole's horrors, making room for networked, sociable singles.

Unfolding some of the strategies contemporary singles use to address the fears associated with being alone and feeling isolated will help us decipher this puzzle. Together with research on social capital, what follows will provide insight into how sociability can benefit single adults. In this way, we can begin to unpack what might have gone through Carole's mind as she gazed upon the nuns playing in the courtyard and, accordingly, think about how singles can improve their well-being.

BEING ALONE

It seems that everyone must have a partner to be part of society, as if the smallest piece in the social puzzle must consist of at least two people. Studies show that one of the prime reported advantages of being married is the human company and reliance found in a marriage.[2] Marriage is therefore considered the most common vaccine against the prolonged isolation that can significantly reduce any individual's well-being.[3]

Megan is over thirty years old and never-married. She has a respectable job and lives comfortably in New York. Megan has friends and colleagues who like her and enjoy her company, but when Sunday comes, she feels trapped. She writes in her blog: "For a long time, I dreaded Sunday mornings as a single person. I would wake up, anxiously aware of my aloneness. I yearned for a partner to be the balm to my self-loathing induced wounds. I longed to share 'Lazy Sundays' with a counterpart. I'd fantasize about groggy morning sex and snuggling and coffee or brunch—or coffee then brunch—strolling hand-in-hand, our hangovers mitigated by infatuation."[4]

Like Megan, many singles face difficulties on the weekends when they do not have the company of their own nuclear family.[5] There are two main reasons for this. First, there is no work, and thus singles have an ample amount of free time in which to occupy themselves. Second, there are fewer people around—no colleagues and clients to meet the need for social interaction. Thus, having a partner and children can help pass the weekend free time while also fulfilling the desire for human communication. When these needs remain unmet, singles might endure psychological distress and impaired well-being.[6]

Sarah experiences similar difficulties on Sundays and writes about the well-known, loneliness-related anxiety common among singles. For Sarah, the feeling of loneliness becomes worse when the families in her community attend church, gather to eat, or go out together. Sarah, who does not have a husband or children, wonders whether she should participate in social and religious activities on her own. She writes:

> I get in the car trying to decide if I have the emotional energy to go and eat alone in a restaurant. It's the Sunday thing to do, to eat out. I decide that a quick sandwich at home might be nice and change lanes to head home instead. The tears are threatening to fall and all the while I'm saying to myself, "It's okay, you're okay. God knows best. He's here. You're not alone.

Don't cry. Don't cry. Don't cry. Jesus, help." This is why I debate going to church every week. I go alone, I sit alone, I leave alone, I eat alone. I'm not a fan of Sundays.[7]

Sarah realizes that she feels awkward and sad when she is out by herself on Sundays and decides to return home, depressed and feeling lonely. Like Sarah, singles might feel fine on their own, but once they engage in certain types of social encounters, they perceive themselves as misplaced and less worthy. In many cases, these feelings reflect society's prejudices. As discussed in the previous chapter, there is ample evidence that society sees singles as a burden or even as a threat. Singles are viewed as more violent, less stable, and needing help.[8] Polanski's horror movie about Carole's single life is a masterpiece because it underscores well-ingrained fears that singles cannot handle being alone and can easily fall into madness. The film ends with Carole killing both her suitor and her sister's landlord, a stark reminder of the ultimate collective fear of the possible consequences of living alone.

Besides the emotional challenge, a single person might face physical/material challenges in doing housework or, in cases of job loss, face sickness or immobility. People with partners, and more so those with partners and children, are assumed to be better off in such circumstances because their immediate families are expected to step in to help.[9] Partners provide an economic safety net in times of unemployment, as well as guaranteed help with sickness- or injury-related difficulties in moving around, eating, or dressing. Therefore, it is easy to understand another of Sarah's thoughts, written one year after her post on Sunday loneliness. Here, Sarah continues to describe her challenges in living alone:

> There are two times and situations when I don't like living alone. The first one is when I can't open something. I had serious thoughts the other day of throwing a brand-new jar of salsa onto the tile floor with some force and then eating around the glass. But, I am woman, and I tapped and twisted and got out towels and hit the edges and emerged victorious, albeit with very sore hands, 5 minutes after I commenced trying to open said jar.

The second time is when I'm sick. There is, quite frankly, nothing worse than being sick and alone. It's not the actual loneliness that makes it so awful, it's the fact that you begin to think you might actually die from lack of nutrition because the thought of getting into an upright position, walking anywhere further than from the bed to the toilet, and then having to smell food while cooking—well, to say the least, it just doesn't appeal to you. So there's no eating for days.[10]

Sarah fears being stranded in times of need and describes her difficulty with mundane tasks like opening a jar. It might be frustrating to need such help. There is no emergency number for opening jars and cans, and singles might feel painfully helpless in times when they need simple but necessary assistance on the spot. Even more challenging are difficulties with mobility or eating, which become more common with age. While many, like Sarah, describe how they successfully deal with single life, they can run into problems when they require immediate help with basic physical needs. In fact, often it is not the fantasy of being together that draws people into marriage but rather the fear of vulnerability—marriage as insurance for times of physical deterioration.

IS MARRIAGE THE SOLUTION?

There is a widespread belief that being married is a safety net for times of distress. However, this notion has been heavily scrutinized.[11] To illustrate this, one can measure the strength of the support system of marriage in cases of disabled individuals, a kind of litmus test. When the capacity of people with disabilities to care for themselves is compromised, their immediate family and closest friends are expected to step in and help, often daily. And while marriage is assumed to provide assistance, an analysis of the European Social Survey indicates that for the over-thirty demographic, the percentage of disabled people among the never-married and divorced is 6.3 percent and 7.2 percent, respectively, compared with 3.1 percent among those married. These numbers only add to previous longitudinal studies showing that having a disability relates to being abandoned.[12] Thus, those who need help are actually more likely to remain alone, or even be left alone, following divorce. In the European Social Survey, the difference between the married and divorced groups is especially alarming, in that people with a disability are 42 percent more likely to be divorced than those without a disability. Apparently, despite the expectation that marriage will act as insurance in times of real need, this does not hold true for many disabled people.

It seems the disabled are but one example of a vulnerable demographic. Those who have lost their jobs are also at further risk of being left alone. Several studies show that the probability of divorce increases following a spouse's job displacement.[13] Instead of being supported, many spouses find themselves in extremely stressful situations that soon end their marriages. Presumably, job loss skews income expectations, which, in turn, change anticipated gains from marriage and make the partner less "worthy," as cruel as it may sound.[14]

Studies show that not only are these disabled or unemployed persons more likely to be divorced, but even if they remain married, the burden falls solely on their partners as relationships with people in outer circles weaken. Some scholars explain that the traditional family unit, with its high expectations of support and undivided attention, can cause individuals to turn inward toward their nuclear family unit and away from resources in outer circles, a phenomenon sometimes referred to as "greedy marriage."[15] Thus, even if the couple stays married, the burden is almost unbearable after the surrounding social resources dry up over the years.

Men are particularly susceptible to the pitfalls of greedy marriage, not least because they become less fiscally generous to their friends and relatives following marriage.[16] This is especially remarkable since studies indicate that married men earn more than single men do.[17] Nevertheless, married men invest fewer resources in their social circles, and therefore they are more vulnerable and have fewer economic and emotional resources of support in times of need.[18]

Eleanore, thirty-eight, recounts a conversation with an older woman she met on a train to Long Island, beginning with the woman's reaction upon learning that Eleanore is single:

LADY: Oh no! Well, who's going to take care of you when you're old?

ME: I don't know for sure. Who's going to take care of you when you're old?

LADY: Well, I have a husband and kids. They'll take care of me.

ME: How do you know that?

And my "How do you know that" question is when I think she wished she had just chosen a different seat. I went on to lay out all the reasons she was no more secure in her old age than I am. You see, life is really uncertain; there just aren't any guarantees. It would be wonderful if every woman who had a husband and/or kids could be assured of a loving, cared-for old age. Unfortunately, that's just not necessarily true....

I went on to explain to her: My friend's elderly aunt—a dynamic spinster lady—recently had a "good, peaceful death." She had no husband or kids but was lovingly cared for in the last weeks of her life by family [and] friends who loved her. That's all we really need: Someone who loves us and is willing and able to care for us.[19]

Eleanore questions the woman's assumption that marriage is the ultimate insurance in times of need. Given the aforementioned statistics, it seems that Eleanore is correct in saying that relying on partners is not a guarantee in times of crisis and, moreover, might weaken other resources for help. This distrust in marriage, especially in modern times, when traditions are constantly questioned, has led many to develop networking units that act much like families and are sometimes even more effective.

THE NETWORKED INDIVIDUAL

Whereas the household was once the cornerstone of one's support system, there has been a shift toward organizing one's life in personal networking units, a phenomenon that is referred to as "networked individualism."[20] This trend has been facilitated by individualization, the growing number of singles at the global level, and technological connectivity, which together allow singles to make social arrangements more independently.[21] Especially among younger singles, the role of friendship in everyday life is strengthened, and in some cases the emotional, social, material, and financial support traditionally provided by the family comes from social networks instead.[22] But this occurs not only among young people: singles of all ages have parents, siblings, and friends in their lives who love and care for them and who can be relied upon in times of need.[23] Indeed, the pattern of receiving support from friends and feeling comfortable in singleness is also emerging among middle-aged singles and seniors.[24]

Back to our litmus test: the social condition of the disabled can lend clear insight into the status of networked individualism. For example, Hunni, thirty, who is single and childless, writes that her friends serve as a support system in dealing with her disability: "I am very lucky to have a good support system of friends and family who help me out when things get bad. With limited mobility at times, and without my own transport, I rely on others to get me places if I have far to go, and [I owe] a huge thank you to everyone who has chipped in to get me where I needed to be."[25]

Hunni does not have a partner or children to help with her disability. Instead, her friends lend a hand. Hunni finds this network especially strong and suggests that its strength derives, in part, from being large enough that the burden does not fall on any one person. Everyone "chipped in," she writes. Indeed, unlike married couples, who naturally turn inward, singles are more poised to help their families and friends and, as a result, to benefit in return. In addition, singles maintain richer and more diverse social lives, while married people invest most of their energy in their spousal relationships. Phil, for example, is forty-seven years old and currently living in Indiana. He said to me in our interview: "I cast a pretty wide net of friends. I have a network of people I can see and socialize with on a regular basis.... Recently I've had so much social stuff going on.... I cast a wide net of friends from different areas, different parts of my life, to make sure there are a lot of social options for me."

Many studies echo Phil's words. It has been found that singles are more likely than couples to socialize and help raise others' children; to enjoy shared experiences that deepen a sense of identity; to care for those who cannot look after themselves; and to benefit from emotional, practical, and material support from wider social circles.[26]

My statistical analysis also indicates that uncoupled people interact more with friends and family. Among the groups tested, never-married individuals were the most social, followed by divorced/separated people, widowed people, cohabiters, and, lastly, married people. It seems that coupled individuals neglect their outer social circles and feel comfortable in their own nests, while singles, no matter which kind, seek more frequently to develop social ties.

One can still argue that many of these studies examine only a specific point in time, leading to the claim that marriage might not be the cause of diminishing social capital. In other words, it is unclear whether married individuals are more likely to neglect their friends, or whether those who tend to neglect their friends while single are more likely to marry.

However, a recent longitudinal analysis of the National Survey of Families and Households supports the former proposition.[27] Over two thousand survey participants were asked over the course of six years to describe the quality of their relationships with friends and family and their frequency of social meetings. At the time of the first sampling, all participants were single and under age fifty. By the end, the sample was divided into three groups: those who were still single, those who had started a relationship within the past three years, and those who had entered a relationship four-to-six years prior. The differences between them were compared, and the results unequivocally proved that those who remained single spent more time with friends, family, peers, and neighbors. Moreover, social withdrawal was consistent among individuals who lived with their partners, regardless of when the relationship began, which implies that such social distancing is not necessarily a temporary effect associated only with the beginning of a relationship.

Interestingly, studies show that greedy marriage has become even greedier in recent decades.[28] When comparing differences in social behavior between couples in 1980 and 2000, researchers found that couples in the year 2000 were less likely than the 1980 group to participate in a broad array of social activities, including visiting friends, working on shared hobbies, and going out. At the same time, singles have become *more* adept at building personal networks. Apparently, married individuals have become increasingly exposed to the risks of loneliness and social isolation over time, whereas singles seem to have been adapting and even flourishing in recent decades.[29]

The move toward greedy marriage is especially evident when comparing singles' Internet usage to that of coupled individuals. My analysis shows that many singles utilize technology and the Internet to connect with friends and family, while couples do so less often. All things being equal, divorced/separated individuals are the most proficient in interacting with friends and family over the Internet of the groups tested (15 percent more than couples), followed by the never-married (12 percent more than couples), while widowed individuals lag.

Networking and community-building can undoubtedly be assisted by the virtual world. While excessive social networking and Internet usage can pose a risk to psychological well-being,[30] these activities also present opportunities to build social capital by acting as channels for meeting others, whether through social networking,[31] communication with others,[32] or contact with special-interest groups.[33] In fact, evidence strongly suggests that for many singles, talking on social networks about one's feelings of loneliness positively affects the social provision they receive.[34] This way, the modern, uncoupled person connects more with others, widens his or her social circle, and finds practical and emotional support.

These adaptation processes among singles, together with technological advancements, help explain the increased number of singles and the reduced stigma of singlehood, which have made room for the emergence of thriving communities of singles. Networks and communities of singles have taken form and gained strength even in religious societies that put heavy emphasis on marriage and establishing a family. One interesting example is that of Orthodox Jewish singles living in Israel, for whom the existence of a singles' community allows them to experience the stage of life between being a young adult and being ready for a family.[35] As a result, whereas the vast majority of single Orthodox Jews exhibit a strong desire to partner and start a family, they also strengthen ties with friends and establish communities of unmarried singles, which facilitates *longer* periods of singlehood. Research is limited on the formation of communities and networks for unmarried individuals from traditional and religious backgrounds, but the increasing prevalence of singleness seems to indicate that, around the world, these groups will continue to grow.

These trends beg the following questions: What do the thriving new singles communities know that research thus far has failed to acknowledge? How exactly does social capital help singles live happily? And does social capital really elevate singles' happiness levels and become a worthwhile substitution for the institution of marriage, or is it merely a temporary and unsatisfactory solution?

THE PARTICULAR IMPORTANCE OF SOCIAL CAPITAL FOR IMPROVING SINGLES' LIVES

The notion of social capital, understood as "the norms and networks facilitating collective action for mutual benefit,"[36] has gained prominence in recent decades, and researchers today are investigating social capital's relation to happiness and well-being.[37] Several studies found that social capital is a robust and direct predictor of well-being.[38] Others reveal a strong correlation between greater life satisfaction and involvement in clubs, nonpolitical societies, and noneconomic organizations.[39]

This is particularly so among older people, for whom social connectedness and perceived social inclusion are both associated with higher levels of mental health.[40]

An analysis of worldwide data sets also suggests that social context variables explain a large portion of cross-country variation in subjective well-being.[41] Studies continue to show that religious social capital, as usually measured by church attendance, also positively corresponds with well-being.[42] Finally, my own cross-country investigation also confirms that in most of the European countries surveyed, social capital correlates strongly with self-reported levels of happiness, as figure 5 illustrates.

Not only does social capital directly affect individual well-being, but it also mediates happiness via secondary factors. For instance, some researchers find that increased social capital improves health by promoting awareness and physical training, which, in turn, raise life satisfaction.[43] Social capital can also lead to increased economic support and improved ability to deal with external stress, thereby increasing individuals' well-being.[44]

These findings are especially important for singles. As detailed above, singles are more socially active, and they develop networked individualism. This may give singles an added advantage related to happiness and well-being, either via direct support or indirect mechanisms such as fitness awareness and economic connections. Forty-year-old Anna, never-married and living in London, writes in her post:

> It's nice to be able to invite friends around, as I am determined not to be typecast a "loner," and I like to see my place as a little social haven where music plays and the wine flows. I want the people I love to feel welcome to come around and see me, as my little pad isn't a shrine or a cocoon for just me. It's my home, and I'd like to think it's a reflection of me as a person.

> So, if you come across me, or a woman like me, who lives alone, please don't think we are unfortunate souls who have had to do this out of circumstance, I have done my research, and most of us choose to live this way! We are happy, we are independent, we are free.... Do feel free to come and visit us, bring some wine, and have a good gossip with us, because it would mean so much![45]

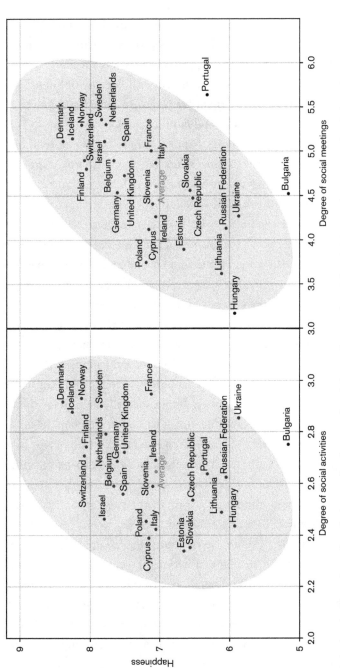

The level of happiness in relation to the degree of social meetings and social activities, at the country level, found among those aged thirty and above. Source: Based on the European Social Survey. Note: Gray ovals signify the 95 percent confidence level.

Anna enjoys living alone but also emphasizes the importance of friends by inviting them into her life. She is aware of the misconception about singles and insists she is happy living this way. Because singles like Anna are more likely to stay in touch with friends, siblings, parents, and communities, they benefit from the emotional and practical support provided by these social and familial circles.[46]

Moreover, not only are singles happier because of closer relationships with the people surrounding them, but they also enjoy greater resilience in the face of adversity. For example, although divorce negatively affects mental health, divorced people—especially those in today's more liberal societies—who take advantage of strong social networks can reduce the stigma and social consequences of divorce and separation. Instead of feeling isolated and abandoned while managing the economic and emotional postseparation challenges, divorced individuals find an opportunity in social networks to share their burden, get advice, and even meet new friends with whom they can go out and spend their leisure time. Indeed, recent studies show that such social networks increase divorced people's well-being and happiness.[47]

Single parents, too, benefit from support by friends and family. In fact, connecting with wider social circles is especially helpful for single parents because they can find other single parents with whom to share child-care responsibilities.[48] Single parents today skillfully adapt to a world that places less emphasis on the centrality of the two-parent family unit, thereby developing diversified social networks that support them in raising their children. Jacqui, thirty-two, argues that she receives more support as a single mother than she would from a partner: "I have to say that I don't use the term 'single parent' as to me it infers loneliness, which in many situations is very inaccurate. With such a wide range of friends and family it is very hard to have a moment to feel lonely or single. In fact, I feel like I have more support as a sole caretaker than I would have had had my circumstances been different."[49] For Jacqui, the support she receives from her surroundings helps her not only in a material sense but also in a deeper, emotional manner. She rarely feels lonely.

My statistical analysis of the European Social Survey confirms Jacqui's assertion. Social capital is an important way to increase singles' well-being, filling most of the "happiness gap" between them and their coupled peers. To fully understand this important finding, we must recall the baseline difference in happiness and well-being between single and married people. The difference is usually measured at less than one point on a 0–10-point scale, around 0.7 points. However, the real figure is even smaller if one accounts for the influence of a priori selection factors, as explained in previous chapters: happier individuals are more likely to marry to begin with. A longitudinal study found that the selection effect accounts for 0.3 points of the difference in life satisfaction between married and never-married persons on a similar 0–10-point scale.[50] This means that people who eventually marry were happier years before. Therefore, the marriage effect—as a cause for greater well-being—stands at only around 0.4 points. Furthermore, as mentioned earlier, even this advantage diminishes and gradually returns to baseline after a two-year "honeymoon," making the long-term advantage much smaller.[51]

Keeping this 0.4-point difference in mind, my analysis—factoring for country-level differences as well as individual-level differences, including age, gender, education, and income—shows that social activities (e.g., community volunteering) and social meetings (e.g., going out with friends) have a strong, positive effect on happiness, providing up to around 0.8–0.9 happiness points. Furthermore, these results are independent of other factors that also increase singles' happiness, such as a healthy lifestyle, meaningful work, and postmaterialist values, as described in the next chapter.

The first conclusion arising from these results is that singles who pursue social interactions more proactively than do couples can bypass them in the happiness index. Single men and women fully engaged in social meetings and activities can pass their average married counterparts by one, and even two, standard deviations, a move of almost 1 point (happier) on the 0-to-10-point scale. Although it might sound like a very small difference, it nonetheless places these singles in the population's upper fifth, even tenth, percentile of happiness and well-being. In other words, singles involved in social undertakings can, and often do, boost their happiness and well-being in significant and sustainable ways. Thus, although singles have a lower baseline of happiness because of discriminatory policies, various benefits that favor couples, and selection mechanisms into marriage (the happier you are, the more likely you are to marry),[52] they can easily overcome these headwinds.

But here comes a second, more complex, question: Given that singles utilize social capital to increase happiness and well-being more than their married counterparts do, are social interactions more *effective* at promoting happiness among single people? That is to say, do married and unmarried people differ in the way that *similar levels* of social capital affect their happiness? Do singles derive greater benefit from every social interaction?

The answer is a resounding yes. My study shows that social capital more profoundly affects singles' happiness compared to that of cohabitators and married individuals. Singles close the "well-being gap" both by being more social and, in some measures, by deriving greater happiness from equal levels of social interaction relative to their coupled peers. To illustrate, take five persons: one is married, the second is a cohabitator, the third has never married, the fourth is divorced, and the fifth is widowed. They are equal in age, education, income, and so on. If all five are very socially active—volunteering in their communities, participating in clubs, and so on—the latter three, those who are single, can gain up to around half a point of happiness more than the married and cohabitating persons.[53] In other words, sociability improves singles' well-being significantly, and fundamentally more than that of their partnered peers, despite the similarities between them save marital status. It seems, then, that singles use social interactions to receive support and to develop their safety nets in more efficient ways.

This finding reverberates throughout many of the interviews I conducted. For example, Dave, forty-nine, from Athens, Georgia, told me that after being divorced, he benefited significantly from various social activities: "I've joined a volleyball club, I've gotten on my bicycle and ridden, I've gone swimming, I've joined choirs, I've gone to church, I've connected with the community in different ways."

Dave reports that these many social activities enrich his life and keep him enthused and energetic. It is mainly a way for him to feel active and more connected after his divorce, not because he wants to meet a potential partner. When I raised these two alternatives in interpreting his various activities, he decisively chose the former interpretation: "Those are good ways to go about meeting people, period."

Studying further, in comparing social meetings (informal social capital) and social activities (formal social capital) as happiness contributors among different marital groups, I found the latter to be more effective. Both single men and single women derive significantly more happiness from formal social activities, such as social clubs and volunteering, than from informal social meetings, such as visiting friends and family, although they derive benefits from both types of social capital and do so more efficiently than their married counterparts.

WHY IS SOCIAL CAPITAL SO IMPORTANT FOR SINGLES' WELL-BEING?

The evidence I have discussed needs to be explained. Why and how do singles use social interactions to increase their well-being? More importantly, what, exactly, does make singles benefit *more* from social capital than couples? In interviewing singles and analyzing their posts and blogs, I found five main explanations, which require unpacking.

First, singles derive more happiness from social capital because they meet more diverse people and engage in a wider variety of activities. As Phil, whom I cited earlier, told me: "I cast a wide net of friends from different areas, different parts of my life." This larger network supports singles in a variety of situations they might find themselves in and, thus, becomes more efficient and offers better coverage in times of need. Furthermore, singles have a more diverse set of confidants than their married counterparts do, especially because singles' confidants are more likely to include nonrelatives. They diversify their social ties because they are more likely to involve their siblings in their adult lives and cultivate meaningful relationships with friends that raise their overall happiness.[54] By diversifying the group of people in whom they can confide, singles create stronger core networks and experience less isolation than their married peers. Agnes, a forty-three-year-old divorced woman from Wisconsin, told me: "I've got a lot of friends, I invest a lot of time into these friendships to counsel my friends, and they turn to me for support and help, so it's a pretty happy [situation]." Indeed, according to one study, stronger and wider networks positively correlate with emotional well-being.[55]

Several researchers describe the numerous ways in which singles interact socially. These ways include such activities as participating in clubs and organizations, working in the community garden, and raising children together.[56] Happy singles alter and diversify their social circles, using various social opportunities to increase their happiness. Some singles proactively diversify their social networks, while others develop such networks naturally, simply by being open to new encounters afforded by not being partnered. Elsie, a never-married woman in her thirties living in New York, writes about such a joyful situation:

The holiday season is rightly noted as a time of year when singles are particularly susceptible to loneliness. Although we don't all want to be coupled, most of us want to be included, and some of us find ourselves subtly or not so subtly butted out of family circles composed of arm-linked couples....

So, it was a pleasant surprise when the ball dropped and instead of feeling like an appendage, I was part of the circle as we all clinked glasses and exchanged hugs. Then we did something I've never done before. We ran up to the roof and, hearing another roof party down the block, called out our

New Year's wishes to these strangers. There was a pause, and then we heard the answering cry, "Happy New Year!"

. . .

In 2010, I want to carry this revelation with me, that life should be about extending ourselves to others in recognition of our common human condition, not organizing our interactions around the artificial boundaries of marriage and the nuclear family. I want to remember that I am single, but I am not alone. I am in this world with millions of other people with the same desires, the same fears, the same struggles, the same satisfactions.[57]

Elsie describes feeling connected to, and celebrating with, a circle of friends on New Year's Eve, a time when she was most susceptible to loneliness. Later, she connects to another circle, opening herself to new social interactions. She is very happy with this ongoing experience and feels part of a larger group of people. Despite being single, she insists that she is not alone.

But the social connectedness is not just about parties on New Year's Eve. The singles I met who were satisfied with their lives were also more likely to build their own social networks and to contribute to their communities by volunteering for civic organizations and charities. That is, happy singles use their time to give generously to others, exactly as Dave described in the interview I cited earlier.

The second explanation for the effectiveness of social capital in raising singles' happiness is the flexibility in building their networks. Researchers note that whereas couples participate in increasingly uniform and conformist social activities, singles become ever more adept at constructing social frameworks that cater to their needs while remaining flexible and open to change.[58] In describing the meaning of "networked individualism," Barry Wellman argues that personal networks, rather than the household unit, are more adaptive to changes and thus become a major, more effective source of support.[59]

Singles arrange such support networks consciously or subconsciously according to the specific needs of the individual, while coupled individuals tend to be more limited by relationship constraints.[60]

Consequently, this adaptiveness increases the ability of social capital to promote greater happiness among singles. Kenneth, a seventy-five-year-old never-married man from Scotland, told me:

> The camaraderie of single people makes me happy.... My friends and I rented a house outside New York City in the woods during the summers, years ago, and really had fun and done dumb things together. You know, dating was okay, but I seriously enjoyed [myself] with that group of friends; they made up for that. So, I think if you have enough friends, you don't necessarily need it. One of my friends has a boat; with one I play tennis. It's sort of just freedom, and I enjoy the excitement of always meeting new people.

The third explanation for the relative potency of singles' social capital is that singles are more attentive to social relationships and make them central to their lives. This is in line with the greedy-marriage theory. Couples turn inward and focus on their relationships, while singles focus on their wider sphere of family and friends.[61] In turn, singles benefit more from holding their social circles in such high esteem. "Consider it a nonromantic, nonsexual crew of people that you rely on, for anything," Phillip, a Parisian divorced man in his fifties, told me. By focusing on their social capital, Phillip and many other singles enhance its quality to a degree that significantly promotes their happiness.[62] In contrast, when couples focus on their relationships, they limit their possibilities for support and might even cause psychological distress, especially at older ages, as explained in chapter 2.[63]

The fourth strength in singles' social capital is related to the use of technological services that are offered nowadays and that make their social capital more efficient. The plethora of online services, technologies, and singles-focused media serve as an extra stream of support, one that is tapped by fewer married people.[64] As mentioned, my statistical analysis shows that singles use technology to socialize more than couples do. The interviews I conducted and the blogs I analyzed show that singles also use it to make their social capital more efficient. Remember Gordon and Vivian? Both met online via the comments section of an article, continued communicating on Facebook, and probably arranged to meet this way. Singles groups on Facebook are flourishing these days, and the very fact that I found so many blogs written by singles on singleness says something about the ways technology enables singles to express themselves and find others with whom they can share their feelings.

In 2017, the *Telegraph* published an article listing the "12 non-dating apps single people need this Valentine's Day."[65] Among them one can find Tourlina, an app geared to female solo travelers, allowing them to connect with other women planning holidays in the same area. Another app is Meetup, which can be used to connect singles with others who share similar interests. The list goes on, even without mentioning WhatsApp, Facebook, Instagram, and the like. In this sense, technology connects singles to others more rapidly, at any time, and in larger circles than ever known before.

The fifth and final advantage of singles' social capital touches upon recent market developments. Markets have adapted to the rise of singlehood with new products, services, and living arrangements targeting singles, such as community spaces in condominiums.[66] In such spaces, they can make more friends and develop social ties. Social events, retirement homes, and activity groups targeted directly to the single market also make it easier for singles to connect with others. In contrast, married individuals, who are not the target audience of these new services, remain outside of this rapidly developing industry that creates ripples of social connectivity.

In summary, singles utilize social capital better than couples because their social networks are more diverse, flexible, sophisticated, efficient, and relatively important to their happiness. Regardless of the precise explanation, social capital holds the key to understanding the rising level of happiness of today's singles.

In the 1960s, Carole stood at arm's length while she watched the joyful nuns playing catch. Today, given a similar scenario, Carole would likely be invited to a wide variety of social activities and opportunities.

Released from the confines of her home and freed from listening to endless complaints about relationships at work, Carole could have simply stepped out and joined any of a plethora of social groups. No more sitting on the sidelines, no acquiescing to religion and its constraints, and no longer a distant observer. Countless social networking sites like Facebook, Meetup, and Tourlina encourage singles like Carole to jump into the social game without the need to find a partner.

New avenues of connection continue to open for a growing group of singles, those who, like Carole, seem to be *single at heart*—that is, they prefer being single.[67] As Anna, cited earlier, writes: "Please don't think we are unfortunate souls who have had to do this out of circumstance, I have done my research, and most of us choose to live this way! We are happy, we are independent, we are free.... Do feel free to come and visit us." It seems that this emerging type of singles, in particular, uses social capital more extensively because they do not expect to marry or to receive support from future partners. Instead, as I discuss in the next chapter, they cherish freedom, creativity, and new experiences. These values signify a new, rapidly emerging type of single: one who wants to sleep alone but increasingly insists on bowling together.

CHAPTER FIVE

Singling in a Postmaterialist World

The invitations are beautifully decorated, and the feeling is highly celebrative. It is definitely going to be a wedding to remember. Some invite their friends, some are joined by their families, while others celebrate on their own. They are excited and dressed up. But, they will not have a spouse standing next to them—they are marrying themselves.

Although still on the fringe, the self-marriage movement is growing. In Kyoto, for example, one can find a two-day, self-wedding package promoted by an agency specializing in travel for singles. The package, reportedly costing around twenty-five hundred American dollars, includes a gown, bouquet, hairstyling, limousine ride to the ceremony, and commemorative photo album. These types of services are thriving now in the United States, East Asia, and Europe. And no worries if you do not want the whole ceremony: one can also find guidance for self-marriage in the form of virtual packages and books.[1]

Self-marriage has also started to appear in the media. In a 2010 episode of the television show *Glee*, Sue Sylvester decides to marry herself, following in the footsteps of Carrie, from *Sex and the City*, who married herself so that she could open a wedding gift registry to replace a lost pair of Manolo Blahnik shoes.[2]

Of course, these ceremonies are somewhat theatrical and highly controversial, yet they express a set of values increasingly shared by young people around the world—namely, individualistic and postmaterialist values.[3] The website Selfmarriageceremonies.com is run by Stanford graduate Dominique Youkhehpaz, a marriage counselor who was self-married at age twenty-two. She marked the occasion with a nose ring so that she could "breath my vows every day."[4] The homepage of Dominique's website describes the principles of self-marriage:

> Self-Marriage is a profound rite of passage into wholeness, trust, self-responsibility, self-liberation, and love sourced from within. It is a ritual of transformation, of proclaiming what is true in your heart and being celebrated as you make it known that you are ready to live your full potential. It is the commitment to radically honor and express your gifts and the precious gift of your life. It is the freedom to live authentically in alignment with your deepest values. It is the dedication to love, no matter what.[5]

This statement calls for singles around the world to be authentic, self-expressive, and independent. It might sound clichéd, but these values are part of a major transformation that human societies have undergone across the world over the past century. Self-marriage is only one example of a fundamental focal change from responsibility to independence and from obedience to self-expression. It is not a semantic modification: this change has rattled societies everywhere. Starting in the developed world and spreading globally into developing nations, it demonstrates a transition away from focusing on the social collective (further divided into families as functional units of work and reproduction) and toward supporting the aspirations of each individual.

Such a shift influences the way we think about every social and interpersonal function in our lives. In particular, changes in the importance of the family—once the bedrock of the larger social structure—played a major part in this shift. Aspirations other than marrying and reproducing have taken center stage for many, forming what theorists call an age of postmaterialism.

By unpacking this shift to the postmaterialist age, and exploring how the newfound values of independence and freedom can enhance singles' well-being, we can examine and challenge the argument that postmaterialist values can be damaging to happiness. In fact, my analysis shows the exact opposite, at least regarding singles. By delving into how individualist and postmaterialist value systems can make singles' lives richer and more fruitful, this chapter provides one of the keys to *singling* happily in today's world.

THE AGE OF POSTMATERIALISM

The term *postmaterialism* was first coined by American social scientist Ronald Inglehart in his book *The Silent Revolution: Changing Values and Political Styles among Western Publics.*[6] Inglehart observes that until the 1970s, materialist values such as physical security and economic growth were universally prioritized. This is especially true against the backdrop of the Great Depression, two world wars, and the Cold War, events that ingrained a global feeling of insecurity and instability.

However, in the 1970s, a silent revolution began, especially in Western countries in which the public's top-priority values came to include a high quality of life. Postmaterialists started to emphasize such goals as creativity, environmental protection, freedom of speech, and human rights. This movement reflected a change from times when survival was precarious to times when survival was secure. Economic prosperity, newly signed peace treaties, and a burgeoning welfare system produced an intergenerational value change. Important movements promoting fair trade, universal political rights, and environmental justice were born and gradually transformed the political and cultural norms of society.

As mentioned in the first chapter, the shift away from materialism encouraged many to embrace individualism and independence[7] and to consider living alone.[8] In times when devastating wars and poor living conditions become distant memories, and economic development and purchasing parity are on the rise, organizing oneself within a family to feel secure and find solace becomes unnecessary. While the children of the Great Depression and the world wars experienced severe material obstacles and, as a result, craved order, economic stability, and military strength, the generations born in the latter part of the twentieth century sought self-expression, fun, freedom, and creativity.[9] And while the former strived for stable family lives and sought to marry early and to stay married, the latter strayed from traditional family values, with many individuals deciding to go solo in order to express their postmaterialist values.[10]

The deinstitutionalization of marriage can be described as having occurred in two stages. First, the role of marriage expanded from fulfilling societal expectations and sustaining survival to providing companionship.[11] In the second stage, the importance of personal choice and self-development (sometimes through transient relationships) increased at the expense of institutional marriage.[12]

Interestingly, these exact two stages were foreshadowed by the psychologist Abraham Maslow in the 1940s and 1950s. In his seminal works on human needs, he indicated that only after one's material and physical needs are fulfilled do other needs become important: first, love and companionship; then, esteem and self-actualization.[13] In this sense, the deinstitutionalization of marriage accurately manifested the shift in focus from materialism to postmaterialism, climbing the ladder of human needs.

SINGLE WOMEN IN A POSTMATERIALIST AGE

One major movement that embodies the values of the postmaterialist revolution is that of women's liberation and feminism, particularly the rise of women's desire for self-actualization, which in turn greatly affected the institution of marriage. Beginning in the 1960s, the second-wave feminism that started in the United States and eventually spread throughout the Western world and beyond had begun emphasizing the values of postmaterialism: freedom and independence gained value, and individualism became the focus of discussion.[14] Yet only the third wave of feminism, which started in the early 1990s, truly liberated the single woman, reconstructing gender roles.[15] In contrast to the first wave, which focused on the legal status of women but still saw women as part of the family unit, and the second wave, which empowered women socially but still only within the context of family, the third wave truly allowed women to live as they wished and challenged the roles of family, sexuality, and labor division.[16] These changing values liberated women and promoted their advancement outside of marriage. Melissa, thirty-five, who lives in New York, writes: "Over the last decade, I've had the pleasure and privilege of following my dreams wherever they've taken me. From chasing on-camera stardom in Illinois and Delaware to living the good Aussie life as a Sydney resident for five months, I have truly enjoyed the freedom that comes with being unattached."[17]

Melissa describes in her blog how being single has enabled her to travel the world and experience living in new places. Being attached to someone could have made that difficult—indeed, a partner comes with his or her own needs, job requirements, visa issues, family ties, and language or cultural barriers.[18] Whatever the reason, being unattached increased Melissa's flexibility, and she feels fortunate.

Such freedom for women is not acceptable, mainstream, or permitted in every national context. In some parts of the world, women are still at the very early stages of transitioning from materialism to postmaterialism. They risk their lives to fulfill their creativity and self-actualization.

For example, in 2012, the *New York Times* published an article about a secret literary society based in Kabul called Mirman Baheer.[19] This group is composed of Afghan women who refuse to marry early and who resist forced marriage. Instead, they educate themselves and write poetry. They told the reporter the story of Zarmina, whose story haunts the women of Mirman Baheer. Zarmina lived outside Kabul and could not visit the literary society as frequently as she would have liked. But almost every week, Zarmina secretly accessed a telephone so she could read her poems to the other members. When her brothers discovered this, they beat her badly. Her parents then decided to marry her off to a man of their choice, but she refused and committed suicide. It was her tragic rebellion against her parents, her family, and society at large.

Zarmina's tragedy, viewed against the background of ongoing social change in Kabul, epitomizes how postmaterialist values go hand-in-hand with women's bitter fight for advancement and self-actualization.[20] This progress then affects marriage patterns. As shown in chapter 1, women across the world are increasingly interested in developing their careers and finishing their studies before marrying, thus delaying family formation and prolonging singledom.[21]

Women's liberation extends even beyond marriage to decisions on motherhood. Increased career resources are associated with women postponing or altogether avoiding having children.[22] An anonymous Canadian blogger, thirty-nine, writes: "I am very ambivalent about having children.... I like my space and my time and my silence. I am a very selfish individual and I'm okay with that."[23] Such "confessions" are becoming more common and socially accepted, indicating the rise of individualistic values. A more gender-equal society that encourages women to advance academically and professionally also reduces the pressure on women to marry and have children.[24]

Many major media outlets, including the BBC, the *Huffington Post*, *The Guardian*, and others, have produced stories about this phenomenon. A recent study of interviews with mothers who regret having children has attracted significant attention.[25] Likewise, the book *The Mother Bliss Lie: Regretting Motherhood* became widely popular, especially in Germany, a country that has experienced a sharp decline in marriage and fertility rates.[26] This plethora of recent writings demonstrates how deciding not to have children has become popular and mainstream. Mainstreaming these ideas gives many women the freedom to be professionally ambitious and mentally experimental and, thus, to forego marriage and family life altogether.

THE POSTMATERIALIST APPEAL OF BEING ALONE

Women's advancement is but one manifestation of the postmaterialism age. Postmaterialism is shared by men and women alike and encompasses values such as creativity, trying new things, and self-actualization. The argument is that when individuals feel secure, they desire to have a unique voice and to fulfill their potential.[27] This leads many to forgo family life. An anonymous blogger, thirty-one, writes:

> In order to go out into the world and be the vivacious, active, creative, and ambitious person that I am, I also need this deeply personal sacred time. And I need a lot of it. In a relationship, a lot of this time seems to, for me, get negotiated away. It disappears under the expectation that being involved with someone means wanting to spend ALL free time together.... It was very difficult, in many of my past relationships[,] to have this private, quiet, reflective time.[28]

Such statements imply a meaning that goes beyond the freedom to travel the world: they focus, instead, on the desire to be creative and active, to try new things, and to fulfill certain ambitions. The presumption is that being in a partnership might hold people back, preventing them from focusing on their goals. In an interview, Angelo, thirty-four, who lives in Germany, uses similar terms in talking about being single. For him, self-expression is interpreted as sexual self-expression, and he emphasizes this aspect: "[Being single is] being free to express myself sexually in every context that is feasible and beneficial, while being emotionally accessible and approachable by all the people I care for and feel for. Commitment tends to put a damper on free expressions."

Angelo, Melissa, and the two cited anonymous bloggers are not alone. My data analysis shows that married people have values that differ from those of unmarried people. Married people, on average, score lower than all other demographics on several postmaterialist measures, including how much they value fun, freedom, creativity, and trying new things—values that, the data shows, go hand-in-hand with higher levels of education, health, wealth, secularism, and social activity. Cohabitators and divorced people score higher on all these variables, while the never-married are a mixed bag: they value fun and freedom more but score similarly to the married group on creativity and trying new things (although, as mentioned in the previous chapter, this may be more reflective of the never-married people who want to get married, not the "singles by choice").[29] Widowed people, too, appreciate freedom much more than married people, although they score lower in valuing fun, creativity, and trying new things.

A link becomes apparent between those who adopt postmaterialist values and those who delay and resist marriage. This phenomenon in general is well-established and is detailed in chapter 1. Not only did the increase in postmaterialism coincide with the decline in marriage, but it also can be held responsible for this deterioration, which occurred through various routes and mechanisms, such as individualism, capitalism, women's self-actualization, and even urbanization. However, the question at the center of our discussion is: how happy are these "postmaterialist singles" in comparison to married people, on one side, versus singles who do not adopt postmaterialist values, on the other side?

DOES POSTMATERIALISM MAKE SINGLES HAPPY?

While it is evident that singles hold postmaterialist values to a larger extent, there is much doubt as to whether singles with such values derive greater life satisfaction and happiness. Moreover, criticism of the more extreme celebrations of these values, such as festive self-marriage ceremonies, is widespread. For example, in 2014, the popular online magazine the *Daily Beast* published a poignant piece about self-marriage, in which the journalist Tim Teeman argues: "Self-marriage is the ultimate brand extension of a self-obsessed, selfish [populace].... It is a joke, and not a funny one. Marrying yourself isn't the answer for single people seeking affirmation or security. It's desperate.... There is nothing that empowering in these ceremonies, no grand feminist statement, no grand personal statement—just a rather pathetic play-acting of symbolism."[30]

Teeman's harsh critique implies being single might be undesirable, but that making it a matter of choice, and even a reason to celebrate, is totally unacceptable. The critique's conclusion is quite straightforward: choosing to be single and adopting a set of individualistic values is selfish, desperate, and mainly sad. Teeman, who received Interviewer of the Year and Journalist of the Year awards at the 2016 NLGJA (the association of LGBTQ journalists), clings to stereotypes shared by other minorities. This is only a continuation of the negative typecasting of singles that portrays them as immature, self-centered and unhappy. [31]

Yet, despite Teeman's criticism of self-marriage, real answers in this debate can come from empirical tests. Does choosing, consciously and even ritually, singlehood over coupledom make people unhappy? Are these self-marriage ceremonies wholly fake? And in general, is this new generation of singles who value individualism and independence truly miserable?

Before addressing potential answers to these questions we must consider four main arguments ostensibly proving that singles who embrace postmaterialist values are unhappy. The first argument suggests that possessing postmaterialist values, such as fun and freedom, does not necessarily lead to greater happiness. In fact, valuing freedom can lead to reduced happiness, not more. This logic is widely apparent in the discourse on capitalism. Some argue that increased freedom was the cause for falling happiness levels in China between 1990 and 2000, when capitalism rose.[32] Similar phenomena were also observed in eastern European countries when they shifted from communism to a market-based system in the 1990s.[33] The given reason in research is that freedom increases competition, stress, and inequality. There is also an argument to be made that singles might be consumed by the constant instability of their solo lives. The freedom in going solo might be tied to a relentless, ultimately empty race to experience new things.

The second argument for why postmaterialist values do not necessarily lead to happiness points out that singles still encounter higher levels of discrimination, even if they manage to overcome the economic, psychological, and behavioral difficulties associated with being unmarried and its accompanying burden of freedom and uncertainty.[34] In fact, those who believe in going solo or who cherish their freedom are more exposed to discrimination. As discussed in chapter 3, even today singlehood is often perceived negatively by both social institutions[35] and individuals.[36] Research shows that people who are happier with their single status and who choose to live accordingly are perceived more negatively than those who are unhappy with their singlehood and who would like to become coupled.[37] As mentioned in the third chapter, singles by choice are often seen as rebellious people who go against mainstream society and thus draw criticism, while singles by circumstances are painted as unfortunate cases that only need help in order to find their soul-mates. It is argued that those who hold postmaterialist values are swimming against the current and thus face harsher social exclusion.

Third, many have argued that holding postmaterialist values and *choosing* to go solo has tremendous negative economic, psychological, behavioral, and physical costs.[38] One study, for example, claims that young people are simply ignorant of the full benefits of marriage, and that postmaterialist values leading them to stay unmarried actually sabotage their well-being.[39] Indeed, there is evidence to suggest that married people are better off financially and seemingly benefit from improved levels of mental and physical health.[40] Thus, those who *believe* in going solo might suffer more from financial, physical, and mental disadvantages simply because they are more likely to remain single longer and less likely to expect to overcome these disadvantages, which appear to be perpetual. For example, if someone pays higher rent because he or she is unmarried (and not sharing the rent with a partner), then the feeling of economic distress can take a heavier toll because there are no real prospects for a situational change.

The fourth argument, drawn from the Maslowian perspective, is that singles with postmaterialist values may suffer from a needs imbalance. Although it may seem reasonable to propose that sacrificing one thing (e.g., a stable relationship) to gain another (e.g., self-actualization) is a fair swap, Maslow's theory would deem such a trade impossible since self-actualization falls on the highest level of the needs triangle and is, therefore, unattainable if one sacrifices lower levels. In other words, there is a hierarchy of needs, one that singles approach incorrectly by satisfying their higher-level needs of freedom and self-actualization without meeting their more basic needs of human interaction and emotional satisfaction. Like workaholics who invest in careers at the expense of family life, postmaterialist singles, according to this argument, pursue new and exciting experiences such as traveling the world while neglecting their elementary emotional needs. This, in turn, might harm their well-being because their lower-level needs are not met.[41]

HAPPY NEVERTHELESS

While individualism and postmaterialism are *causes* of the rise of singlehood, my research shows how these values can also *benefit* singles. That is, singles with postmaterialist values are also better equipped to deal with singlehood. Even if holding postmaterialist values can somewhat reduce the well-being of singles, the benefits are nonetheless large enough to offset the disadvantages. This might explain why an increasing number of people choose to go solo in our postmaterialist age. Sasha, thirty-four, gives some insight into the matter by listing the benefits that relate to postmaterialist values:

> This year, I have been thinking that I am grateful for still being single, which, honestly is not what I would have said last year. I took this year off to travel and I did the journey alone.... So, this leads me to thinking about reasons to be grateful for being single this Thanksgiving.... A relationship can be very time-consuming. When you are single, you have all your free

time outside of work and other obligations to discover what brings you joy. Use it and be grateful for it! Being single gives you the opportunity to create more joy in your life without depending on someone else to provide it for you. Freedom to travel and explore alone.[42]

Sasha underwent a transformation from struggling with being single to experiencing joy and gratitude by embracing postmaterialist values: freedom, an appreciation of personal growth, and discovering new things. She devotes time to herself rather than to a "time-consuming relationship." It seems that she now actually prefers being single, at least for the time being. Rick, sixty-nine, is single and lives in Oregon. In our interview, he describes his own perspective on being single: "[Being single] you get to have your own individual perspective. Really, the most amazing part about this game is that you get to play it any way you want. It's totally your choice."

My data analysis backs up Sasha's newfound inner peace and Rick's playful perspective. It shows that postmaterialist beliefs are consistently associated with greater happiness among singles. Accounting for secondary variables such as gender, education, and wealth, happiness correlates strongly with postmaterialist values.

For example, a never-married person who gives the highest scores to freedom or fun is around 10 percent happier than a never-married person who thinks these values are unimportant (i.e., gives it the lowest score). Similarly, valuing creativity and trying new things is associated with a 15 percent happiness advantage for a never-married person. These patterns are shared among every other singles group, including widowed, divorced, and separated individuals, all of whom gain happiness by holding postmaterialist values.

More importantly, singles gain more from postmaterialist values even when their levels are similar to those of couples. In other words, not only are singles who hold higher levels of postmaterialist values significantly happier, but they also derive greater benefit from every additional unit of postmaterialism (as reported by respondents on a scale of 1 to 6). For example, consider a married woman and a widow: Both are equal in all major characteristics (education, income, etc.), and both value trying new things (e.g., they answer "6" in the survey). My analysis indicates that, on average, the widow gains 10 percent more happiness when compared to her married counterpart. In general, for all postmaterialist values measured, all unmarried groups who hold the maximum levels of postmaterialist values are roughly 0.4 standard deviations happier than married individuals with identical levels. This gain compares to the difference between someone experiencing racism, ageism, or chauvinism versus someone who does not, and this applies for each postmaterialist value measured separately.

Furthermore, since unmarried individuals, on average, hold higher scores in measurements of postmaterialist values than couples to begin with, they naturally gain an additional advantage. Not only do they benefit more from every additional point on the postmaterialist scale, but they also have "more points" to gain from.

These results therefore suggest that postmaterialist values greatly contribute to increasing singles' happiness. In fact, possessing a significantly postmaterialist set of values enables singles to make gains in happiness that may reverse their initial disadvantage compared to married people. Arlene, a thirty-three-year-old from Scotland, writes in a letter to *BBC Magazine*:

> I am perfectly happy to be single.... I am free to do whatever I want and when I want. I'm responsible for my everyday living, my luxuries in life, my way of living and my own happiness. I think nowadays there is too much expectation on being part of a couple. Why should I chase that? I was born as an individual and encouraged as I grew up to think for myself. So, I certainly don't think I am missing out in anything. I say to all my friends, I love being single and can never see a time I will think any different.[43]

Arlene's assertion is neither snide nor aggressive, simply a statement of fact. She loves single life. Having adopted values that differ from those of her peers or the previous generation, Arlene sees singleness as a gift, not a sentence. Instead of being constrained by marriage, she finds that her single status sets her free.

Especially noteworthy is that no significant difference exists between married and cohabiting people concerning happiness garnered from postmaterialist values. Even though cohabitating couples hold higher levels of postmaterialist values, they do not boast a happiness advantage when compared to their married counterparts. This is arguably because, unlike nonpartnered singles, the living situations and social structures of cohabitators resemble those of married individuals. Apparently, postmaterialist values serve the single population better, echoing the importance of freedom for uncoupled individuals who want to travel and explore, similarly to what Melissa and Sasha both describe in their blogs. Of course, the reality is not so dichotomous, and there are many who ascribe moderate importance to postmaterialist values. Yet the principle is always the same: postmaterialist values greatly benefit singles.

HOW AND WHY DOES POSTMATERIALISM BENEFIT SINGLES?

The aforementioned criticism and the questions raised in this chapter demand some elaboration. Why does embracing postmaterialist values help singles narrow the gap in well-being between them and their married friends—and how? Rising numbers of singles indicate they are deriving something good from their situations. Although the link between postmaterialist values and their benefits is not so intuitive, the movement that cherishes singlehood is nevertheless growing rapidly. They might all be wrong, but my findings do show they are onto something. There are several possible explanations for how and why postmaterialist values actually benefit singles and contribute to their well-being.

The first explanation is that postmaterialist values immunize singles against society's prejudices. It seems that singles with a postmaterialist outlook care less about norms and traditions and are less inclined to compare themselves to the rest of society. In a sense, this stance is inherent to postmaterialism because valuing freedom and trying new things contradicts adherence to norms and traditions. Indeed, an additional analysis I conducted shows a significant and negative correlation between postmaterialist values and the belief that adhering to norms is important. Thus, postmaterialist values not only promote the solo lifestyle but also free singles from feeling judged by others. This is particularly important, since singles are viewed negatively by society.[44] Heron, who has been self-married since 2002, writes: "For years I had noticed really high needs for validation, attention, and affection.... Since my Marriage to Self, I have felt a deep sense of peace and safety, belonging, and just plain love. My centering is within myself."[45]

Before he self-married, Heron felt like he was wearing an ill-fitting suit. Perhaps he could not quite place the source of the irritation, but something was wrong. He did not feel comfortable being single. The self-marriage did not change anything, but it seems to serve as Heron's declaration to the world: "I am who and what I am—and I am fine with it."

A second reason that postmaterialism may benefit the unwed is that singles, consciously or unconsciously, define and satisfy their familial needs without cohabitating or marrying. In this sense, freedom and creativity, for example, are not only high in the hierarchy of needs, as Maslow describes,[46] but also define the lower layers of needs, reinventing the meaning of being loved and having companionship. Indeed, research shows that singles increasingly find companionship through alternative families and communal arrangements.[47] Thus, the exact same postmaterialist values that encourage them to go solo also open them to alternative living arrangements (these novel arrangements are discussed in detail later in this book). In this sense, although postmaterialist singles might place greater importance on the upper levels of the needs hierarchy and, in many instances, readily devote more time and resources to them,[48] this does not mean that they neglect the need for feeling loved and for belonging. Intan, thirty-eight, an Indonesian woman who broke up with her boyfriend and moved to Berlin with their son in 2015, said to me in an interview: "I think my needs are pretty much completed. What do you need from a partner actually? Let's say, sex. Well, I have sex. Companionship?

I have my friends.... Are there any other things needed from a relationship? In my mind I can get sex and companionship from the way I am living now. So, it's not that big a deal."

Intan feels her needs are being satisfied by friends and sex-mates. Instead of deriving life satisfaction from marriage, singles like Intan find it in a new, more experimental and fluid way through technology, communities, and big urban centers. Differences regarding the latter are particularly noticeable between married and never-married people, among whom there is often an urban-suburban split.[49] In another interview, Joseph, never married, thirty-two, describes the importance of living in a big city like Berlin: "I am surrounded by lots of academics, and there are a lot of people who live really progressive or new life models; they are not looking for a specific partner or are not looking for a partner at all. If you think about people with low education, or from the countryside, they are mostly more traditional and conservative. I accept it, but it is not my first goal to achieve."

Joseph, who was born in Bonn and moved to Berlin a few months before the interview, sees Berlin as a hub for new life models that make partnership unnecessary, even obsolete. Singles are drawn more to such urban environments, where they can not only limit the pressure caused by comparing themselves to others but also benefit from a rich and diverse range of opportunities for social interaction and circles of belonging.[50] Based on their quests for new things and the value they place on freedom, singles explore innovative ways of living and continuously reinvent their lifestyles. These experiments create a variety of opportunities, not only for entertainment but for actually satiating their lower strata of needs, too.

A third explanation is that postmaterialist values are compounded by factors that further promote happiness. For instance, postmaterialist singles may be more inclined to engage in sports, thereby improving their health and, by extension, enhancing their well-being. One study reveals a clear relationship between postmaterialism and participation in certain physical leisure activities,[51] particularly running and other solo sports.[52] The logic behind this is that those who feel materially safe want to develop and challenge themselves, often doing so through aerobic sports that further cultivate physical and mental health.

Individuals who appreciate creativity and trying new things may also be more inclined to engage in social activities outside of work, such as by enrolling in classes or joining clubs, thereby fostering additional levels of happiness (according to the analysis presented in the previous chapter). Again, postmaterialism becomes a way of living and not simply a cognitive worldview. Consequently, it creates an ecosystem that promotes higher well-being. Chloe, thirty-six, lives in the United Kingdom. In our interview, she said:

> Out of relationships, I feel more myself. I feel happy and enjoy independence. Being in a relationship simply makes me too complacent. But I want to push myself, to go to places, to meet people, and to do things.
>
> With a partner, I find that I get kind of lazy in my social interactions. You see, I'm quite a social person, but in relationship that eventually becomes quite a negative thing. [But as a single], you're starting to feel: "Do something, even with traveling"—I was traveling to Australia, which would have been probably impossible being together with someone.

Chloe describes herself as "social," but any sort of attachment makes her feel constrained. Precisely because she feels complacent, her social dynamism grinds to a halt as soon as she ties herself to another individual. Without the "anchor" of a relationship, however, Chloe feels free to sail the boat of her life along new routes and explore exciting new directions.

To that end, it seems that the global shift toward self-development and postmaterialism[53] actually presents an increased opportunity for raising singles' happiness levels. The evidence in this chapter shows that postmaterialist views do not undermine happiness by preventing marriage[54] or by making a person look pitiful, as Teeman argues.[55] Rather, postmaterialist values benefit singles by encouraging them to deflect social judgment, find alternatives for companionship, and engage in activities that make them feel good about being uncoupled. While the rise of postmaterialist values leads to reduced rates of marriage and, by extension, to reduced financial, legal, and social privileges of those who go solo, these very same values may be key to *raising* the well-being of singles in many other ways.

Admittedly, values are not easily adopted or discarded, and it might be harder to develop postmaterialist values than to engage in social activities as recommended in the previous chapter. However, in many cases, it is possible for singles to employ, consciously or unconsciously, behaviors and undertakings that align with postmaterialist values, such as adventurous trips, experimental workshops, cognitive therapy sessions, and even symbolic ceremonies such as self-marriage. These activities only scratch the surface, but they might be enough to provide singles with a mental advantage. Essentially, discussions on postmaterialist values should start at an early age and thus might help prepare adult singles in more comprehensive and fundamental ways. The understanding that postmaterialist values can increase the well-being of singles opens a path for novel ways to educate the next generation of singles and prepare them for the option of solo living.[56]

While the self-marriage movement might remain a curiosity, Dominique Youkhehpaz and her self-married fellows enlighten us with a new way of viewing singlehood. Teaching the values of independence, creativity, personal freedom, and trying new things might serve well those 25 percent of American children (and others throughout the world) who are predicted never to marry.[57] In particular, this call surely needs to reverberate in faraway cities like Kabul, where women like Zarmina still struggle for marriage independence.

CHAPTER SIX

Work Hard, (but) Play Hard

Walking around the Palace of Versailles, you will notice an impressive sculpture almost three meters, or nine and a half feet, in height: Proteus, accompanied by two seals, is chained by Aristaeus and struggles to break free. Installed in 1714, it is considered the most important work of the sculptor Sébastien Slodtz, who attempted to capture this dramatic, mythological moment. Aristaeus, son of Apollo, had lost his love, Eurydice, who had died after being bitten by a serpent. Aristaeus bound Proteus to extract advice from him. He wanted to know how to recover from the curse that Eurydice's companion nymphs had leveled against his bees. They held Aristaeus accountable for her death.[1]

In this drama, Proteus continues to struggle; the love affair of Aristaeus is none of his business, nor is the fact that Aristaeus's bees are dying. The son of Poseidon, god of the sea, Proteus is a shepherd, a prophet, and a shape-shifter. Some ascribe to him a specific domain in the Greek hierarchy and call him the god of "elusive sea change," which suggests the constantly changing nature of the sea or the liquid quality of water. In modern times, the psychologist Carl Jung defined him as a personification of the unconscious, who, because of his gift of prophecy and shape-changing, has much in common with the central but elusive figure of alchemy, Mercurius.[2] Proteus's power to predict the future and explain the will of the gods attracts several heroes in the Greek mythology, who seek him out for advice. But he does not like to be bothered and constantly uses his shape-shifting powers to escape.

According to the myth, Aristaeus follows his mother's advice: "The only way to get Proteus to listen to you is to hold on no matter what form he assumes." He grips Proteus with force, trying to hold him down. But Proteus continues to struggle; he wants to maintain his privacy. He takes various animal forms, as well as that of fire and even water. But he fails. He must guide Aristaeus in order to be set free.

Ironically, although Aristaeus released Proteus in the end, the white marble sculpture still holds Proteus tied to this embarrassing moment of being chained centuries later—frozen, unable to assume any other form. Maybe Proteus would have wanted this, for his message to be preserved for future generations: be careful, for no matter how flexible you are and how much freedom you seek, others will try to take advantage of you for their own benefit.

Two hundred and sixty-two years after Slodtz's creation was installed at Versailles, Proteus's legacy came to life, in 1976, in the term *protean career*. Douglas Hall coined the term to describe the shift from an organizational career to an individualistic one, which consists of a person's varied experiences in education, training, and work. According to Hall, the protean person seeks a personal career track as part of the search for self-fulfillment, changing fields of expertise and moving from one workplace to another. For this emerging new character, the criterion of success is internal, not external.[3]

Indeed, most people see their work in one of three ways. Some see it as a *job* that provides financial rewards and is necessary for subsistence and paying the bills. Others see work as a *career* that fulfills the necessity of earning an income, but which comes with the added value of permitting an individual to seek advancement and to feel successful and capable. The third group sees work as a *calling*, where workers choose their professions for reasons of personal enjoyment and fulfillment or with a focus on creating change and/or contributing to a wider cause.[4]

In recent years, the importance of work to self-fulfillment has been emphasized even more, and the idea of having a *job* is becoming less appealing compared to a protean career or calling. Throughout the twentieth century, globalization and market harmonization caused increasing competition and pushed many industries to seek ways to raise workers' utilization and enhance their time effectiveness.[5] This pressure, along with the increasing pace of work, placed unreasonable demands on workers, negatively shaping their personal lives as well as their mental and physical health.[6] Recently, however, we have witnessed a backlash against these trends that has catalyzed a demand to change the nature of work. Individuals are increasingly unwilling to work hard without a feeling of self-fulfillment. This is especially apparent among the younger generations; post–baby boomers have higher expectations from work than their parents and tend to favor highly engaged employers, opportunities for professional development, and goal-oriented work.[7] Employers have responded accordingly, shaping a new business culture that empowers all employees to make employment decisions based on the search for self-fulfillment.[8]

In turn, self-fulfillment has become an important pathway to happiness. Self-fulfillment, or the fulfillment of one's hopes, dreams, and ambitions, is now a direct and authentic measure of our happiness.[9] Whether this has to do with meeting personal goals, or with seeking deeper meaning in life, self-fulfilled individuals are typically happier.[10] Particularly with the rise of individualism, much of the world has witnessed a change in the social order that has placed self-fulfillment at center stage.[11] Today, many individuals primarily seek a way to feel needed and meaningful to others, and they emphasize this aspect in judging their life-satisfaction. No wonder, then, that therapists and mental-health professionals use the pursuit of self-fulfillment as an essential tenet of well-being and psychotherapeutic treatment.[12]

Identifying with a type of work that belongs to the "protean" category can, therefore, be one of the sources of life satisfaction. One British study, for example, found that those in the education and health sectors are, overall, highly satisfied with their jobs despite being less satisfied with their paychecks. According to this study, the reason for their satisfaction lies in the sense of social contribution and achievement they feel in their work.[13]

WORK AND THE UNMARRIED

How does all of this relate to creating a happy singlehood? My study shows that work is essential in explaining the making of happy singles. Happy singles, and especially long-term, never-married happy singles, increase their well-being by seeking self-fulfillment through their careers rather than through the creation of a nuclear family.

My statistical analysis shows that job satisfaction contributes to the overall happiness of singles more than it does to that of married individuals. It is important to note that "job satisfaction" in this instance does not mean job convenience or a large paycheck. I exclude those factors from the analysis. Job satisfaction is much deeper and relates to deriving meaning and self-fulfillment from work.

To make the issue more tangible, consider a married person and a never-married person who are identical in terms of age, education, income, health, and so on, and who both experience the highest level of job satisfaction. In such a case, the gap in overall happiness between the never-married person and the married person is reduced by more than 70 percent. Yes, by that much. The rest, as was discussed earlier, is attributable to the selection process into marriage (happier people choose to marry, rather than marriage contributing to happiness). After accounting for such selection mechanisms, it is possible to say that the never-married person is in fact happier because of his or her satisfying job.

The importance of job satisfaction to the well-being and happiness of singles is common among more than simply the never-married. It is equally valued by divorced and widowed individuals, albeit to a lesser extent. In these latter two cases, the gap in happiness is bigger (recall the penalty for exiting marriage, discussed earlier), and thus the impact of a satisfying job on reducing the gap is around 50 to 60 percent.

In the interviews I conducted, I found an explanation for this impact. Jane, who lives apart from her husband in upstate New York, provides one example. She is sixty-two and works in the health-care industry, and in our interview she thought back to her old life as a housewife and compared it to her current life. She said:

> I think it's most important in life to have a job that you like. That is most important—then you feel good about yourself. I was a housewife. I spent ten years driving the car, taking my children from one school to another school. I spent all day doing something, and at the end of the day, I was waiting for everybody to go to sleep so I could sit by myself, to write in my journal—have some time. But I had to wake up in the morning to start again. You are doing something, but then you sit by yourself and you think, "Why?"

Jane wondered about the meaning of her life as a housewife who took care of the children and waited all day for a few moments of alone time that she could devote to writing. In contrast, today's Jane emphasizes that her job as a nurse is important for her and how happy she is to have it. It makes her feel good about herself. Later in the interview, she testified that she does not look forward to retirement; quite the opposite, she absolutely understands why people continue working into their seventies and eighties. She said, "Now, I can do things.... I have to be pushed. I am really not surprised that a lot of Americans said they work until they are seventy, eighty."

The importance of a meaningful job in feeling good, independent, and satisfied with life recurred throughout the interviews, not only among older singles but also among young, unmarried individuals. Shawn, a thirty-two-year-old living in Long Beach, California, who never married, told me, "As long as you're seeking self-fulfillment in other areas of life, like work, then you'll feel a bit more like you can choose or choose not to be single." It seems that being married, for Shawn, is only one option in achieving a sense of self-fulfillment.

Deriving self-fulfillment in other realms of life, such as work, gives him the freedom to stay single if he wishes.

Louise's story is striking. We had our interview in her beautifully decorated bookstore, where customers can also order food and coffee or just sit and relax on the soft couches scattered around. Louise was married seventeen years and, out of necessity, worked in jobs she did not like. Now, forty-four-year-old Louise is divorced and living in Brussels. She opened her bookstore after her divorce to fulfill one of her dreams. She says: "I really love my bookstore, because for me it is the first time in my life I did what I chose to do.... Here, I really wanted to do something for combining food and books. It is the first time for me that I'm acting like a self-entrepreneur, and it's very satisfying because I realized that I could do something like this. I never imagined I would have done this before. It brings me a lot of satisfaction."

Louise does not see her bookstore only as a job she likes or even only as something she finds meaning in. Rather, by opening this bookstore, Louise learned she can be independent. For her, it is a life accomplishment, even an important component of her identity. She looks at herself now as an owner of a business, a "self-entrepreneur." Indeed, I repeatedly heard from all groups of singles how they see their singlehood as an opportunity to redefine themselves.

More than all other demographics, singles, and highly individualistic singles in particular, tend to value meaningful work because it actualizes their capabilities, brings them a sense of freedom, and makes them feel worthy.[14] As a result, singles whose work has added meaning or value for them gain more satisfaction in life.[15] Furthermore, another statistical analysis I conducted shows that singles value life accomplishments on average more than married individuals do and, therefore, stand to gain more from investing in their careers.[16] Indeed, Louise tells me time and again how happy she is since leaving her husband and opening her bookstore.

This has a lot to do with the motivations for career choice. Family-oriented individuals, or those who enter family relationships earlier, may select job security and stable income over something that provides them with added meaning, because they assume the responsibility of financially supporting others.[17] In contrast, never-married singles (divorced and widowed individuals join them once they start living alone again and their children can support themselves) do not usually have these obligations and have the freedom to choose a less-secure career path that may be more emotionally rewarding. An anonymous female blogger, age thirty-five, writes about the importance of work and career advancement, stressing the advantage of being single: "You can focus on your career, and give it your all. You can grow as a professional, chart out your career path without any pauses or breaks—typically associated with marriage and moving to a new city or having kids."[18]

This blogger insists that her single lifestyle contributes to achieving her life goals. For her, family life is full of "pauses or breaks" that potentially would distract her from focusing on the career she wants, a situation very similar to what Jane described as having happened when she was a housewife and needed to look after her family.

In a sense, this blogger raises the issue of work-family conflict. For married people, self-fulfillment in life is based on two central pillars: work and career, on the one hand, and family life, on the other. However, the two might clash at times and come at the expense of each other. Of course, this is not always the case, and some will even say that family life and job satisfaction support one another. But studies show that many married couples struggle to balance work with their commitment to their spouses (going out together, visiting spouses' families and friends, celebrating spouses' life events, etc.).[19] This is even before having children, a situation that makes this juggling more difficult.[20]

In contrast, many singles are happier with their singleness, and find their lives enriched, when they are unbound by family responsibilities and can fully invest in their careers. Some singles even hold on to their independence and choose not to enter relationships *because* they want to avoid the work-family conflict. In any case, there are typically fewer restraints and pressures preventing singles from investing in their careers without feeling guilty. Even divorced singles with children feel the work-family conflict to a lesser extent, because they often share childcare responsibilities with their exes and, sometimes, with their exes' new spouses. Lena, fifty-five, works in an Israeli theater. She has divorced three times, and after twenty-one years of living alone, she says in an interview, "We have a ring in the theater that only people who are really invested in work get. I got one on my fiftieth birthday, and I wear it on my left hand, like a wedding ring, because I'm married to the theater. And that's my most permanent marriage."

Lena expresses a passion for her work that is more permanent, and maybe even more important, than her three marriages. As a single parent for more than twenty years, testifies that she loves her daughter and maintains good relationships with her three ex-husbands. But the ring she received from her colleagues symbolizes the marriage she cherishes most: her work at the theater.

However, being "married" to work is not always simple or romantic. There are other realms of life, such as friends, hobbies, and so on. Singles who devote time to their careers might glean satisfaction from their work, but they also might face job burnout and work-life conflicts. This puts singles at risk, and we should carefully consider how happy singles avoid the pitfalls of overdevotion to work.

SINGLES' WORK-LIFE CONFLICT

Job burnout is a type of stress characterized by elevated levels of exhaustion, cynicism, and inefficacy. Recent studies show that unmarried individuals are more prone to symptoms of job burnout than those who are married.[21] Within the singles population, men in general, and especially people who never married, are particularly at risk of job burnout, while women in general, and especially divorced people, experience moderate levels.[22]

Job burnout occurs more often among singles because they tend to place high importance on their professional lives at the expense of other activities. Singles certainly do not wish to neglect friends and family, but the driving need to be perceived as a successful and dynamic professional might overtake social activities and engagement.[23] Thus, while work may serve as a source of pride and happiness, it can also create barriers to achieving a balanced and healthy life and, ultimately, lead to reduced well-being.

In addition, by placing such high value on their careers, single people have more at stake in their jobs. Challenges in this sole realm of focus can prove daunting. The pressure to succeed is greater, and the risk of losing one's sense of self-fulfillment because of underperformance is higher. By comparison, many married couples assign high importance to their roles as spouses and parents.[24] Therefore, work is not their only source of satisfaction; they have a "safety net." Of course, singles also gain a lot from the concentration on their career, more than couples do, but their emotional well-being should not be without a safety net of its own.

In the opposite case, singles might involve themselves in a wide variety of sporting, volunteer, community, and family-related activities, dividing their social lives into far more pieces than coupled individuals who focus primarily on themselves and their nuclear families.[25] Their multiple roles can be a source of extra conflict for these singles, something couples do not experience. Singles can thus feel underwater from balancing so many activities, raising the specter of inter-role conflict and job burnout.[26]

Besides the pressure that singles may put on themselves, their work-life balance may be negatively affected by employers and policies discriminating against those without partners or families. As discussed in chapter 3, singles are often expected to work harder than their married colleagues while gaining fewer benefits.[27] Thus, emotional and physical exhaustion among singles is evident in today's workplace because of ignorance about their needs, and because of pervasive, yet seldom scrutinized, discrimination against singles. Abe, thirty-one, who was born in Milledgeville, Georgia, and still lives in his hometown, said in our interview: "A single person is seen as somebody who can work later hours, longer hours, earlier hours, things outside the standard workday. Whereas, for family people, it's more expected of them to have more standard work hours, nine to five with an hour lunch break. For me, it may be working until ten or eleven o'clock at night or start working at six o'clock in the morning—or whatever it might be—because I don't have a partner or somebody else whose life is dependent on me maintaining a consistent schedule to some degree."

Abe describes a situation wherein unmarried people with no children are at particularly high risk. He points out the assumption that, since singles do not have traditional familial responsibilities, they can meet higher work expectations. Indeed, today's treatment of singles in the workforce overlooks the notion that many of them have very rich lives and might be balancing numerous social roles when allocating their nonwork hours. It is a misconception that singles have less of a social life to balance. In many cases, the opposite is true, and singles lead a much more involved and varied life than coupled individuals.

My statistical analysis further shows that although singles derive a greater benefit from job satisfaction, they feel they are not being paid appropriately considering their efforts when compared to married colleagues. This is especially true for the never-married group, who are 9 percent more likely to believe they are not paid appropriately. This finding is unsurprising considering employers' neglect and singles' high workload, as Abe describes. Indeed, even if singles decide to invest themselves in their work, employers should reward them appropriately.

More striking is that singles feel that the balance between their personal lives and their jobs is less satisfactory than that of married individuals. One could assume that married individuals are the ones who find the balance difficult because of family responsibilities, but it is actually singles who suffer more from this problem. This is especially true for widowed individuals and divorced people, who are 31 percent and 22 percent more likely, respectively, to think their work and lives are out of balance compared to those of married people.

It seems that a main issue here is a misunderstanding of what *work-life balance* means for different people, especially singles. In fact, it is common for researchers, reporters, and policy makers to talk about *work-family* balance instead of *work-life* balance in today's marriage-focused society. The vast majority of attention is directed to the nuclear family and translates *life* as "family" without people even noticing.[28]

Yet a person's identity includes various components, such as leisure and educational activities, community involvement, household repair and maintenance, and friendship development.[29] In this sense, the family is but one domain among many that deserve attention and time allocation. Even in the family domain, singles are the ones who care for aging parents, more than married individuals do, a fact that is widely ignored by the average employer.[30]

Thus, both employers and singles themselves should be careful about balancing singles' work with other activities and insist on workloads equal to those of their married peers. Although they do not necessarily have the responsibilities of the traditional nuclear family, happy singles are those who know how to balance work with other aspects of life and give themselves space to develop in several directions, while alleviating potential conflict with work.

WORK HARD, PLAY HARD: HOW HAPPY SINGLES BALANCE WORK

According to the interviews I conducted, happy singles employ certain strategies to cope with work stress and improve their quality of life and happiness. Specifically, I have found that happy singles broaden their understanding of the work-life balance in at least six ways.

The first strategy is to balance work with a healthy array of leisure activities. This can involve serious, substantial hobbies (e.g., gardening or dancing) or casual leisure that is more short-lived and requires minimal special training or investment (e.g., going to the cinema or visiting a museum). Sheila, thirty-one, who lives in London, is in the middle of hectic studies that will lead to her master's degree, while maintaining an intense schedule at work. Yet as a single, she keeps herself in good spirits and insists on balancing her busy schedule with hobbies and a general sense of discovery: "I think having all that extra space to learn about your own place in life, and hobbies, to learn about yourself as an individual again—I think it's great. I think it's a lot of discovery, rediscovering things from when I was younger, finding new things, and having a greater sense of adventure. So, there isn't one thing that I do with my free time, but there's a whole lot of crap to do."

Sheila feels energized in our interview. Part of it is what she calls "a greater sense of adventure." She has never married and does not have a long-term relationship. Instead, she is focusing on her career but makes sure to broaden her activities and find new hobbies. This way of living is certainly not unique to young singles. In fact, it was the older interviewees I met, more than anyone else, who insisted on the importance of leisure activities to balance their intense, yet satisfying, work time.

The second way to balance work is to foster enriching educational activities. For several happy singles I interviewed, a good work-life balance includes time devoted to education and learning, outside of the formal work environment. Highly individualistic singles were especially interested in noncompulsory learning, reading, or taking a course about their fields of work. Others pursued extra degrees or certificates and occupied themselves with general self-improvement. Haim, fifty-two, a never-married man who works in agriculture in northern Israel, explains how hard he works during the day. However, he tells me, when he returns home he relaxes and prefers delving into something interesting rather than being stressed out with family issues. He testifies, "So, I have absolutely no problem being by myself—there are so many good books, so much good music, and this stupid Internet that has changed our lives. You don't realize it—you start to read something, and three hours pass, just like that."

Third, every individual who is attempting to maintain a work-life balance also needs to take into consideration his or her health and appearance needs. Finding time to visit the gym and exercise after work, and making time to cook and eat well, are essential parts of a happy single's routine. The combination of these factors is important for physical and mental health. For some, maintaining their health and appearance may include praying and meditating. In fact, my interviews revealed that spiritual and mindfulness practices are a recurrent, highly important theme in maintaining a happy single lifestyle, especially within a stressful work environment. For example, Abigail, a forty-four-year-old never-married woman who lives in Portland, Oregon, told me how practicing mindfulness exercises before and after work helps her in feeling positive on the job: "I have an active gratitude practice. I write down three things in the morning and three things in the evening. The mornings are easy; and then what happens is that I think: Oh God, I've got to come up with three more things I'm grateful for [after work]. You train yourself to be very attuned or attentive to small moments that you can be thankful for. It's kind of that idea that... if you're looking for reasons to be grateful, you'll have reasons to be grateful."

Mindfulness, spirituality, and, in some situations, religion can be used to increase singles' happiness at work.[31] Several studies show a strong, positive relationship between mindfulness and job satisfaction, and a strong inverse relationship with work burnout.[32] Spiritual health in Islam, for example, can be achieved through the calming effect of prayer or meditation.[33] For divorced people, who are reportedly more vulnerable to being lonely, studies show that mindfulness-based cognitive therapy is effective for reducing anxiety and depression.[34] Studies in South Korea have found that spirituality and religious beliefs moderate the effects of loneliness and depression among older singles.[35] Research from India reveals that it is not only religious practice or belief in a greater power that improves the happiness of singles and the elderly: spirituality, or the practice of dharma, is also an important predictor of stress reduction and increased well-being.[36] All these variations of spirituality and mindfulness are highly efficient in reducing stress at work. This is in addition to the widely practiced routine of many happy singles, who train and exercise at the gym or outdoors.

The fourth aspect of work-life balance for singles to consider is household management. Working long hours can eat into the time required for housekeeping tasks. Singles who live alone need to manage their bills, buy food, and deal with repairs, home improvements, and other services, many times on their own, not to mention that sometimes they also assume multiple social responsibilities. Even if money is not an issue, finding the time to complete these tasks can prove burdensome. To maximize one's work-life balance, this extra burden must be considered. One idea on how to deal with this comes from Heather, who suggested to her church community, in a comment she posted in a blog: "Wouldn't it be nice if others would see the need of an unmarried person and fill it? The single person who owns a home could use some help taking care of some repairs, or a car repair, or something similar."[37]

Heather's words can be linked to the idea of "time banks," where singles who find the time to volunteer in their local communities, clubs, congregations, or other types of groups can receive help in other areas.[38] A sense of community paired with social exchange has a positive effect on the subjective well-being of singles who avail themselves of community resources that compensate for the time they devote to work.

But it is also a matter of attitude. Happy singles turn their spare time on the weekends into joyful time that combines with housekeeping. Anna, who is in her thirties and lives in the United Kingdom, writes:

> I rarely iron, as usually I don't need to, and if I do need to do it, it's usually on a sunday afternoon with the music blaring. Ironing kareoke can be the best! I also usually dance around shaking my tush as I hoover[,] as once again the stereo is on full pelt. There is nobody to moan about the washing up not being done, and no one to have a hissy fit if you don't pick up your jeans off the floor. Truth time, I have occasionally done some chores in the nude! Imagine your mum walking in on that![39]

The fifth strategy for balancing work is to "select" a family for oneself. Focusing on a specific family—siblings, parents, more distant relatives, or even friends and their children—strengthens singles in their dealings with employers and coworkers who overload them with more tasks under the assumption that they are free of family responsibilities. The fact that work-life balance is commonly understood to center on spouses and children is highly damaging for singles. However, happy singles feel at liberty to choose their families. With this chosen family, happy singles develop a different stance and a specific reason not to work extra hours.

Most importantly, of course, they benefit from interactions with and mutual support from their designated family members.[40] Sheila, mentioned above, describes how she balances her intense work with leisure activities, as well as with time invested in friends and family. She says: "Being single certainly inspires you to invest more in the friendships and other relationships you have, like with your family.... When you really invest in [nonromantic relationships], especially as an adult, you really get something else out. Like, my relationships with my parents, my friends, and my brother have been phenomenal, because I have the space and time for them."

Sheila intentionally devotes more time to her friends and family. She leverages the free time she has outside of work to deepen her connections with those surrounding her. Singles, and particularly those who live alone, are very likely to be solely responsible for their time outside of work, so purposely investing more in their chosen relationships is even more important for their well-being than for married couples, cohabitators, and parents, all of whom are naturally consumed by their nuclear family.

The sixth strategy I found turns the work environment into a social one. Happy singles connect to other people at work and constantly find new friends among colleagues. Currently, many employers, and even singles themselves who focus on attaining professional status, are prone to downplay the importance of friendships. However, happy singles are those who find friends everywhere, even in their work environments.

Suzie, thirty-seven and never-married, holds two jobs and works long hours. To achieve balance, she connects with people at work. She said to me in our interview: "I work five days a week and I work roughly twelve hours per day, in one job, three days a week. But my job involves my friends and my creativity, so even though I'm there thirty-six hours a week, I'm there with people I like. I'm doing something I love.... At least once a night, somebody I know will come out to have a chat time."

Indeed, having friends at work helps happy singles in securing a good work-life balance. To that end, a new app was recently launched named NeverEatAlone. It allows people at work to log in and find someone from their workplace with whom to eat lunch. This app has been very successful, and many employers have adopted it to increase social inter-action among employees and to ensure that no one eats alone. The com-pany's website tells the story of Marie, the founder: "After joining UBS, Marie felt lonely at work and noticed that she was spending most of her breaks with the same colleagues. She decided to change that and started to knock on the doors of different departments in order to meet new col-leagues. It gave her the opportunity to discover their work and get to know people who shared her passion (for meditation and yoga). She ended up meeting with the CEO! Marie realized that helping employees meet makes everyone better off as it leads to a happier workplace."

No doubt, finding friends at work revolutionizes the notion of the workplace as an alienating space. Marie not only eliminated the emo-tional distance between colleagues at work but also disrupted the hier-archy at her organization in meeting with the CEO.

TOWARD A SINGLE-FRIENDLY WORK SPACE

What links these six work-life balance factors is the ability to put work in perspective. Whether finding time for the gym, attending a weekly dance club, practicing mindfulness before and after work, or making a friend at work, happy singles are those who manage their working time to allow participation in these activities.

Of course, being able to work from home or having flexible hours might provide immediate solutions to the challenges facing the modern, multitasking single who has multiple commitments. While some report that working from home, or telecommuting, can ultimately create extra work-family interference for those with family at home,[41] these options might prove promising to singles who stand to benefit from the elasticity of a more flexible work time.

Even those singles who cannot afford or do not enjoy working from home or having flexible hours should negotiate with their employers to have time for outside activities. Recall the chapter on singlism (discrimination against singles): It is also up to singles and those who care about them to educate employers about singles' needs despite the seeming reverence for family life. Singles should feel free to explain the importance of recreational outlets and social events to their lives and well-being.

The climax of the battle between Aristaeus and Proteus still stands, sculptured in marble, inside the Gardens of Versailles. It continues to symbolize how some people, singles especially, require freedom and the ability to shape-shift in order to focus on their inner selves. Like Louise, who left her husband and founded her bookstore after working seventeen years in dull jobs, many singles do not want to be bound to the shore. They belong to the kingdom of the ever-changing sea, or rather they prefer the realm of the creative, aspiring subconscious. Following Proteus, many singles look for their "protean careers" and benefit considerably from them. Changing forms, keeping themselves free of distractions, allows singles to develop their self-expression and to find their own personal prophecy. Jane's writing and Lena's theater work are products of committing to their inner aspirations. Some singles, such as the anonymous blogger quoted previously, even purposely avoid "dropping the anchor" in order to continue sailing.

But it seems that Aristaeus, and many others, will forever keep trying to tie Proteus down. They are not mean; they just see Proteus as a tool for their own use. But Proteus, whose name is derived from the Greek word *protos* (meaning "original," "uncompounded"), will keep going back to the sea, swimming freely, accompanied by his herd of seals. As Philostratus writes in *Life of Apollonius of Tyana*, "I need hardly explain to readers of the poets the quality of Proteus and his reputation as regards wisdom; how versatile he was, and for ever changing his form, and defying capture, and how he had the reputation of knowing both past and future."[42]

CHAPTER SEVEN

The Future of Happy Singlehood

The legend of Edai Siabo is still being told every year in Papua New Guinea. Edai, a young man from the village of Boera, lived among the Motu people in a dry area where it was extremely hard to grow enough crops to feed everyone. One day, Edai was fishing peacefully when a great eel, the embodiment of the Spirit of the Sea in Papua mythology, appeared and dragged him under the water. The eel instructed Edai in how to build a canoe and how to sail westward to trade with others. Following these instructions, Edai built a canoe and filled it with clay cooking pots that his wife prepared, hoping to trade them for some food. Braving the dangers of the unknown, Edai boarded his canoe and sailed toward the horizon.

Most of the Motu believed they would never see Edai again. But months later, Edai appeared in the distance with his canoe full of food for the harsh dry season. The Motu people understood they could not rely solely on themselves anymore. Instead, they discovered trade and intertribal transactions. Since then, they have thrown a yearly festival to celebrate this first coastal trading voyage, known as Hiri.[1]

Living in today's world, trade seems so natural to us—almost trivial. We think nothing of picking up an item in a store and reading the stamp Made in Mexico, or Vietnam, or any other place in the world.

We are surrounded by a web of resources that provides everything we need, desire, or even imagine. We understand that no one place can do it all. Manufacturing all of a country's goods within a single country is considered a mark of a failed economic system.[2] Of course, it is possible for a country to achieve a degree of self-sufficiency, but it requires the citizens of that country to minimize their needs, perhaps even to survive in privation like the Motu people before they discovered trade and understood the advantages of engaging in a network of commerce.

To some people, the institution of marriage is similar. For them, marriage can no longer be the sole supplier of physical, social, emotional, and mental needs. Instead, these needs require a varied network of exchanges to be satisfied. While this is still not a widely shared belief, more and more people have come to understand that traditional marriage, which means living with the same person and trusting him or her to be the main provider for almost all of one's needs, throughout a half century or more, is simply impossible.

Consider the rise in life expectancy. Only a hundred years ago, the average American lived to about fifty years of age. Today this number is just under eighty.[3] Living so much longer makes individuals think about the variety they want in their lives and whether one partner can provide it. People not only live longer but also have more needs, seek more experiences, and want to capitalize on more opportunities. They expect more from the world and, in turn, expect more from their partners and want them along for the ride throughout a wide variety of experiences.[4] The burden of serving as the sole provider for someone else's expanding wishes can prove overwhelming, even to a strong, committed individual.

As an alternative to the traditional model, contemporary singles discover that trading a variety of human interactions enriches their lives and raises their well-being. Instead of living in a "greedy" and isolating couplehood, people start adopting social webs as a way of living.[5] Individuals become networked individuals and their needs are fulfilled by several sources, not exclusively from within the nuclear family.[6]

Yes, there were advantages in the closed system of the Motu. Above all, it seemed safer: sailing to other tribes and trading with them was a risky bet, however inevitable. Similarly, for young individuals, marriage seems safe at first. Many of them see the model of the self-sufficient family unit as the best way to live happily ever after because it is assumed to be a predictable and reliable system that addresses all their needs continuously. However, many come to realize that they develop over the years and change their tastes, often in a way unsynchronized with their partners' changes. They learn that marriage simply does not fit them, because they need a more flexible, open-ended system to reflect their life evolution. Otherwise, they simply "starve"—sexually, emotionally, and intellectually. It is hard to sustain such a self-sufficient system in the long run, and it is, in fact, riskier for them to live this way.

Many people instead adopt single living and develop a networked life. This increasingly popular choice challenges the marriage institution at an ever-increasing pace. Looking ahead, singles will soon comprise most of the adult population in many countries, and singlehood will be the mainstream in public discourse. In such a reality, varying or dividing the exchange of emotional, intellectual, and even sexual goods is likely to take a larger and more positive role in the lives of singles. Some researchers name this coming reality an age of "posttraditional intimacy."[7] This term does not mean that intense emotional exchange or sexual interactions will disappear; rather, there will be multiple streams that form such exchanges. These streams will be unfixed and carry changing, protean forms all the time. The pyramid of society built with the family at its base will morph into more horizontal social networks.

It is useful to lay out some of the components of such a reality. These components represent only the beginning of a whole new social order that is still hardly imaginable. Edai needed more than just a great idea to discover new ways to provide food for his people. In addition to a new canoe and new clay cookware for Edai to trade with, the Papua myth uses the eel, the great Spirit of the Sea, to show how drastic this change was. Edai even needed to be submerged in the ocean, an act often symbolizing a dive into the subconsciousness, personally and collectively.[8] Similarly, understanding and internalizing new trends in a postmarital world requires a fundamental shift in the perception of intimacy exchange and social organization. Humbly bowing to the future, I hope to engender discussion on how a society built on a seemingly self-sufficient family unit may transform into a society of networks and a web of human forces that provide for its nodes all they need and much more.

THE FUTURE OF SINGLES AND FRIENDSHIPS

Continuing this line of thinking brings one to reevaluate the role of friendship in an age of singlehood. The friendship institution is as old as the marriage institution. In an age of singlehood, however, the friendship institution will come to the fore to fill the void that marriage can no longer fill. For many, meaningful friendships will become a life goal just as important, if not more so, than getting married.

Given the prevalence of single living in Japanese society, one researcher highlights the role of interpersonal relationships as a predictor of happiness for the residents of Tokyo, especially in middle age. The study forecasts that "friendship support may become more important as a predictor of ... happiness relative to family support."[9] Another recent study suggests friendship as a critical source of social support, particularly in elder care.[10] But whereas previous studies have found that the importance of friendship increases with age as more people lose longtime partners,[11] it seems more relevant today to consider the expanded importance of friendship at all ages.

Indeed, friendship can serve as a basic building block for the future of the single lifestyle, since it is not exclusive by nature. Friendships can thus afford several channels through which to establish intimacy and interpersonal relations. Like voyages for trade, these friendships will yield routes to physical, emotional, social, and intellectual exchange in an ever-branching web of interactions. Such connections will not only be more diverse, but they will also be more central to singles' lives, serving as major means for addressing their needs. Thus, a new type of stronger, more intense, and even more formally established friendship is expected to be part of an ecosystem surrounding singles.

I got a glimpse of this idea when I interviewed Lorraine, forty-seven, a never-married woman from Texas, who told me: "I don't think you need to get married to have a successful life or to enjoy life. I think that you can have friends and everything you need without being married." Another example is that of Kim, seventy-five, a never-married woman from Georgia, in the United States. I envied Kim's energy right out of the gate. In the interview, she described the many relationships she'd had throughout her life, involving men and women as well as nuns and priests. People came into and went out of her life, but when mentioning her long-term friend, she became serious: "I have a best friend, who is a female. We've been friends for more than forty years." It was clear that this relationship was the most stable one she had had—one she is still enjoying, a relationship she has nurtured with great tenderness over the years.

Of course, friendships can fulfill only certain needs, but the array of such addressed needs can be quite broad, including social company, emotional support, and intellectual stimulation. Some predict that the offerings of friendship will widen even more with the growing trends of delaying marriage, remaining single, and separating, with friendship becoming a source of physical care and financial provision.[12]

This kind of friendship will only grow stronger and become more popular in the future; moreover, associated legal and societal pacts will emerge because of the increasingly larger role friendship will play. While many singles prefer living alone, it is easy to contemplate that it will be more common for friends to rely heavily on each other and move in together, beyond what seems typical now. The clear financial, physical, social, and emotional benefits make this an attractive choice at different stages of singles' lives.[13] Such living arrangements will require legal pacts and even social rituals. Accordingly, there will be a new marital/personal status: cohabiting friends who are *not* in a romantic relationship. This category gets largely overlooked in social surveys, since it is traditionally limited to young adults.[14] But as marriage becomes increasingly delayed and infrequent, cohabitating with friends will require a separate social category.

Legal and social frameworks for this growing demographic seldom exist, but one researcher proposes the concept of a "civil friendship."[15] Currently, friends who care for each other and live together essentially act as a family unit but with limited, if any, legal recognition. The idea, then, is to introduce civil friendship pacts that would legally sanction the relationship between interdependent friends based on commitments to care for and support each other, agreed upon beforehand. This suggests a legally recognized relationship analogous to marriages and civil unions, one that would need to be made available to prevent cases of discrimination against such single friends.[16]

With the legal protection of civil friendship pacts, cohabitating and interdependent single friends would be guaranteed important protections and rights regarding tax benefits, employee and workers' rights, hospital visitation, financial and inheritance benefits, and more. Given the recent pace of change in public attitudes toward same-sex marriage and LGBTQ individuals—who campaigned for the aforementioned rights once granted only to heterosexual married couples—an international movement of singles who seek the same rights with their friends seems not only likely but also bound to eventually succeed.[17] Thus, in a time when the role of friendship is being reconceptualized, the burgeoning singles demographic is likely to spur many of the upcoming changes.[18]

In addition to the legal framework provided for cohabitating friends, we can expect to see the culture of friendship develop institutions and events of its own. One of the first such indicators occurred in Paraguay in 1958, when Dr. Ramón Artemio Brach founded the World Friendship Crusade and, together with his colleagues, initiated the first World Friendship Day. The driving idea was to create a specific day equal to those honoring mothers, fathers, other relationships, and even trees. Friendship is simply too important to be omitted from this list.[19] Indeed, more than half a century later, in 2011, the United Nations declared July 30 to be Friendship Day, although it is observed on different dates around the world.[20]

Notably, since 2015, Facebook has promoted what it designates as Friends Day, on February 4, the anniversary of its founding. The website creates automatic personal media collages for friends who have interacted with each other on the site. While this celebration undoubtedly has the business advantage of increasing user traffic across Facebook, the immediate by-product is an emphasis on the values of friendship.[21] Undeniably, the idea of Friends Day and friendship anniversaries generated some positive responses and comments in the media and the news. Especially remarkable is the rate at which a new practice or observance seems to be taking hold without much surprise. Anniversaries were once reserved only for couples, but now friends are also marking milestones, whether online with the help of a social network or with actual gifts, ceremonies, and celebrations. One reported example is that of Leela Hatfield and Alie Martell, both twenty-seven and living in New York, who threw a friendship twentieth-anniversary party (unofficially called a friendiversary). "Friendship milestones are usually overlooked, but we wanted to celebrate our anniversary and share it with all our friends," said Alie, the managing editor at *Cosmopolitan* magazine.[22]

These new trends stand to improve the well-being of singles. In fact, research already indicates that friendship has a powerful role in predicting and maximizing happiness.[23] In the future, we could potentially see a time when cultures allow singles to regard their friendships as being as strong as couples' partnerships. In this respect, thoughtful, meaningful, and long-term friendships could take the place of marriage, particularly for singles by choice. The cultural implications here are dramatic, but given the falling status of marriage, the idea that friendship could evolve to help fill the void left by the diminishing number of marriages is not too radical.

American journalist and writer Edna Buchanan is well-known for her valuation of friendship. As she puts it: "Friends are the family we choose for ourselves."[24] Although one can interpret this quotation in many ways, it carries an additional meaning with regard to this discussion. As concepts of intimacy develop in young adulthood, people differentiate between romantic partners and friends.[25] Yet as friendship replaces marriage for long-term singles, the perceived social support and level of intimacy between friends may begin to more closely resemble those of a romantically involved couple.[26]

Maybe the main concern in this discussion on friendship is how sexual needs can be addressed in a world where friendships replace marriage altogether. But this is exactly the secret of widening the circles of exchange. Having a large pool of available singles in urban communities, for example, already creates a situation in which singles who want intimacy on a certain level, or casual sex, can easily find it. Juan, fifty, who lives in Los Angeles and is a never-married gay man, said in our interview: "I think it keeps me carte blanche ["blank card," or "unlimited"] when it comes to being on apps like Grindr and Scruffs [gay-dating and -sexting apps]. You know, as a single guy, I am able to have a different flavor of the week, or even a different flavor of the day, whereas if I was in a relationship I wouldn't be able to have that much playtime."

Juan enjoys allocating his time to different types of intimate encounters. For him, a relationship takes valuable time that he would rather devote to meeting new people, and he sees his life as filled with "different flavors." Without a doubt, casual sex is becoming more acceptable: Data from the United States reveals that since the 1970s, Americans have become more tolerant of sex outside of marriage, and that casual encounters are more accepted and common.[27] The percentage of those surveyed who believed premarital sex among adults was "not wrong at all" was 29 percent in the early 1970s, 42 percent in the 1980s and 1990s, 49 percent in the first decade of the twentieth century, and 58 percent in the early 2010s. Although public discourse may discourage casual sex and treat it as potentially risky and psychologically damaging, more recent evidence shows this is not the case.[28] In fact, in some instances, and in particular when singles do not hold traditional gender-role beliefs, people generally have a positive attitude toward casual encounters.[29]

Obviously, one can imagine a world where singles' sexual and emotional transactions are coldhearted and empty, but a new reality is manifested in the interviews I conducted. Singles form circles of sex-friends that are treated affectionately, with frequent meetings that make their interactions pleasant, full of warmth and laughter. Side by side, they develop a network of emotionally connected friends that support each other, sometimes becoming a fully functioning, lively community.

THE FUTURE OF SINGLES AND COMMUNITIES

While singles receive support from family and friends, and while they socialize with circles of people, enjoying a diverse range of relationship statuses, some of the most meaningful support can come from other singles organized in groups. Singles stand to gain by establishing communities of like-minded individuals who offer support and camaraderie via shared attitudes, interests, beliefs, and goals. This is particularly important for singles who benefit more from social capital, as discussed in chapter 4.

Today, singles' communities are few and far between, resembling mostly ad hoc groupings of young singles in inner cities. Not only do such communities exclude many older singles, but they are also mostly transient: Singles date and marry and move in and out of these groups. Thus, even young singles, who feel safe in these communities, look ahead and see they must escape and marry before their "community membership expires," either because they get too old or other community members marry and leave, dismantling the group altogether.

The future seems brighter, however. In Sweden, which boasts a high percentage of singles, an association has been established called Filos, which supports alternative forms of close relations such as shared meals and communal events. Of course, some participants are looking to find a mate, but the association is not focused on pairing people. Instead, Filos organizes shared activities and affords members the opportunity to create social bonds. To some extent, the organizers see their association as mitigating the need for family.[30]

Another example for this kind of singles community comes from Zurie, thirty, who lives on the outskirts of Brussels: "The sense of community here is really, really strong. It's almost like a family.... I like living in a city, because I like walking out my door and having a million things at my fingertips. But despite this being such a small village, you still have that. If I walk down to Stefan's, there's, like, six people on the way." Zurie has developed a sense of community with other singles in her own small town. Being around like-minded singles removes any pressure to marry. Loneliness evaporates because, as she describes, she can barely walk down the street without encountering other people who are like her. The "sameness" gives her confidence and a strong sense of belonging.

Tony, thirty-five, lives in the suburbs of New York City. He tells me about living in a singles community: "I have a lot of friends who live in, not an actual commune, but a quasi-communal situation where there's always lots of people around, people I have known for many years and have close relationships with." During our interview it became apparent that Tony's community features a unique, somewhat unspoken code described by Tony as both accepting of permanent singleness and allowing the freedom for any lifestyle one chooses. Such communities, which are only now starting to spread, let single adults develop a web of exchanges around which they can organize their lives and social networks instead of focusing on dating and forging family units. As friends shift the traditional limits of relationships, society can move into an age where nonromantic social circles are more central. In such an era, singles communities will develop a permanent status, and the bonds between singles will no longer feel transient.[31]

Furthermore, more singles-specific events can be provided in these communities. For example, a greater opportunity will exist to promote political activities. As singles communities strengthen and grow, their influence and lobbying potential will expand. They will make known their needs and be able to garner support and funding for singles events, holidays, celebrations, and even community centers.

In fact, some singles communities are already taking an activist role in advocating marital-status equality. These groups, such as the Unmarried Equality Movement, bring unmarried and single people together to pursue equality and fairness in health care, housing, parenting, immigration, taxation, and other legal and social issues.

Another prominent route through which singles are creating supportive communities is the Internet. After extensively writing about and researching the topic of singles, Bella DePaulo used her blog to describe the need for an online singles community based on the questions and requests she received.[32] In her blog, she mentioned receiving inquiries from other single people and single activists seeking virtual communities of like-minded people. In response, she founded a Facebook group named Community of Single People. Potential members are approved only after indicating a clear understanding that the group is not for romantic purposes. In fact, the first line of the group description clearly states, "This group has nothing to do with dating."

Two years after DePaulo's blog post, the Community of Single People boasts a couple thousand members who share thoughts, ideas, and posts related to single life, with no more than a few hours passing between each post. Members discuss topics ranging from self-approval to happy single living, offering each other support on these and a wide variety of other issues. The interactions are almost exclusively positive and encouraging.

The very existence of such virtual groups indicates the growing strength and influence of singles broadly united under a set of issues. At this stage, the international and far-reaching nature of an online singles community remains imperative, since it is less common to find local singles groups that have nothing to do with dating. Their rarity seems to stem not from a lack of need but from the struggle to gain legitimacy in societies preoccupied with marriage. However, the nascent singles movement foreshadows a period where the single identity will gain increasing prominence. With the evolution of a full-bodied identity for singles, and a cause behind which to unite, society can expect the arrival and development of more singles communities.

In parallel, several media sources have noticed the increasing pull toward singles communities for the unmarried of all ages, and publishers and news outlets now consider and rank singles' quality of life in different places. While older lists of the "best cities to live in" for singles focus on dating economics and the likelihood of meeting a partner, some of the newer lists take friendship and fun into account, such as one from *Forbes* that addresses both singles at heart and those who want to find a mate.[33] Some updated lists go into further detail, ranking cities by nightlife options, percentage of single persons, the cost of going out, and other factors.[34]

While these lists in and of themselves do not tell much about communities in the ranked cities, they demonstrate promise for the creation and growth of singles communities. By indicating where it is cheaper or easier to go out, socialize, and live (not just date) as a single, and by recording where large numbers of singles live, these lists highlight locations with the greatest potential for community development. Moreover, these lists and the traffic they generate illustrate that singles today are seeking more positive lifestyles, and that deciding where to reside may be influenced by community-related factors.

Indeed, the emergence of singles communities is critical to singles' well-being and to creating an age of happy singlehood. The power of communities to facilitate the happiness of different social groups is well-established by research on the population at large showing that a sense of community can positively affect the subjective well-being of adults.[35] In contrast, an absence of community is associated with feelings of loneliness, depression, isolation, and alienation.[36]

In other contexts, studies confirm that a sense of community is important for minority groups. For example, social support and community involvement are proven to predict the life satisfaction of Indian immigrants in Canada,[37] minorities in Australia,[38] several groups of immigrants in Spain,[39] and refugees in several national contexts.[40] These studies show that communities help minorities by providing a sense of belonging; strengthening their identities; and creating a source of social, practical, physical, and emotional support. For minorities, communities are especially critical in assisting them with overcoming racism, ethnicism, and other prejudice. In this sense, singles are an excluded group that, like minorities, stands to gain on many fronts from organizing into communities. By grouping together and offering each other support, advice, and company, singles can build a more positive future less affected by singlism.

Such communities are already apparent but are still developing, and they may take many different forms in the future. For example, singles may organize around specific shared interests, and each community may be characterized by different ways of interacting according to its own unique system and rules. In other cases, singles might congregate in certain geographical areas and urban centers. Geographically based communities require further explanation regarding housing options and municipal services that might be needed in the future. The following section details some suggestions to this end.

THE FUTURE OF SINGLES AND URBAN PLANNING

Housing and urban planning have been based for a long time on the assumption that nuclear families are the standard. Thus, cities and neighborhoods evolved to cater to this population by constructing highways, suburbs, and larger houses.[41] Inner-city buildings were created to accommodate family lifestyles, with public areas set aside for playgrounds and kindergartens. Apartments featuring large kitchens and multiple bedrooms were also designed to cater to family units.[42]

Following the rise of singlehood, however, such housing and urban settings are less suitable for the new demographic compositions in many cities, particularly in big cities that attract large numbers of solo-goers. As discussed in chapter 1, singles frequently move to cities in search of friends, communities, employment, and dating opportunities.[43] While such moves were once a trend seen mainly among younger singles, the recently divorced and separated, too, are now moving to cities.[44] For these singles, who mostly prefer to live alone, the lack of appropriately sized apartments, suitable public spaces, and adequate accommodations is a troubling issue, thereby increasing demand on urban planners to revitalize these areas.

Moving forward, the growing singles population, particularly in urban communities, will fuel the search for creative solutions that accommodate this demographic change. Urban planning is already adjusting, and several solutions have been offered. One space-conscious option is to convert existing spaces, buildings, and dwellings into smaller apartments and studios. Singles do not need large kitchens or big living rooms. Instead, old apartments can be split and converted into smaller apartments tailored to singles, who often dine out and socialize with friends in public spaces. The high demand for such apartments has already initiated market-oriented conversions around the world, a process expected to accelerate in the near future.[45]

Microhousing and furnishing design also offer potential solutions.[46] By using clever designs and space-saving techniques, architects and interior designers create livable, stylish, and comfortable homes in spaces significantly smaller than five hundred square feet. Policy makers will have to adjust accordingly, however, since many cities limit the minimum size of a rentable house. In New York, for instance, the minimum was four hundred square feet until recently, making many micro-dwelling options effectively illegal.[47]

Another way in which planning can adapt to the shift toward singlehood is by prioritizing construction of new apartments in the inner city that cater to people who want to live alone. The logic is simple: residential densification will allow affordable housing for singles, together with proximity to city services. The demand is there for studios and one-bedroom apartments, and planners as well as developers have begun to cater to this need. However, the idea of building blocks of small apartments has yet to attract enough interest, and demand is still higher than supply. The problem lies mainly in the speculative nature of developing multiunit high-rises. Several models have been proposed to deal with this issue, including the *demand aggregation model*, which involves a two-sided market maker that brings buyers and sellers together and facilitates trade, in a model similar to those of Uber and Airbnb, before the construction begins.[48] A similar design is the *deliberative development model*, wherein the prospective residents, rather than a developer, become the proponents and funders of the project.[49] Both models are becoming more feasible based on emerging singles communities. Knowing each other through shared activities, events, and dinners, it is easier for singles to organize a large pool of purchasers who collectively push for developing a new housing project.

These ideas are becoming prevalent in many singles communities and manifest the reality in which singles live side-by-side and support one another. In my interview with Lina, forty-six, who has never married and who lives in Frankfurt, Germany, she said:

> If I compare the people that I grew up with—all my friends: they all got married, they all have kids. Now I live in a community where my friends don't have kids and aren't married. Either they live together because they're not married, or they don't have a partner and they don't have kids. And they're all my age group. They're not going to have any kids. I don't really know what direction it's going, but when we talk amongst ourselves, it is definitely, like: "Oh, we're going to have to live together to find a way to support each other." Because at the end of the day, there won't be kids taking care of us.

One reporter tells her own story that gives a glimpse into what might be normal in the future. Like Lina, and like others cited in the stories in chapter 4, Kiran Sidhu is in her early forties and has a group of single, childless female friends from school and university days. Regardless of their reasons for remaining single, she and her friends understood that in the absence of nuclear families, they want to live with each other in one property. By doing so, Kiran and her friends intend to look after one another's physical needs. They also plan to provide for each other socially by engaging in activities together. In an article published by *The Guardian*, Kiran discloses they have already talked about hiring a yoga instructor on a weekly basis, and about how their skills and interests will complement those of each other. One is great at cooking, another really likes gardening, and Kiran is proud of her decorating abilities. Perhaps most importantly, they are happy to care for their respective emotional needs. "Since my friends and I came up with our alternative, old-age plan, getting old no longer feels like a daunting prospect, and I no longer shy away from it—instead it feels hopeful and promising," she writes.[50]

Cohousing has already been suggested as a policy solution for aging communities that can benefit from the mutual support and shared spaces.[51] But in the near future, cohousing will be common among younger singles as well. Research already shows that cohousing tends to attract less-conventional households, working women, and people with new ideas of gender roles.[52] Thus, even in cohousing communities not specifically designed for singles, the traditional family unit is not always the norm, making it easier for singles to assimilate. Singles then benefit from a supportive community that can fill the role normally assumed by a spouse. Cohousing further appeals to singles by offering a balance between the privacy of living in one's own residence combined with a sense of community, support, and safety.[53]

As mentioned in chapter 3, a company named WeLive, the less-known sister of WeWork, has opened coliving, microapartment blocks in the desirable areas of Crystal City near Washington, DC, and lower Manhattan. Importantly, the rent includes a variety of amenities, such as shared spaces and even tea and coffee. Events are also organized for residents, who are already testifying about the friendships they have made by living in such an environment. This evolving new way of living offers many advantages to singles, such as increasing the supply of small apartments and creating opportunities for living alone while also developing a sense of community. James Woods, WeLive's chief executive officer, testifies in an interview: "We are seeking to build diverse communities.... People who are open to all kinds of interactions and are willing to give up a private space in return for a communal experience."[54] In addition, taking care of bills, utilities, and maintenance issues via the all-in-one amenities fee accommodates time-pressed singles, especially those unable to rely on another person for housing-related issues during daytime or working hours.

Finally, special attention should be given to replanning suburbs. Space is limited in cities, and as the number of singles increases, the demand will grow for singles housing outside of metropolitan centers.[55] Suburbs and rural areas are usually more affordable and provide important relief for singles who have only one income and cannot afford to live alone in central areas.[56] As Zurie mentioned in an interview cited earlier in the chapter, living among fellow singles in her small town makes her feel at ease with her singleness, an arrangement that holds a great deal of potential for developing singles housing in small towns and suburbs.

Thus, residential communities are expected to be developed outside of cities. This type of project creates a community of people living in adjacent homes with a shared communal space. In this sense, residential communities are somewhat like gated communities. However, sharing and companionship are what differentiate the two.[57] Gated communities are often home to high-value properties and result more from a culture of fear and a desire for safety. Their residents seek strictly controlled entrances, which are sometimes staffed by private security guards. Residential communities, however, are characterized by positive relationships between neighbors, a culture of mutual aid, group decision-making about shared spaces, and a promotion of friendships and social activities.[58]

Ram Carmi, one of the most prominent architects in Israel, designed a "suburban kibbutz" in the city of Bet Shemesh called Tammuz, a town located between Jerusalem and Tel Aviv. Visiting Tammuz, one can see two public spaces: The first is a round plaza that opens onto the beautiful mountain landscape. It serves all communal events. The second is a large lawn, around which daily life takes place and all communal buildings stand. There is a small dining room, secretaries, and social clubs. In the summer, the residents of Tammuz, singles and families alike, gather to eat on the lawn. "It's been 18 years since these buildings were built and I have great satisfaction to see that it really works," says the architect in charge.[59]

Living far away from central areas, however, requires improvements to the appeal and variety of housing choices that will attract singles. Most pertinent, for example, are the issues of distance and isolation. Long commutes to work or to gatherings with friends are not desirable, especially since many singles are interested in nighttime activities.

Heading into the future, improving public transport to urban centers will be important for many singles living alone. Public transport is especially relevant to older adults, to singles with mobility issues, and to those without access to a car. Planning communities for singles in small towns is not an easy task, but some have already started creating shared spaces for artists or youth volunteering and hubs for young tech entrepreneurs.[60] This social and physical infrastructure centered on singles' needs can easily draw singles who seek cheaper housing combined with employment opportunities.[61]

THE FUTURE OF SINGLES AND CONSUMERISM

Singles are clearly an emerging and increasingly central market that is forcing businesses to react accordingly by adjusting products, services, and advertising.[62] As a result of their many activities, singles' consumer preferences differ from those of married individuals.[63] Consumer expenditure reports reveal that singles spend larger proportions of their incomes on clothes, food, restaurants, leisure, and entertainment, and that singles expenditures are increasing.[64] In terms of purchase patterns, singles have also been found to be more tolerant of risk, less price-conscious, more brand-focused, and drawn to convenience when it comes to consumption and buying.[65] The combination of these characteristics is expected to fundamentally affect markets in the coming years.

Businesses desiring to crack the singles market have started to provide goods and services for singles, such as smaller packages of the same products sold to families.[66] Entrepreneurs have also started to identify activities and goods of particular importance to singles, including gym equipment, leisure activities, and social events.[67] Singles, in turn, benefit from a wider variety of services that meet their needs, a selection sure to grow in the future.

One prominent sector adapting to changing demographics is restaurants and food service. This industry has adjusted to the solo consumer in three ways: It has become more accessible, varied, and healthy. First, according to a British study, single-person households are overrepresented in the "kitchen evaders" category.[68] Over the last few decades, the general population has dedicated less time to cooking because of increased work hours and other pressures on time. The singles population is at the front of this movement because the efficiency in cooking for one person is low.[69] Thus, singles are drawn to the convenience-food industry more than any other demographic, and as a result these foods have become even more efficient and accessible. The popularity of prepared meals in single- or two-serving sizes is expected to rise further, resulting in price decline and greater availability.

Second, singles are attracted by the opportunity to be particular about what they eat, even on short notice.[70] They take advantage of the fact that the convenience-food market has risen in tandem with individualism and postmaterialism, as shown in chapter 5. Therefore, tailored dishes especially fit the singles population, particularly younger singles, because they are more conscious of their preferences, want to experience new tastes, and look for authentic, community-based food more than couples do.[71]

Third, the food market is also expected to offer healthier takeout food, especially for singles. This is because the singles group is not only more conscious about eating habits but also willing to spend more money on high-quality food.[72] My analysis shows that eating vegetables, fruits, and other healthy foods is more prevalent among singles, especially among the never-married. Thus, singles are expected to lead the market in raising awareness of healthy, nutritious food.

Another industry that is expected to adapt to singles is tourism. To the single person who may be especially interested in travel as a way of seeking adventure and self-fulfillment, the apparent lack of potential travel partners can be intimidating and make travel less affordable.[73] While it is widely acceptable for young people to travel in groups or with friends, it can be more difficult to find travel partners past the average age when people marry, when people begin to prefer traveling with partners and families.[74] However, travel companies have begun offering solutions to meet the needs of middle-aged and senior singles, encouraging joint travels that help singles minimize costs and that provide a sense of security. Others organize groups of solo travelers but make no attempts at matchmaking. In fact, these companies answer the need of solo travelers who prefer freedom and flexibility but a more packaged, structured type of holiday.[75]

Some companies are advertising directly to those who wish to travel alone. The company G Adventures, for instance, cites the advice of travel writer Freya Stark to appeal to single customers:

> To awaken quite alone in a strange town is one of the pleasantest sensations in the world. You are surrounded by adventure. You have no idea of what is in store for you, but you will, if you are wise and know the art of travel, let yourself go on the stream of the unknown and accept whatever comes in the spirit in which the gods may offer it. For this reason, your customary thoughts, all except the rarest of your friends, even most of your luggage—

everything, in fact, which belongs to your everyday life, is merely a hindrance. The tourist travels in his own atmosphere like a snail in his shell and stands, as it were, on his own perambulating doorstep to look at the continents of the world. But if you discard all this, and sally forth with a leisurely and blank mind, there is no knowing what may not happen to you.[76]

G Adventures and other companies recognize the potential pleasures of traveling alone and seek to empower singles accordingly and thereby fulfill their wishes. They focus on the increasing number of solo travelers by offering singles-friendly tours to assuage potential fears and guarantee them the company of like-minded individuals. Many companies are even reducing or eliminating single-occupancy charges as a result. Indeed, the offerings for the solo traveler are expected to diversify and increase in number, including trips centered on sports, culture, history, cruises, and more.

Furthermore, singles' engagement in their social lives creates a growing prospect for businesses and products affording opportunities for singles to meet. For example, social networking services such as Meetup have added singles groups to their settings. There is also an increasing number of events, clubs, and social activities catering to singles who are not necessarily looking for a relationship. In other words, singles increasingly need organized gatherings without the pressure, overtones, or assumptions that automatically accompany a dating event.[77]

Finally, the advertising and marketing worlds are also adapting to singles' needs. Although marketing strategies have traditionally stigmatized singles by trying to capitalize on anxieties, fears, and negative stereotypes,[78] some marketers are shifting their approach now, aiming to tap into this market. They have begun taking advice from special consultants on how to advertise to singles without stigma.[79] This advice includes instructions on offering convenience, using time-sensitive promotions, and avoiding unnecessary labeling or stereotyping through overtargeting. Some marketing strategists are going even further, with the American Marketing Association recommending that companies market directly to singles on Valentine's Day in order to carve out a niche in couples' mainstream marketing.[80]

While such advice is plainly intended to increase profit, it also evidences an increasing awareness of negative stereotypes. As a result, more confident, unmarried presenters will appear in coveted market advertising, which will portray singles in an empowering light. In turn, singles in the future will likely experience less discrimination, less stereotyping, and more recognition.

Of course, the relationship between marital status and consumer habits varies among different groups of singles.[81] For example, singles by choice, or "new singles,"[82] who are typically characterized as more individualistic and pleasure-seeking, may spend more on entertainment and leisure. Singles by circumstance, on the other hand, may spend less frivolously because of economic constraints, particularly following divorce or widowhood. Even so, these differences have scarcely been researched, and the time has come to study them. Such studies will help businesses and society at large to more comprehensively understand variations within the singles population.

THE FUTURE OF SINGLES AND TECHNOLOGY

The rise of the singles demographic is well-timed with unprecedented advances in technological innovation, probably not coincidentally. For a dynamic population like singles, technology offers efficient ways to network that overcome the constraints of the immediate family. Edai made a breakthrough for the Motu people by using technology. He built a canoe that took him to other tribes and helped establish the Motu trading network. Similarly, today's technology overcomes time and space constraints, allowing singles to expand their reach. New technologies facilitate the choice to enter or exit different types of relationships, making them malleable and diversified.[83]

Indeed, while many people find happiness via dating apps and websites, others making use of technology are not looking for a relationship. Instead, a growing number of singles use technology to seek various types of intimacy and social opportunities.[84] This may include long- or short-term romance, a one-night stand, or a platonic level of closeness. For those looking to socialize with old or new friends, social networks can help them keep in touch with distant friends or relatives[85] and can even help them increase their levels of familiarity and intimacy by sharing their interests, hobbies, and personal content more efficiently.[86]

But what if the technologicalization of relationships could be taken even further? Currently, dating and friendship technologies act as a means of connecting *humans* together to satisfy social, emotional, and physical needs. An interesting question going forward is whether technology can augment or even replace certain needs for which men and women normally rely on each other.

While the idea of replacing human interactions with technology might seem far from mainstream, the possibility must be considered carefully. After all, huge leaps in technology have created impressive robots that can be used in ways unimaginable only a few years ago. The focus of robotics research has recently moved toward the development of socially intelligent robots,[87] and socially assistive robots have been used for several years in mental health care as companions, play partners, and coaches.[88] Robots can also assist in providing care to older adults and by improving the emotional intelligence of children.[89] In addition, it is now clear that technology and robots can help with menial household tasks and chores while addressing manual and physical needs such as cleaning and cooking.

But given the expected advances in robotics, can humanoid robots also satisfy the *emotional* and *social* needs of singles?

The integration of intelligent technology in facilitating robo-sexuality and, more recently, robo-romanticism has made a significant leap in the last few years.[90] For example, a Chinese engineer, Zheng Jiajia, made headlines when he held a marriage ceremony for himself and the humanoid robot he designed and built.[91] According to Jiajia, he dated

Yinging—the name he gave to his robot—for two months before putting on his finest clothes and "marrying her" in a ceremony with his friends and his mother present. The wedding was not recognized in China, however, and the public reaction was mixed. But judging by Jiajia's report, it seems that spending time with a robot is answering at least some of his needs.

Zheng Jiajia is not alone. In Barcelona, a company called Synthea Amatus is at the forefront of the industry after having launched one of the world's first artificially intelligent robots that can provide romantic and sexual companionship. Using advanced technologies similar to the voice-activated systems of Apple's Siri and Amazon's Alexa, artificially intelligent robots, such as the one produced by Synthea Amatus, can hold conversations with their users and respond positively to human touch.[92]

In Japan, robots have already been given a more central part in the family and society.[93] The Japanese government is even encouraging the integration of robots into family life, as part of Innovation 25, a program with an eye on the year 2025.[94] The policy program is designed to use technology to care for an aging and sick population, helping families with the burden of working long hours and assisting elders. But almost ironically, the advances in robotics have resulted in a growing culture of Japanese singles spending more time with circuited companions than do families.[95]

The BBC reporter Rupert Wingfield-Hayes met Erica, a humanoid robot developed by Professor Hiroshi Ishiguro, outside the city of Kyoto in western Japan. Rupert describes his first impressions:

> It doesn't quite come across in photos, but when you're standing in the room with her, Erica is uncannily human-like. When I walk around her, she turns to look at me. She blinks her eyes as if she's trying to focus on me.
>
> "I like Chihuahua dogs," she tells me. "How about you? Do you have a dog?"
>
> When I tell her I do, she sighs with apparent satisfaction, content it seems that we share a love of animals.

A few minutes later I notice my companions are giggling at Erica's answers. Apparently she finds my poor Japanese funny and is making fun of me.[96]

Although relations with robots are still faced with fierce rejection and even violent attacks,[97] the robo-romantic actualization seems unstoppable. The rise of human-robot relationships was foreseen by David Levy in his book *Love and Sex with Robots*. Levy not only predicts that such relationships will be common by the middle of the twenty-first century but also explains their numerous benefits to individuals and society. In his words, if the "natural human desire can be satisfied for everyone who is capable of loving, surely the world will be a much happier place."[98] Levy considers the many ways people experience love, affection, and desire, and predicts that technological advances will meet many emotional needs, particularly of individuals who are not in a relationship. In the first ten years following the publication of Levy's book, the tech industry had already witnessed leaps in the fields of humanoid robots and artificial intelligence, with the production of technology that can more accurately capture human emotions.[99]

Levy is not alone. Other researchers have speculated on and explored how robots can conceivably replace humans, establishing a field of robo-ethics.[100] Others, in the academic journal *International Journal of Social Robotics*, explore how far humans are willing to go with the automation of social interactions. In early 2017, the prestigious *Annual Review of Psychology* published an article about robot-human interactions.[101] There is no definitive answer in this piece or in others, but nonetheless the call has been sounded for further development and research of robots, not only for technological purposes, but also for psychological and sociological ones.

While the development of robotics raises important ethical and theoretical questions, the effects on the singles population are expected to be enormous. The advances in robot technology—coupled with the possibility that society is likely to increasingly accept meaningful relationships with circuited companions, as happened with the adoption of assistive artificial intelligence—are bound to challenge the notions of family and traditional values.[102] Researchers argue that the changes in attitudes toward robot-human sexual and romantic relations will occur quickly.[103] Levy, for example, foresees legal provisions for robot-human marriage in the coming decades.[104] His ideas are supported by legal opinions declaring that, in theory, a robotic person capable of understanding, deciding, and expressing intention could be capable of entering a legal marriage contract.[105]

Other researchers conclude that the initial reluctance toward social robots may be replaced by acceptance if they are shown to improve or add value to people's lives.[106] After several phases of adaptation, so goes the prediction, most users will allow social robots to be part of their everyday lives.[107]

Following such developments, one could argue that a single person who enters a relationship with a robot may no longer be classified as "single" per se. Robots might render insignificant some of the challenges in being single, perhaps making the definition of singlehood more fluid compared to couplehood. Robots will be programmed and designed to meet singles' needs and desires, enough to make us question the "single" category.

In fact, every person, regardless of his or her romantic or sexual desires, could find some level of comfort or benefit—emotionally, physically, or sexually—from robots. Couples might also find themselves using a robot to enrich their relationships. The only difference might be that this kind of relationship will be without the same responsibilities and pressures inherent in a relationship with humans. In this sense, the categories of marriage and family are expected to crumble even more.

No doubt, the process of integrating technology into interpersonal relationships will gather momentum in the coming years. According to many scientists and some of the world's most venerated futurists, we are on track to reach an age of *technological singularity,* in which the pace of artificial superintelligence results in unpredictable and unimaginable changes to civilization at a rate surpassing human imagination.[108]

The idea of a robotic or posthuman age was once the subject of science fiction around the world.[109] However, progress in engineering and computing has led inventors, philosophers, and writers to broach the subject differently. Moore's law has shown that the number of transistors that can be placed in a dense integrated circuit doubles approximately every two years, a law that has held true since the 1970s, leading to the exponential growth in technological capability.[110] Observing this pace of change, scientists at Massachusetts Institute of Technology anticipate that robots will evolve into a new series of artificial superintelligent species starting around 2030–2040.[111]

What will this progress in reaching the techno-human singularity do to singles? This is, of course, a question no one can answer yet. We cannot predict how such a future will play out exactly, and it is perhaps naive to assume that technological advancements will continue without any danger. But even before the *actual* spread of humanoid robots, our social norms are already shifting because of the *potential* of this spread. One pattern is clear: social concepts of what constitutes the "acceptable" will change as our interactions with technology become varied and more complex.

THE FUTURE OF HAPPY SINGLEHOOD

Edai, who left the Motu people to establish new routes of trading and human interaction, made himself vulnerable to great danger and severe criticism. For him, it was not only a physical effort but also a mental leap—going underwater and connecting with something bigger than his everyday reality. Imagining the future of singles and, more than that, accepting the coming reality are almost unnatural to us. But such days loom large, and we must begin thinking about singles' future and researching its implications for society at large.

Whether that future has to do with the growing role of friendships, new singles communities, innovative housing and urban planning, shifting markets and patterns of consumerism, or technological advancements and relationships with robots, society must adapt to a new reality in which familial norms and culture are modified by these advances. The idea that every human being inherently or evolutionarily needs to pair off, either to satisfy basic needs or to promote survival, may eventually be replaced by singles who would rather be on their own, interacting with friends and fellow singles in more fluid and flexible communities and perhaps even assisted by highly intelligent technology.

Like the process experienced by the Motu people, this is expected to result in a highly significant change in the fabric of society, and its implications strike at the very core of the social structure. But we might as well celebrate this change, perhaps even throw a yearly festival marking the rise of happy singlehood, exactly as the Motu people annually celebrate the first coastal trading voyage, the Hiri.

Conclusion

What Can States, Cities, and Social Institutions
Do for Singles?

Previous chapters make it clear that the rise of the single population is undeniable, despite the social disadvantages, stigmas, and prejudices single people have encountered. In fact, we are on the verge of living in a society of singles. The reasons are numerous, and it seems that the convergence of the various social forces that lead to singlehood will only accelerate in the near future. Not only is the proportion of married people to single people changing, but the norms and functions of society are also fundamentally shifting to be more inclusive of singles. Singles themselves, without any formal announcement, are also starting to cultivate happy singlehood. They do so by joining supportive social environments, subscribing to postmaterialist values, learning to defy social pressure, and occupying themselves in meaningful ways. This is the everyday praxis of happy singles nowadays, even if they are not entirely aware of it.

Importantly, this book does not oppose marriage. Some studies have even shown a partial causation effect in which being married leads to a better quality of life (although other studies refute these claims and the debate still continues).[1] The point here, however, is that singleness is increasingly part of our lives and will be part of future generations' lives. Marriages end much more often than we think, and when they do, those coming out of broken marriages or coping with spouses' deaths are unprepared for life as singles and subject to a steep decline in their happiness. Others might want not to marry in the first place because of the numerous reasons mentioned in chapter 1 so they simply choose to remain single. Either way, all of us need to learn how to embrace singleness, no matter what we think of the marriage institution, simply because it is an inevitable reality.

However, instead of accepting singleness, even celebrating it, many forces still push against it. A great many benefits derived from marriage are "unearned" and unjustifiably drive people into marriage, sometimes against their wishes. In other words, the institution itself grants married people special status and advantages that may persuade otherwise reluctant individuals to enter a permanent, legal union.[2] In some places, this push is so harsh that it ends in tragedies like the death of Zarmina, whose story was told in chapter 5. In other places, the push is subtler, yet often ends in a painful separation process, even in liberal societies.

Trying to coerce people into marriage, or hasten marriage, will apparently not lead to increased rates of "wedded bliss." To the contrary, singles are only growing in number, so it seems. Therefore, the unjustified push and benefits should be severely scrutinized, as they are products of social norms that reject a growing part of society.

This raises the need to consider the steps that governments, local authorities, and policy makers should take to secure the welfare of the singles population. It is not a neglected minority anymore but, rather, a majority that, albeit diverse, needs to be addressed.

In recent years, world-renowned economists such as Amartya Sen and Joseph Stiglitz, major international institutions such as the Organization for Economic Cooperation and Development, and high-profile politicians such as the former French president Nicolas Sarkozy have promoted the idea of measuring policy making and federal administration according to their effects on people's happiness.[3] This idea is actually not so new: the American Declaration of Independence already lists the "pursuit of happiness" as an unalienable right of American citizens. However, the actual application of the pursuit of happiness to policy making is only now gaining traction. Given this recent emphasis on happiness, it is necessary to explore what role governments, municipalities, urban planners, and academics can play in raising happiness, or even simply allowing the pursuit of it, among singles.

It seems that this challenge has a multilayered answer. First, policy makers and governments must recognize the injustice against singles and prevent subsequent discrimination. Negative stereotypes and perceptions of singles often lead policy makers to create policies that encourage relationship formation. Apparently, municipalities and policy makers assume that those whom they pledged to protect behave in irrational and detrimental ways. Therefore, "to secure domestic tranquility," policy makers feel compelled to push citizens in the "correct" direction. But the reality is that these policies prove ineffective, because people remain single anyway. Outwardly, singles believe in their way of living; they did not come to live this way by coincidence or without logic. Hence, coaxing people into marriage is not only unjust and immoral but also represents poor governance and inefficiency.[4] Some marriage initiatives are even offensive and may well have caused harm to those who felt pressured into marriage; these initiatives may also have prompted resentment against those who decided to go solo. Apparently, a traditional married relationship is not necessarily what makes single people happy, certainly not when incentivized by governments. Therefore, awareness of these decadent policies should be raised, and policy changes should be put on the public agenda.

Second, governments and social institutions seeking to preserve and improve singles' happiness must not only fight the ubiquitous negative stereotypes surrounding them but also actively encourage the study and development of happy singlehood.[5] Since the early 1970s, American school curricula have been designed to include gender, ethnic, and environmental studies.[6] All of them are worthy enterprises that shatter misconceptions, broaden perspectives, and promote benevolent views of ignored and disadvantaged populations. However, because marriage is so ingrained in the social discourse, the importance of educating students about singlehood and preparing them for single life is still missing from most countries' curricula. Given that a quarter of today's children will never marry, and that 40 to 50 percent of those who do will divorce,[7] it is essential to equip children with a social and psychological "toolbox" that will enable them to be happy singles. Learning about singleness in schools and supporting high-quality solo lifestyles through the health and welfare ministries, exactly as is done with family life, are essential to our society. Social workers, psychologists, and doctors should be trained to serve the singles population. Additionally, special community centers and information points should be set up. Today's children need these services for their own benefit as well as for the welfare of the many singles who will surround them in the future.

Third, urban planners and municipalities should accelerate their offerings for the single population. Urban planners and developers should be encouraged to apply different models of co-residency, including collective housing for singles,[8] neighborhoods with cohousing projects,[9] and intergenerational living arrangements.[10] Designing new housing projects and even entire neighborhoods around the single population can dramatically improve singles' lives.[11] Municipalities may offer to organize singles communities and urban centers; relax city regulations to allow projects like microhousing; and facilitate services for the singles population with places to meet, socialize, and develop shared interests.

Finally, academia plays a crucial role in advancing knowledge about singlehood. Until now, much of the research in the academic world was based on the obsolete assumption that marriage should, and would, dominate adult life. As a result, singles are underrepresented and even misrepresented in scholarship and policy papers.[12] Future research on how singles adapt to single living is therefore merited and necessitates the development of a singles-studies field.[13] By better understanding the psychological, social, and even physical repertoire of happy singles, it will be possible to make recommendations on how to improve single living. Expanded scholastic concentration on singles could guide law-makers in creating frameworks for how to increase the well-being of the fast-growing singles population. Additionally, psychological, sociological, educational, economic, and technological research on the subject could provide keys to enhancing the welfare of both married and single individuals. Directions for research could include studies of intergroup relations between singles and couples; singles' means of emancipation and self-development; market needs and consumerist patterns of singles; efficient ways to improve transportation and municipal services for singles; teaching practices to prepare for solo living; and much more.

. . .

Walking through my childhood neighborhood, I look again at the lighted windows, minutes before Shabbat. I smell the same wonderful aromas of all the Friday night meals from decades ago. So much seems the same.

But now I know something has changed. Society is more diverse today. Many of the people I see in my childhood neighborhood remained single, endured divorce, or lost their partners. The hunchbacked man and his son, whom I saw in my boyhood place of worship, are still shy and keep to themselves, but they do not look weird anymore, not to me, and probably not to many others surrounding them. Reality has changed and keeps evolving at an ever-faster pace. Looking around, I wonder how many people of the older generation would have wanted this for themselves if only happy singlehood had been more prevalent decades ago, before they married.

Now we at least have some room for optimism. Society has started to be open and accepting about singleness, allowing many the "pursuit of happiness" in their own way.

Continuing walking, I watch the children, those who are like my younger self, standing on their tiptoes and looking out into the streets. How do we make sure they will grow up happily? Just "happily," with no presumptions whatsoever about its meaning. It can be "happily ever after" for a brave knight and a beautiful princess (or vice versa) or, quite likely, happily never-married, happily divorced, or happily widowed. It is our obligation to afford these clean and tidy children, currently gazing at the world with curious wonder, the opportunity to grow up in a society that embraces whatever marital status they choose. Society has advanced so much in accepting women, sexual minorities, and ethnicities; we surely can take this one additional step. Just one more step.

NOTES

INTRODUCTION

1. Bella M. DePaulo and Wendy L. Morris, "The Unrecognized Stereotyping and Discrimination against Singles," *Current Directions in Psychological Science* 15, no. 5 (2006): 251–54.

2. Todd M. Jensen, Kevin Shafer, Shenyang Guo, and Jeffry H. Larson, "Differences in Relationship Stability between Individuals in First and Second Marriages: A Propensity Score Analysis," *Journal of Family Issues* 38, no. 3 (2017): 406–32; Megan M. Sweeney, "Remarriage and Stepfamilies: Strategic Sites for Family Scholarship in the 21st Century," *Journal of Marriage and Family* 72, no. 3 (2010): 667–84.

3. Stephanie S. Spielmann, Geoff MacDonald, Jessica A. Maxwell, Samantha Joel, Diana Peragine, Amy Muise, and Emily A. Impett, "Settling for Less out of Fear of Being Single," *Journal of Personality and Social Psychology* 105, no. 6 (2013): 1049.

4. John T. Cacioppo and William Patrick, *Loneliness: Human Nature and the Need for Social Connection* (New York: W. W. Norton, 2008).

5. Ibid.; Berna van Baarsen, Tom A. B. Snijders, Johannes H. Smit, and Marijtje A. J. van Duijn, "Lonely but Not Alone: Emotional Isolation and Social Isolation as Two Distinct Dimensions of Loneliness in Older People," *Educational and Psychological Measurement* 61, no. 1 (2001): 119–35.

6. Shelley Budgeon, "Couple Culture and the Production of Singleness," *Sexualities* 11, no. 3 (2008): 301–25; Richard Fry, "A Rising Share of Young Adults

Live in Their Parents' Home," in *Social Demographic Trends Project* (Washington, DC: Pew Research Center, 2013); Eric Klinenberg, *Going Solo: The Extraordinary Rise and Surprising Appeal of Living Alone* (New York: Penguin, 2012).

7. Wendy Wang and Kim C. Parker, *Record Share of Americans Have Never Married: As Values, Economics and Gender Patterns Change*(Washington, DC: Pew Research Center, 2014).

8. National Bureau of Statistics of China, "China Statistics: National Statistics" (Beijing: National Bureau of Statistics of China, 2013).

9. Eurostat, "Urban Europe—Statistics on Cities, Towns and Suburbs," (Luxemburg: Publications Office of the European Union, 2016); Euromonitor, *Downsizing Globally: The Impact of Changing Household Structure on Global Consumer Markets* (London: Euromonitor, 2013).

10. Paul R. Amato, "Research on Divorce: Continuing Trends and New Developments," *Journal of Marriage and Family* 72, no. 3 (2010): 650–66; Wendy Wang and Kim C Parker, *Record Share of Americans Have Never Married: As Values, Economics and Gender Patterns Change* (Washington, DC: Pew Research Center, 2014).

11. Eric Klinenberg, *Going Solo: The Extraordinary Rise and Surprising Appeal of Living Alone* (New York: Penguin, 2012).

12. Terrence McCoy, "Do It for Denmark!" Campaign Wants Danes to Have More Sex: A Lot More Sex," *Washington Post*, March 27, 2014, www.washingtonpost.com/news/morning-mix/wp/2014/03/27/do-it-for-denmark-campaign-wants-danes-to-have-more-sex-a-lot-more-sex/?utm_term=.d8e6eef47764.

13. Philip Brasor and Masako Tsubuku, "A Rise in Vacancies Won't Mean Drops in Rent," July 2, 2016, www.japantimes.co.jp/community/2016/07/02/how-tos/rise-vacancies-wont-mean-drops-rent/#.WmN_R6iWbg8.

14. Vivian E. Hamilton, "Mistaking Marriage for Social Policy," *Virginia Journal of Social Policy and the Law* 11 (2004): 307–71.

15. C. Marshall and G.B. Rossman, *Designing Qualitative Research* (Newbury Park, CA: Sage, 2006); S.F. Rallis and G.B. Rossman, *Learning in the Field: An Introduction to Qualitative Research,* 3rd ed. (Thousand Oaks, CA: Sage, 2011); A.L. Strauss and J. Corbin, *Basics of Qualitative Research* (Thousand Oaks, CA: Sage, 1990).

16. A.L. Strauss and J. Corbin, *Basics of Qualitative Research* (Thousand Oaks, CA: Sage, 1990).

17. Ari Engelberg, "Religious Zionist Singles: Caught between 'Family Values' and 'Young Adulthood,'" *Journal for the Scientific Study of Religion,* 55, no. 2 (2016): 349–64.

18. Similarly to the 1990 US census, for example, in which cohabitation with a partner who is not a spouse was included as a possible and separate category, see Casey E. Copen, Kimberly Daniels, Jonathan Vespa, and William D. Mosher, "First Marriages in the United States; Data from the 2006–2010 National Survey of Family Growth" (Hyattsville, MD: Department of Health and Human Services, Centers for Disease Control and Prevention, National Center for Health Statistics, 2012); Lynne M. Casper and Philip N. Cohen, "How Does Posslq Measure Up? Historical Estimates of Cohabitation," *Demography* 37, no. 2 (2000): 237–45.

19. Tim B. Heaton and Renata Forste, "Informal Unions in Mexico and the United States," *Journal of Comparative Family Studies* 38, no. 1 (2007): 55–69; Teresa Castro Martin, "Consensual Unions in Latin America: Persistence of a Dual Nuptiality System," *Journal of Comparative Family Studies* 33, no. 1 (2002): 35–55; Brienna Perelli-Harris, Monika Mynarska, Caroline Berghammer, Ann Berrington, Ann Evans, Olga Isupova, Renske Keizer, Andreas Klärner, Trude Lappegard, and Daniele Vignoli, "Towards a Deeper Understanding of Cohabitation: Insights from Focus Group Research across Europe and Australia," *Demographic Research* 31, no. 34 (2014): 1043–78.

20. Matthew D. Bramlett and William D. Mosher, "Cohabitation, Marriage, Divorce, and Remarriage in the United States," *Vital Health Statistics* 23, no. 22 (2002): 1–32; Andrew J. Cherlin, "The Deinstitutionalization of American Marriage," *Journal of Marriage and Family* 66, no. 4 (2004): 848–61; Anke C. Zimmermann and Richard A. Easterlin, "Happily Ever After? Cohabitation, Marriage, Divorce, and Happiness in Germany," *Population and Development Review* 32, no. 3 (2006): 511–28.

21. Jane Lewis, *The End of Marriage?* (London: Institute for the Study of Civil Society, 2000); Patricia M. Morgan, *Marriage-Lite: The Rise of Cohabitation and Its Consequences* (London: Institute for the Study of Civil Society, 2000); James A. Sweet and Larry L. Bumpass, "Young Adults' Views of Marriage Cohabitation and Family" (working paper no. 33, National Survey of Families and Households, Center for Demography and Ecology, University of Wisconsin-Madison, 1990).

22. Patricia M. Morgan, *Marriage-Lite: The Rise of Cohabitation and Its Consequences* (London: Institute for the Study of Civil Society, 2000).

23. Gavin W. Jones, "The 'Flight from Marriage' in South-East and East Asia," *Journal of Comparative Family Studies* 36, no. 1 (2005): 93–119.

24. Ruut Veenhoven, "The Utility of Happiness," *Social Indicators Research* 20, no. 4 (1988): 333–54.

25. S.M. Chiang, *The Philosophy of Happiness: A History of Chinese Life Philosophy* (Taipei: Hong Yie Publication Company, 1996); Georg Wilhelm Friedrich Hegel and Robert F. Brown, *Lectures on the History of Philosophy: Greek Philosophy* (Oxford: Oxford University Press, 2006); Darrin M. McMahon, "From the Happiness of Virtue to the Virtue of Happiness: 400 BC–AD 1780," *Daedalus* 133, no. 2 (2004): 5–17; Wladyslaw Tatarkiewicz, "Analysis of Happiness," *Philosophy and Phenomenological Research* 38, no. 1 (1976): 139–40.

26. Luo Lu, "Understanding Happiness: A Look into the Chinese Folk Psychology," *Journal of Happiness Studies* 2, no. 4 (2001): 407–32.

27. Shigehiro Oishi, Jesse Graham, Selin Kesebir, and Iolanda Costa Galinha, "Concepts of Happiness across Time and Cultures," *Personality and Social Psychology Bulletin* 39, no. 5 (2013): 559–77.

28. Cassie Mogilner, Sepandar D. Kamvar, and Jennifer Aaker, "The Shifting Meaning of Happiness," *Social Psychological and Personality Science* 2, no. 4 (2010): 395–402.

29. Yew-Kwang Ng, "Happiness Surveys: Some Comparability Issues and an Exploratory Survey Based on Just Perceivable Increments," *Social Indicators Research* 38, no. 1 (1996): 1–27.

30. Adam Okulicz-Kozaryn, Zahir Irani, and Zahir Irani, "Happiness Research for Public Policy and Administration," *Transforming Government: People, Process and Policy* 10, no. 2 (2016): 196–211.

31. Martin E.P. Seligman, *Authentic Happiness: Using the New Positive Psychology to Realize Your Potential for Lasting Fulfillment* (New York: Simon and Schuster, 2004); Martin E.P. Seligman and Mihaly Csikszentmihalyi, *Positive Psychology: An Introduction* (New York: Springer, 2014).

CHAPTER 1. THE AGE OF SINGLEHOOD

1. Xiaqing Zhao and Hooi Lai Wan, "Drivers of Online Purchase Intention on Singles' Day: A Study of Chinese Consumers," *International Journal of Electronic Marketing and Retailing* 8, no. 1 (2017): 1–20.

2. Tiffany Hsu, "Alibaba's Singles Day Sales Hit New Record of $25.3 Billion," *New York Times,* November 10, 2017.

3. *Singular Magazine,* "National Singles Day Returns to West Hollywood," January 1, 2016.

4. Zhongwei Zhao and Wei Chen, "Changes in Household Formation and Composition in China since the Mid-twentieth Century," *Journal of Population Research* 25, no. 3 (2008): 267–86.

5. Wei-Jun Jean Yeung and Adam Ka-Lok Cheung, "Living Alone: One-Person Households in Asia," *Demographic Research* 32, no. 40 (2015): 1099–112.

6. Euromonitor, *Downsizing Globally: The Impact of Changing Household Structure on Global Consumer Markets* (London: Euromonitor International, 2013).

7. Eric Klinenberg, *Going Solo: The Extraordinary Rise and Surprising Appeal of Living Alone* (New York: Penguin, 2012).

8. Wendy Wang and Kim C. Parker, *Record Share of Americans Have Never Married: As Values, Economics and Gender Patterns Change* (Washington, DC: Pew Research Center, 2014).

9. Pew Research Center, *Parenting in America: Outlook, Worries, Aspirations Are Strongly Linked to Financial Situation* (Washington, DC: Pew Research Center, 2015).

10. Reiko Hayashi, *Social Security in Japan* (Tokyo: National Institute of Population and Social Security Research, 2016).

11. Roslyn Appleby, "Singleness, Marriage, and the Construction of Heterosexual Masculinities: Australian Men Teaching English in Japan," portal: *Journal of Multidisciplinary International Studies* 10, no. 1 (2013): 1–21; Masahiro Morioka, "A Phenomenological Study of 'Herbivore Men,'" *Review of Life Studies* 4 (2013): 1–20; James E. Roberson and Nobue Suzuki, eds., *Men and Masculinities in Contemporary Japan: Dislocating the Salaryman Doxa* (London: Routledge, 2005).

12. Masahiro Morioka, "A Phenomenological Study of 'Herbivore Men,'" *Review of Life Studies* 4 (2013): 1–20.

13. Alexandra Harney, "The Herbivore's Dilemma," *Slate,* June 2009.

14. Kathleen Kiernan, "Unmarried Cohabitation and Parenthood in Britain and Europe," *Law & Policy* 26, no. 1 (2004): 33–55.

15. Peter J. Stein, "Singlehood: An Alternative to Marriage," *Family Coordinator* 24, no. 4 (1975): 489–503.

16. Gary R. Lee and Krista K. Payne, "Changing Marriage Patterns since 1970: What's Going On, and Why?" *Journal of Comparative Family Studies* 41, no. 4 (2010): 537–55.

17. Census of India, *Houselisting and Housing Census Data* (New Delhi: Government of India, Ministry of Home Affairs, 2011); Premchand Dommaraju, "One-Person Households in India," *Demographic Research* 32, no. 45 (2015); Hyunjoon Park and Jaesung Choi, "Long-Term Trends in Living Alone among Korean Adults: Age, Gender, and Educational Differences," *Demographic Research* 32, no. 43 (2015): 1177–208; Christophe Guilmoto and Myriam de Loenzien, "Emerging, Transitory or Residual? One-Person Households in

Viet Nam," *Demographic Research* 32, no. 42 (2015): 1147–76; Chai Podhisita and Peter Xenos, "Living Alone in South and Southeast Asia: An Analysis of Census Data," *Demographic Research* 32, no. 41 (2015): 1113–46; Hyunjoon Park and Jaesung Choi, "Long-Term Trends in Living Alone among Korean Adults: Age, Gender, and Educational Differences," *Demographic Research* 32, no. 43 (2015): 1177–208.

18. Shelley Budgeon, "Couple Culture and the Production of Singleness," *Sexualities* 11, no. 3 (2008): 301–25; Euromonitor, *Downsizing Globally: The Impact of Changing Household Structure on Global Consumer Markets* (London: Euromonitor International, 2013).

19. Euromonitor, *Single Living: How Atomisation—the Rise of Singles and One-Person Households—Is Affecting Consumer Purchasing Habits* (London: Euromonitor International, 2008).

20. Mohammad Jalal Abbasi-Shavazi, Peter McDonald, and Meimanat Hossein Chavoshi, *Changes in Family, Fertility Behavior and Attitudes in Iran* (Canberra, Australia: Demography and Sociology Program, Research School of Social Sciences, 2003).

21. Amir Erfani and Kevin McQuillan, "Rapid Fertility Decline in Iran: Analysis of Intermediate Variables," *Journal of Biosocial Science* 40, no. 3 (2008): 459–78.

22. UAE Interact, *Marriage Fund Report* (Abu Dhabi, United Arab Emirates: Ministry of Information and Culture, 2015).

23. Hoda Rashad, Magued Osman, and Farzaneh Roudi-Fahimi, *Marriage in the Arab World* (Washington, DC: Population Reference Bureau, 2005).

24. Government, United Arab Emirates, *Marriage Fund Report* (Abu Dhabi, United Arab Emirates: Ministry of Information and Culture, 2017), http://beta.government.ae/en/information-and-services/social-affairs/marriage.

25. Hoda Rashad, Magued Osman, and Farzaneh Roudi-Fahimi, *Marriage in the Arab World* (Washington, DC: Population Reference Bureau, 2005); Paul Puschmann and Koen Matthijs, "The Demographic Transition in the Arab World: The Dual Role of Marriage in Family Dynamics and Population Growth," in *Population Change in Europe, the Middle-East and North Africa: Beyond the Demographic Divide*, ed. Koenraad Matthijs, Karel Neels, Christiane Timmerman, Jacques Haers, and Sara Mels (New York: Routledge, 2016), 119.

26. Stephanie Coontz, *Marriage, a History: How Love Conquered Marriage* (New York: Penguin, 2006).

27. Organization for Economic Cooperation and Development, *Fertility Rates (Indicator)* (Paris: OECD, 2017).

28. Joshua Goldstein, Wolfgang Lutz, and Maria Rita Testa, "The Emergence of Sub-replacement Family Size Ideals in Europe," *Population Research and Policy Review* 22, no. 5–6 (2003): 479–96.

29. World Bank, *Total Fertility Rate (Births per Woman)* (Washington, DC: World Bank, 2016).

30. P. Hogan, "The Effects of Demographic Factors, Family Background, and Early Job Achievement on Age at Marriage," *Demography* 15, no. 2 (1978): 161–75; Gavin W. Jones, "Delayed Marriage and Very Low Fertility in Pacific Asia," *Population and Development Review* 33, no. 3 (2007): 453–78.

31. Jiehua Lu and Xiaofei Wang, "Changing Patterns of Marriage and Divorce in Today's China," in *Analysing China's Population* (New York: Springer, 2014), 37–49.

32. Xuanning Fu and Tim B. Heaton, "A Cross-national Analysis of Family and Household Structure," *International Journal of Sociology of the Family* 25, no. 2 (1995): 1–32; Frances E. Kobrin, "The Fall in Household Size and the Rise of the Primary Individual in the United States," *Demography* 13, no. 1 (1976): 127–38.

33. Robert T. Michael and Nancy Brandon Tuma, "Entry into Marriage and Parenthood by Young Men and Women: The Influence of Family Background," *Demography* 22, no. 4 (1985): 515–44; Philip E. Ogden and François Schnoebelen, "The Rise of the Small Household: Demographic Change and Household Structure in Paris," *Population, Space and Place,* 11, no. 4 (2005): 251–68; Philip E. Ogden and Ray Hall, "The Second Demographic Transition, New Household Forms and the Urban Population of France during the 1990s," *Transactions of the Institute of British Geographers* 29, no. 1 (2004): 88–105; Peter A. Morrison, *Demographic Factors Reshaping Ties to Family and Place* (Santa Monica, CA: Rand Corporation, 1990).

34. Vern L. Bengtson and Norella M. Putney, "Who Will Care for Tomorrow's Elderly? Consequences of Population Aging East and West," in *Aging in East and West: Families, States, and the Elderly,* ed. Vern L. Bengtson, Kyong-Dong Kim, George Myers, and Ki-Soo Eun (New York: Springer, 2000), 163–85; Antonio Golini and A. Silverstrini, "Family Change, Fathers, and Children in Western Europe: A Demographic and Psychosocial Perspective," in *The Family on the Threshold of the 21st Century: Trends and Implications,* ed. Solly Dreman (New York: Psychology Press, 2013), 201.

35. Jennifer M. Ortman, Victoria A. Velkoff, and Howard Hogan, *An Aging Nation: The Older Population in the United States* (Washington, DC: US Census Bureau, Economics and Statistics Administration, US Department of Commerce, 2014).

36. Organization for Economic Cooperation and Development, *Life Expectancy at 65 (Indicator)* (Paris: OECD, 2017).

37. Ellen A. Kramarow, "The Elderly Who Live Alone in the United States: Historical Perspectives on Household Change," *Demography* 32, no. 3 (1995): 335–52; Jim Oeppen and James W. Vaupel, "Broken Limits to Life Expectancy," *Science* 296, no. 5570 (2002): 1029–31; Steven Ruggles, *Living Arrangements of the Elderly in America, 1880–1980* (Berlin: de Gruyter, 1996).

38. Axel Börsch-Supan, *Survey of Health, Ageing and Retirement in Europe (Share) Wave 6* (Munich: SHARE-ERIC, 2018).

39. Renee Stepler, *Led by Baby Boomers, Divorce Rates Climb for America's 50+ Population* (Washington, DC: Pew Research Center, 2017).

40. Adam Ka-Lok Cheung and Wei-Jun Jean Yeung, "Temporal-Spatial Patterns of One-Person Households in China, 1982–2005," *Demographic Research* 32, no. 44 (2015): 1209–38; Wei-Jun Jean Yeung and Adam Ka-Lok Cheung, "Living Alone: One-Person Households in Asia," *Demographic Research* 32, no. 40 (2015): 1099–112.

41. K. Bolin, B. Lindgren, and P. Lundborg, "Informal and Formal Care among Single-Living Elderly in Europe," *Health Economics* 17, no. 3 (2008): 393–409; Elena Portacolone, "The Notion of Precariousness among Older Adults Living Alone in the U.S.," *Journal of Aging Studies* 27, no. 2 (2013): 166–74.

42. Vanessa L. Fong, *Only Hope: Coming of Age under China's One-Child Policy* (Stanford, CA: Stanford University Press, 2004).

43. Census of India, "Houselisting and Housing Census Data," *Houselisting and Housing Census Data* (New Delhi: Government of India, Ministry of Home Affairs, 2011).

44. "Bare Branches, Redundant Males," *The Economist*, April 18, 2015, www.economist.com/asia/2015/04/18/bare-branches-redundant-males.

45. Fred Arnold and Liu Zhaoxiang, "Sex Preference, Fertility, and Family Planning in China," *Population and Development Review* 12, no. 2 (1986): 221–46; Christophe Z. Guilmoto, "Economic, Social and Spatial Dimensions of India's Excess Child Masculinity," *Population* 63, no. 1 (2008): 91–117; Shelley Budgeon, "Couple Culture and the Production of Singleness," *Sexualities* 11, no. 3 (2008): 301–25; Monica Das Gupta, "Selective Discrimination against Female Children in Rural Punjab, India," *Population and Development Review* (1987): 77–100; Chai Bin Park and Nam-Hoon Cho, "Consequences of Son Preference in a Low-Fertility Society: Imbalance of the Sex Ratio at Birth in Korea," *Population and Development Review* (1995): 59–84.

46. Eurostat, *Eurostat Regional Yearbook* (Brussels: European Commission, 2017).

47. Soon Kyu Choi and Ilan H. Meyer, *LGBT Aging: A Review of Research Findings, Needs, and Policy Implications* (Los Angeles: Williams Institute, 2016).

48. Elizabeth A. Cashdan, "Natural Fertility, Birth Spacing, and the 'First Demographic Transition,'" *American Anthropologist* 87, no. 3 (1985): 650–53; John C. Caldwell, "Toward a Restatement of Demographic Transition Theory," *Population and Development Review* (1976): 321–66.

49. Ronald Inglehart and Christian Welzel, *Modernization, Cultural Change, and Democracy: The Human Development Sequence* (Cambridge: Cambridge University Press, 2005); Wolfgang Lutz and Vegard Skirbekk, "Policies Addressing the Tempo Effect in Low-Fertility Countries," *Population and Development Review* 31, no. 4 (2005): 699–720.

50. Zillah R. Eisenstein, ed., *Capitalist Patriarchy and the Case for Socialist Feminism* (New York: Monthly Review Press, 1979); Ann Ferguson and Nancy Folbre, "The Unhappy Marriage of Patriarchy and Capitalism," *Women and Revolution* 80 (1981): 10–11.

51. Rosalind Chait Barnett and Janet Shibley Hyde, "Women, Men, Work, and Family," *American Psychologist* 56, no. 10 (2001): 781–96; Ronald Inglehart and Christian Welzel, *Modernization, Cultural Change, and Democracy: The Human Development Sequence* (Cambridge: Cambridge University Press, 2005).

52. Hans-Peter Blossfeld and Johannes Huinink, "Human Capital Investments or Norms of Role Transition? How Women's Schooling and Career Affect the Process of Family Formation," *American Journal of Sociology*, 97, no. 1 (1991): 143–68; Agnes R. Quisumbing and Kelly Hallman, *Marriage in Transition: Evidence on Age, Education, and Assets from Six Developing Countries* (New York: Population Council, 2005), 200–269.

53. Hans-Peter Blossfeld and Alessandra De Rose, "Educational Expansion and Changes in Entry into Marriage and Motherhood: The Experience of Italian Women," *Genus* 48, no. 3–4 (1992): 73–91.

54. Steve Derné, Meenu Sharma, and Narendra Sethi, *Structural Changes Rather Than the Influence of Media: People's Encounter with Economic Liberalization in India* (New Delhi: Sage India, 2014).

55. Jill Reynolds, *The Single Woman: A Discursive Investigation* (London: Routledge, 2013); Jill Reynolds and Margaret Wetherell, "The Discursive Climate of Singleness: The Consequences for Women's Negotiation of a Single Identity," *Feminism & Psychology* 13, no. 4 (2003): 489–510.

56. May Al-Dabbagh, "Saudi Arabian Women and Group Activism," *Journal of Middle East Women's Studies* 11, no. 2 (2015): 235.

57. Alanoud Alsharekh, "Instigating Social Change: Translating Feminism in the Arab World and India," *QScience Connect* (2016): 2; Sylvia Vatuk, "Islamic Feminism in India," in *Islamic Reform in South Asia,* ed. Filippo Osella and Caroline Osella, 346–82 (Cambridge: Cambridge University Press, 2013).

58. Nada Mustafa Ali, "Feminism in North Africa," *The Wiley Blackwell Encyclopedia of Gender and Sexuality Studies* (Hoboken, NJ: Wiley Blackwell, 2016); Melissa Jackson, "A Season of Change: Egyptian Women's Organizing in the Arab Spring," *Undercurrent* 11, no. 1 (2015).

59. Veronica V. Kostenko, Pavel A. Kuzmuchev, and Eduard D. Ponarin, "Attitudes towards Gender Equality and Perception of Democracy in the Arab World," *Democratization* 23, no. 5 (2015): 1–28.

60. Paul Puschmann and Koen Matthijs, "The Demographic Transition in the Arab World: The Dual Role of Marriage in Family Dynamics and Population Growth," in *Population Change in Europe, the Middle-East and North Africa: Beyond the Demographic Divide,* ed. Koenraad Matthijs, Karel Neels, Christiane Timmerman, and Jacques Haers (London: Routledge, 2016), 119.

61. Michael A. Messner, "'Changing Men' and Feminist Politics in the United States," *Theory and Society* 22, no. 5 (1993): 723–37.

62. Laurie A. Rudman and Kimberly Fairchild, "The F Word: Is Feminism Incompatible with Beauty and Romance?" *Psychology of Women Quarterly* 31, no. 2 (2007): 125–36; Laurie A. Rudman and Julie E. Phelan, "The Interpersonal Power of Feminism: Is Feminism Good for Romantic Relationships?" *Sex Roles* 57, no. 11–12 (2007): 787–99.

63. Elizabeth Gregory, *Ready: Why Women Are Embracing the New Later Motherhood* (New York: Perseus Books Group, 2012).

64. Joelle Abramowitz, "Turning Back the Ticking Clock: The Effect of Increased Affordability of Assisted Reproductive Technology on Women's Marriage Timing," *Journal of Population Economics* 27, no. 2 (2014): 603–33.

65. Ya'arit Bokek-Cohen and Limor Dina Gonen, "Sperm and Simulacra: Emotional Capitalism and Sperm Donation Industry," *New Genetics and Society* 34, no. 3 (2015): 243–73.

66. Robert E. Emery, *Marriage, Divorce, and Children's Adjustment* (New York: Sage, 1999).

67. Richard E. Lucas, Andrew E. Clark, Yannis Georgellis, and Ed Diener, "Reexamining Adaptation and the Set Point Model of Happiness: Reactions to

Changes in Marital Status," *Journal of Personality and Social Psychology* 84, no. 3 (2003): 527.

68. Jody Van Laningham, David R. Johnson, and Paul Amato, "Marital Happiness, Marital Duration, and the U-Shaped Curve: Evidence from a Five-Wave Panel Study," *Social Forces* 79, no. 4 (2001): 1313–41.

69. Vaughn Call, Susan Sprecher, and Pepper Schwartz, "The Incidence and Frequency of Marital Sex in a National Sample," *Journal of Marriage and the Family* 57, no. 3 (1995): 639–52; Helen E. Fisher, *Anatomy of Love: The Natural History of Monogamy, Adultery and Divorce* (New York: Norton, 1992).

70. Andrew E. Clark, Ed Diener, Yannis Georgellis, and Richard E Lucas, "Lags and Leads in Life Satisfaction: A Test of the Baseline Hypothesis," *Economic Journal* 118, no. 529 (2008); Anke C. Zimmermann and Richard A. Easterlin, "Happily Ever After? Cohabitation, Marriage, Divorce, and Happiness in Germany," *Population and Development Review* 32, no. 3 (2006): 511–28.

71. Alois Stutzer and Bruno S. Frey, "Does Marriage Make People Happy, or Do Happy People Get Married?" *Journal of Socio-Economics* 35, no. 2 (2006): 326–47.

72. Richard E. Lucas, "Time Does Not Heal All Wounds: A Longitudinal Study of Reaction and Adaptation to Divorce," *Psychological Science* 16, no. 12 (2005): 945–50.

73. Richard E. Lucas, "Adaptation and the Set-Point Model of Subjective Well-Being: Does Happiness Change after Major Life Events?" *Current Directions in Psychological Science* 16, no. 2 (2007): 75–79; Pasqualina Perrig-Chiello, Sara Hutchison, and Bina Knöpfli, "Vulnerability Following a Critical Life Event: Temporary Crisis or Chronic Distress? A Psychological Controversy, Methodological Considerations, and Empirical Evidence," in *Surveying Human Vulnerabilities across the Life Course* (New York: Springer, 2016), 87–111.

74. Andrew E. Clark and Yannis Georgellis, "Back to Baseline in Britain: Adaptation in the British Household Panel Survey," *Economica* 80, no. 319 (2013): 496–512; Paul Frijters, David W. Johnston, and Michael A. Shields, "Life Satisfaction Dynamics with Quarterly Life Event Data," *Scandinavian Journal of Economics* 113, no. 1 (2011): 190–211; Kelly Musick and Larry Bumpass, "Reexamining the Case for Marriage: Union Formation and Changes in Well-Being," *Journal of Marriage and Family* 74, no. 1 (2012): 1–18; Judith P.M. Soons, Aart C. Liefbroer, and Matthijs Kalmijn, "The Long-Term Consequences of Relationship Formation for Subjective Well-Being," *Journal of Marriage and Family* 71, no. 5 (2009): 1254–70.

75. Casey E. Copen, Kimberly Daniels, Jonathan Vespa, and William D. Mosher, *First Marriages in the United States: Data from the 2006–2010 National Survey of Family Growth* (Hyattsville, MD: Department of Health and Human Services, Centers for Disease Control and Prevention, National Center for Health Statistics, 2012); Eurostat, *Marriage and Divorce Statistics* (Luxembourg: European Commission, 2017); Pamela Engel, "Map: Divorce Rates around the World," *Business Insider,* May 25, 2014.

76. Robert E. Emery, Mary Waldron, Katherine M. Kitzmann, and Jeffrey Aaron, "Delinquent Behavior, Future Divorce or Nonmarital Childbearing, and Externalizing Behavior among Offspring: A 14-Year Prospective Study," *Journal of Family Psychology* 13, no. 4 (1999): 568.

77. Paul R. Amato and Bruce Keith, "Parental Divorce and Adult Well-Being: A Meta-analysis," *Journal of Marriage and the Family* (1991): 43–58; Paul R. Amato, "Explaining the Intergenerational Transmission of Divorce," *Journal of Marriage and the Family* 58, no. 3 (1996): 628–40; Larry L. Bumpass, Teresa Castro Martin, and James A. Sweet, "The Impact of Family Background and Early Marital Factors on Marital Disruption," *Journal of Family Issues* 12, no. 1 (1991): 22–42.

78. Nicholas Wolfinger, "Want to Avoid Divorce? Wait to Get Married, but Not Too Long," *Family Studies,* July 16, 2015.

79. Fakir Al Gharaibeh and Nicole Footen Bromfield, "An Analysis of Divorce Cases in the United Arab Emirates: A Rising Trend," *Journal of Divorce & Remarriage* 53, no. 6 (2012): 436–52; Andrew Cherlin, *Marriage, Divorce, Remarriage* (Cambridge, MA: Harvard University Press, 2009).

80. Albert Esteve and Ron J. Lesthaeghe, *Cohabitation and Marriage in the Americas: Geo-Historical Legacies and New Trends* (New York: Springer, 2016).

81. Nicole Hiekel and Renske Keizer, "Risk-Avoidance or Utmost Commitment? Dutch Focus Group Research on Cohabitation and Marriage," *Demographic Research* 32, no. 10 (2015): 311.

82. Amanda J. Miller, Sharon Sassler, and Dela Kusi-Appouh, "The Specter of Divorce: Views from Working-and Middle-Class Cohabitors," *Family Relations* 60, no. 5 (2011): 602–16.

83. Arielle Kuperberg, "Reassessing Differences in Work and Income in Cohabitation and Marriage," *Journal of Marriage and Family* 74, no. 4 (2012): 688–707; Elina Mäenpää and Marika Jalovaara, "The Effects of Homogamy in Socio-economic Background and Education on the Transition from Cohabitation to Marriage," *Acta Sociologica* 56, no. 3 (2013): 247–63; Jarl E. Mooyaart and Aart C. Liefbroer, "The Influence of Parental Education on Timing and Type

of Union Formation: Changes over the Life Course and over Time in the Netherlands," *Demography* 53, no. 4 (2016): 885–919.

84. Masahiro Yamada, "Parasaito shinguru no jidai [The Age of Parasite Singles]," *Tokyo: Chikuma Shobo* (1999); Masahiro Yamada, "Parasite Singles Feed on Family System," *Japan Quarterly* 48, no. 1 (2001): 10.

85. Youna Kim, *Women and the Media in Asia: The Precarious Self* (London: Palgrave Macmillan, 2012), 6–32.

86. Masahiro Yamada, "Parasite Singles Feed on Family System," *Japan Quarterly* 48, no. 1 (2001): 10.

87. Juliet Stone, Ann Berrington, and Jane Falkingham, "The Changing Determinants of UK Young Adults' Living Arrangements," *Demographic Research* 25, no. 20 (2011): 629–66.

88. Kathryn Edin and Joanna M. Reed, "Why Don't They Just Get Married? Barriers to Marriage among the Disadvantaged," *Future of Children* 15, no. 2 (2005): 117–37.

89. Hyunjoon Park, Jae Kyung Lee, and Inkyung Jo, "Changing Relationships between Education and Marriage among Korean Women," 한국사회학 47, no. 3 (2013): 51–76.

90. Richard Fry, "A Rising Share of Young Adults Live in Their Parents' Home," in *Social Demographic Trends Project* (Washington, DC: Pew Research Center, 2013).

91. Eric Klinenberg, *Going Solo: The Extraordinary Rise and Surprising Appeal of Living Alone* (New York: Penguin, 2012).

92. S. Niranjan, Saritha Nair, and T.K. Roy, "A Socio-demographic Analysis of the Size and Structure of the Family in India," *Journal of Comparative Family Studies*, 36, no. 4 (2005): 623–51; Tulsi Patel, *The Family in India: Structure and Practice* (New York: Sage, 2005).

93. David Levine, *Family Formation in an Age of Nascent Capitalism [England]*, Studies in Social Discontinuity (New York: Academic Press, 1977).

94. Henrike Donner and Goncalo Santos, "Love, Marriage, and Intimate Citizenship in Contemporary China and India: An Introduction," *Modern Asian Studies* 50, no. 4 (2016): 1123–46.

95. Wim Lunsing, Tamako Sarada, Masahiro Yamada, Shumon Miura, Tamako Sarada, and Kiyo Yamamoto, "'Parasite' and 'Non-parasite' Singles: Japanese Journalists and Scholars Taking Positions," *Social Science Japan Journal* 6, no. 2 (2003): 261–65.

96. Anne Stefanie Aronsson, *Career Women in Contemporary Japan: Pursuing Identities, Fashioning Lives* (New York: Routledge, 2014); John McCreery,

Japanese Consumer Behaviour: From Worker Bees to Wary Shoppers (New York: Routledge, 2014).

97. Japan Family Planning Association, *Biannual Survey* (Tokyo: National Institute of Population and Social Security Research, 2014).

98. Andrew D. Gordon, "Consumption, Consumerism, and Japanese Modernity," in *The Oxford Handbook of the History of Consumption,* ed. Frank Trentmann, 485–504 (Oxford: Oxford University Press, 2012).

99. Richard Grassby, *Kinship and Capitalism: Marriage, Family, and Business in the English-Speaking World, 1580–1740* (Cambridge: Cambridge University Press, 2000).

100. Maggie Gallagher and Linda Waite, *The Case for Marriage* (New York: Random House, 2000).

101. Sharon Boden, *Consumerism, Romance and the Wedding Experience* (London: Palgrave Macmillan, 2003); Colin Campbell, *The Romantic Ethic and the Spirit of Modern Consumerism* (Hoboken, NJ: Blackwell, 2005).

102. Ellen A. Kramarow, "The Elderly Who Live Alone in the United States: Historical Perspectives on Household Change," *Demography* 32, no. 3 (1995): 335–52.

103. Christina M. Gibson-Davis, Kathryn Edin, and Sara McLanahan, "High Hopes but Even Higher Expectations: The Retreat from Marriage among Low-Income Couples," *Journal of Marriage and Family* 67, no. 5 (2005): 1301–12.

104. Irina Khoutyz, "Academic Mobility Programs as Part of Individual and Professional Development in a Globalized World: Uncovering Cultural Dimensions," in *Handbook of Research on Individualism and Identity in the Globalized Digital Age,* ed. F. Sigmund Topor, 168 (Hershey, PA: IGI Global, 2016).

105. Jianguo Liu, Thomas Dietz, Stephen R. Carpenter, Carl Folke, Marina Alberti, Charles L. Redman, Stephen H. Schneider, Elinor Ostrom, Alice N. Pell, and Jane Lubchenco, "Coupled Human and Natural Systems," *AMBIO: A Journal of the Human Environment* 36, no. 8 (2007): 639–49.

106. Bella M. DePaulo, *Singled Out: How Singles Are Stereotyped, Stigmatized, and Ignored, and Still Live Happily Ever After* (New York: St. Martin's Griffin, 2007).

107. Helen Katz, *The Media Handbook: A Complete Guide to Advertising Media Selection, Planning, Research, and Buying* (New York: Routledge, 2014).

108. Annette Pritchard and Nigel J. Morgan, "Sex Still Sells to Generation X: Promotional Practice and the Youth Package Holiday Market," *Journal of Vacation Marketing* 3, no. 1 (1996): 68–80; Philip Roscoe and Shiona Chillas, "The State of Affairs: Critical Performativity and the Online Dating Industry," *Organization* 21, no. 6 (2014): 797–820.

109. Dana L. Alden, Jan-Benedict E.M. Steenkamp, and Rajeev Batra, "Brand Positioning through Advertising in Asia, North America, and Europe: The Role of Global Consumer Culture," *Journal of Marketing* 63, no. 1 (1999): 75–87; Stuart Ewen, *Captains of Consciousness: Advertising and the Social Roots of the Consumer Culture* (New York: Basic Books, 2008).

110. Breana Wilson and Esther Lamidi, *Living Alone in the U.S., 2011*, FP-13–18, (Bowling Green, OH: National Center for Family & Marriage Research, 2013), http://ncfmr.bgsu.edu/pdf/family_profiles/file138254.pdf.

111. Hans-Peter Blossfeld and Johannes Huinink, "Human Capital Investments or Norms of Role Transition? How Women's Schooling and Career Affect the Process of Family Formation," *American Journal of Sociology* 97, no. 1 (1991): 143–68; Hans-Peter Blossfeld and Alessandra De Rose, "Educational Expansion and Changes in Entry into Marriage and Motherhood: The Experience of Italian Women," *Genus* 48, no. 3–4 (1992): 73–91.

112. Wolfgang Lutz and Vegard Skirbekk, "Policies Addressing the Tempo Effect in Low-Fertility Countries," *Population and Development Review* 31, no. 4 (2005): 699–720.

113. Robert T. Michael, Victor R. Fuchs, and Sharon R. Scott, "Changes in the Propensity to Live Alone: 1950–1976," *Demography* 17, no. 1 (1980): 39–56; Samuel Andrew Stouffer, *Communism, Conformity, and Civil Liberties: A Cross-section of the Nation Speaks Its Mind* (Piscataway, NJ: Transaction, 1955).

114. Lawrence Bobo and Frederick C Licari, "Education and Political Tolerance: Testing the Effects of Cognitive Sophistication and Target Group Affect," *Public Opinion Quarterly* 53, no. 3 (1989): 285–308.

115. Frederick D. Weil, "The Variable Effects of Education on Liberal Attitudes: A Comparative-Historical Analysis of Anti-Semitism Using Public Opinion Survey Data," *American Sociological Review* 50, no. 4 (1985): 458–74.

116. Premchand Dommaraju, "One-Person Households in India," *Demographic Research* 32, no. 45 (2015); Hyunjoon Park and Jaesung Choi, "Long-Term Trends in Living Alone among Korean Adults: Age, Gender, and Educational Differences," *Demographic Research* 32, no. 43 (2015): 1177–208; Christophe Guilmoto and Myriam de Loenzien, "Emerging, Transitory or Residual? One-Person Households in Viet Nam," *Demographic Research* 32, no. 42 (2015): 1147–76; Chai Podhisita and Peter Xenos, "Living Alone in South and Southeast Asia: An Analysis of Census Data," *Demographic Research* 32, no. 41 (2015): 1113–46; Wei-Jun Jean Yeung and Adam Ka-Lok Cheung, "Living Alone: One-Person Households in Asia," *Demographic Research* 32, no. 40 (2015): 1099–112.

117. Lisa R. Silberstein, *Dual-Career Marriage: A System in Transition* (New York: Psychology Press, 1992).

118. Richard E. Kopelman, Jeffrey H. Greenhaus, and Thomas F. Connolly, "A Model of Work, Family, and Interrole Conflict: A Construct Validation Study," *Organizational Behavior and Human Performance* 32, no. 2 (1983): 198–215; Lisa R. Silberstein, *Dual-Career Marriage: A System in Transition* (New York: Psychology Press, 1992).

119. Sarah Badger, Larry J. Nelson, and Carolyn McNamara Barry, "Perceptions of the Transition to Adulthood among Chinese and American Emerging Adults," *International Journal of Behavioral Development* 30, no. 1 (2006): 84–93; Rachel Gali Cinamon, "Anticipated Work-Family Conflict: Effects of Gender, Self-Efficacy, and Family Background," *Career Development Quarterly* 54, no. 3 (2006): 202–15.

120. David Card, "The Causal Effect of Education on Earnings," *Handbook of Labor Economics* 3 (1999): 1801–63; Biwei Su and Almas Heshmati, "Analysis of the Determinants of Income and Income Gap between Urban and Rural China," *China Economic Policy Review* 2, no. 1 (2013): 1–29.

121. Ellen A. Kramarow, "The Elderly Who Live Alone in the United States: Historical Perspectives on Household Change," *Demography* 32, no. 3 (1995): 335–52.

122. Hyunjoon Park and Jaesung Choi, "Long-Term Trends in Living Alone among Korean Adults: Age, Gender, and Educational Differences," *Demographic Research* 32, no. 43 (2015): 1177–208.

123. Robert T. Michael, Victor R. Fuchs, and Sharon R. Scott, "Changes in the Propensity to Live Alone: 1950–1976," *Demography* 17, no. 1 (1980): 39–56; Kathleen McGarry and Robert F. Schoeni, "Social Security, Economic Growth, and the Rise in Elderly Widows' Independence in the Twentieth Century," *Demography* 37, no. 2 (2000): 221–36.

124. Yoav Lavee and Ruth Katz, "The Family in Israel: Between Tradition and Modernity," *Marriage & Family Review* 35, no. 1–2 (2003): 193–217.

125. Eli Berman, "Sect, Subsidy, and Sacrifice: An Economist's View of Ultra-Orthodox Jews," *Quarterly Journal of Economics* 115, no. 3 (2000): 905–53; Tally Katz-Gerro, Sharon Raz, and Meir Yaish, "How Do Class, Status, Ethnicity, and Religiosity Shape Cultural Omnivorousness in Israel?" *Journal of Cultural Economics* 33, no. 1 (2009): 1–17.

126. Ron J. Lesthaeghe and Lisa Neidert, "The Second Demographic Transition in the United States: Exception or Textbook Example?" *Population and Development Review* 32, no. 4 (2006): 669–98; Wendy Wang and Kim C.

Parker, *Record Share of Americans Have Never Married: As Values, Economics and Gender Patterns Change* (Washington, DC: Pew Research Center, 2014).

127. Albert Esteve, Ron Lesthaeghe, Julieta Quilodrán, Antonio López-Gay, and Julián López-Colás, "The Expansion of Cohabitation in Mexico, 1930–2010: The Revenge of History?" in *Cohabitation and Marriage in the Americas: Geo-Historical Legacies and New Trends,* ed. Albert Esteve and Ron Lesthaeghe (New York: Springer, 2016).

128. Organization for Economic Cooperation and Development, *Fertility Rates (Indicator)* (Paris: OECD, 2017); Daniele Vignoli and Silvana Salvini, "Religion and Union Formation in Italy: Catholic Precepts, Social Pressure, and Tradition," *Demographic Research* 31, no. 35 (2014): 1079–106.

129. Albert Esteve, Ron Lesthaeghe, Julieta Quilodrán, Antonio López-Gay, and Julián López-Colás, "The Expansion of Cohabitation in Mexico, 1930–2010: The Revenge of History?" in *Cohabitation and Marriage in the Americas: Geo-Historical Legacies and New Trends,* ed. Albert Esteve and Ron Lesthaeghe (New York: Springer, 2016).

130. Alicia Adsera, "Marital Fertility and Religion in Spain, 1985 and 1999," *Population Studies* 60, no. 2 (2006): 205–21.

131. Benoît Laplante, "The Rise of Cohabitation in Quebec: Power of Religion and Power over Religion," *Canadian Journal of Sociology* 31, no. 1 (2006): 1–24.

132. Albert Esteve, Ron Lesthaeghe, and Antonio López-Gay, "The Latin American Cohabitation Boom, 1970–2007," *Population and Development Review* 38, no. 1 (2012): 55–81.

133. Justin Farrell, "The Young and the Restless? The Liberalization of Young Evangelicals," *Journal for the Scientific Study of Religion* 50, no. 3 (2011): 517–32.

134. Ziba Mir-Hosseini, "Muslim Women's Quest for Equality: Between Islamic Law and Feminism," *Critical Inquiry* 32, no. 4 (2006): 629–45.

135. Laura Levitt, *Jews and Feminism: The Ambivalent Search for Home* (London: Routledge, 2013).

136. Amita Sharma, "Feminism in India—a Fractured Movement," *History* 4, no. 2 (2015).

137. Tanya Zion-Waldoks, "Politics of Devoted Resistance Agency, Feminism, and Religion among Orthodox Agunah Activists in Israel," *Gender & Society* 29, no. 1 (2015): 73–97.

138. Brian H. Smith, *The Church and Politics in Chile: Challenges to Modern Catholicism* (Princeton, NJ: Princeton University Press, 2014).

139. Renato M. Liboro and Richard T. G. Walsh, "Understanding the Irony: Canadian Gay Men Living with HIV/AIDS, Their Catholic Devotion, and Greater Well-Being," *Journal of Religion and Health* 55, no. 2 (2016): 650–70.

140. Leonard Gargan, "Stereotypes of Singles: A Cross-cultural Comparison," *International Journal of Comparative Sociology* 27 (1986): 200.

141. Anthea Taylor, *Single Women in Popular Culture* (London: Palgrave Macmillan, 2012), 6–32.

142. Jane Arthurs, "Sex and the City and Consumer Culture: Remediating Postfeminist Drama," *Feminist Media Studies* 3, no. 1 (2003): 83–98.

143. Evan Cooper, "Decoding *Will and Grace:* Mass Audience Reception of a Popular Network Situation Comedy," *Sociological Perspectives* 46, no. 4 (2003): 513–33.

144. Shane Gunster, ""All about Nothing': Difference, Affect, and *Seinfeld,*" *Television & New Media* 6, no. 2 (2005): 200–223.

145. Janine Hertel, Astrid Schütz, Bella M. DePaulo, Wendy L Morris, and Tanja S. Stucke, "She's Single, So What? How Are Singles Perceived Compared with People Who Are Married?" *Zeitschrift für Familienforschung / Journal of Family Research* 19, no. 2 (2007); E. Kay Trimberger, *The New Single Woman* (Boston: Beacon Press, 2006).

146. Shane Gunster, "All about Nothing": Difference, Affect, and *Seinfeld,*" *Television & New Media* 6, no. 2 (2005): 200–223; Vesela Todorova, "Arab Women Find a Voice in Turkish Soap Operas," *The National,* November 2013; Anqi Xu and Yan Xia, "The Changes in Mainland Chinese Families during the Social Transition: A Critical Analysis," *Journal of Comparative Family Studies* (2014): 31–53.

147. Jonathan Matusitz and Pam Payano, "Globalisation of Popular Culture: From Hollywood to Bollywood," *South Asia Research* 32, no. 2 (2012): 123–38.

148. Robert Jensen and Emily Oster, "The Power of TV: Cable Television and Women's Status in India," *Quarterly Journal of Economics* 124, no. 3 (2009): 1057–94.

149. Alberto Chong and Eliana La Ferrara, "Television and Divorce: Evidence from Brazilian Novelas," *Journal of the European Economic Association* 7, no. 2–3 (2009): 458–68.

150. Harry Charalambos Triandis, *Individualism & Collectivism* (Boulder, CO: Westview Press, 1995).

151. Arjun Appadurai, *Modernity at Large: Cultural Dimensions of Globalization* (Minneapolis, MN: University of Minnesota Press, 1996).

152. Russell B. Clayton, Alexander Nagurney, and Jessica R Smith, "Cheating, Breakup, and Divorce: Is Facebook Use to Blame?" *Cyberpsychology, Behavior, and Social Networking* 16, no. 10 (2013): 717–20.

153. Russell B. Clayton, "The Third Wheel: The Impact of Twitter Use on Relationship Infidelity and Divorce," *Cyberpsychology, Behavior, and Social Networking* 17, no. 7 (2014): 425–30.

154. Juliet Stone, Ann Berrington, and Jane Falkingham, "The Changing Determinants of UK Young Adults' Living Arrangements," *Demographic Research* 25, no. 20 (2011): 629–66.

155. Rita Afsar, *Internal Migration and the Development Nexus: The Case of Bangladesh* (Dhaka: Bangladesh Institute of Development Studies, 2003); Alice Goldstein, Guo Zhigang, and Sidney Goldstein, "The Relation of Migration to Changing Household Headship Patterns in China, 1982–1987," *Population Studies* 51, no. 1 (1997): 75–84; Mary M. Kritz and Douglas T. Gurak, "The Impact of Immigration on the Internal Migration of Natives and Immigrants," *Demography* 38, no. 1 (2001): 133–45; Chai Podhisita and Peter Xenos, "Living Alone in South and Southeast Asia: An Analysis of Census Data," *Demographic Research* 32, no. 41 (2015): 1113–46.

156. Abbasi-Shavazi, Mohammad Jalal, and Abbas Askari-Nodoushan, "Family Life and Developmental Idealism in Yazd, Iran," *Demographic Research* 26, no. 10 (2012): 207–38.

157. Madhav Sadashiv Gore, *Urbanization and Family Change* (Bombay: Popular Prakashan, 1990).

158. Kenneth T. Jackson, *Crabgrass Frontier: The Suburbanization of the United States* (Oxford: Oxford University Press, 1985); Philip E. Ogden and Ray Hall, "Households, Reurbanisation and the Rise of Living Alone in the Principal French Cities, 1975–90," *Urban Studies* 37, no. 2 (2000): 367–90.

159. Hyunjoon Park and Jaesung Choi, "Long-Term Trends in Living Alone among Korean Adults: Age, Gender, and Educational Differences," *Demographic Research* 32, no. 43 (2015): 1177–208; Georg Simmel, *The Metropolis and Mental Life* (New York: Free Press, 1903); Wei-Jun Jean Yeung and Adam Ka-Lok Cheung, "Living Alone: One-Person Households in Asia," *Demographic Research* 32, no. 40 (2015): 1099–112.

160. Gill Jagger and Caroline Wright, *Changing Family Values* (Taylor & Francis, 1999); James Georgas, "Changing Family Values in Greece from Collectivist to Individualist," *Journal of Cross-cultural Psychology* 20, no. 1 (1989): 80–91.

161. Peter L. Callero, "Living Alone: Globalization, Identity, and Belonging," *Contemporary Sociology: A Journal of Reviews* 44, no. 5 (2015): 667–69; John

Eade, *Living the Global City: Globalization as Local Process* (London: Routledge, 2003).

162. Agnese Vitali, "Regional Differences in Young Spaniards' Living Arrangement Decisions: A Multilevel Approach," *Advances in Life Course Research* 15, no. 2 (2010): 97–108.

163. Robert T. Michael, Victor R. Fuchs, and Sharon R. Scott, "Changes in the Propensity to Live Alone: 1950–1976," *Demography* 17, no. 1 (1980): 39–56.

164. Zhongwei Zhao and Wei Chen, "Changes in Household Formation and Composition in China since the Mid-twentieth Century," *Journal of Population Research* 25, no. 3 (2008): 267–86.

165. Kathleen Sheldon, *Courtyards, Markets, and City Streets: Urban Women in Africa* (Boulder, CO: Westview Press, 2016).

166. Melissa Blanchard, "Sending Money or Purchasing Provisions? Senegalese Migrants' Attempts to Negotiate a Space for Autonomy in Long-Distance Family Relations," *Journal des africanistes* 84 (2014): 40–59.

167. Emily J. Shaw and Sandra Barbuti, "Patterns of Persistence in Intended College Major with a Focus on Stem Majors," *NACADA Journal* 30, no. 2 (2010): 19–34.

168. Hasan Mahmud, "Migrants Sending Money and the Family" (presented to *XVIII ISA World Congress of Sociology* Yokohama, Japan, July 14, 2014).

169. Albert Saiz, "Immigration and Housing Rents in American Cities," *Journal of Urban Economics* 61, no. 2 (2007): 345–71; Matthew R. Sanderson, Ben Derudder, Michael Timberlake, and Frank Witlox, "Are World Cities Also World Immigrant Cities? An International, Cross-city Analysis of Global Centrality and Immigration," *International Journal of Comparative Sociology* 6, no. 3–4 (2015): 173–97.

170. Stephen Castles, Hein de Haas, and Mark J. Miller, *The Age of Migration: International Population Movements in the Modern World* (New York: Guilford, 2013).

171. Robyn Iredale and Kalika N. Doloswala, "International Labour Migration from India, the Philippines and Sri Lanka: Trends and Policies," *Sri Lanka Journal of Social Sciences* 27, no. 1 (2016); Eleonore Kofman and Parvati Raghuram, "Gendered Migrations and Global Processes," in *Gendered Migrations and Global Social Reproduction* (New York: Springer, 2015), 18–39.

172. Soon Kyu Choi and Ilan H. Meyer, *LGBT Aging: A Review of Research Findings, Needs, and Policy Implications* (Los Angeles: Williams Institute, 2016); Eurostat, *Eurostat Regional Yearbook* (Brussels: European Commission, 2017).

173. Amparo González-Ferrer, "Who Do Immigrants Marry? Partner Choice among Single Immigrants in Germany," *European Sociological Review* 22, no. 2

(2006): 171–85; Katarzyna Grabska, "Lost Boys, Invisible Girls: Stories of Sudanese Marriages across Borders," *Gender, Place & Culture* 17, no. 4 (2010): 479–97.

174. Stephen P. Casazza, Emily Ludwig, and Tracy J Cohn, "Heterosexual Attitudes and Behavioral Intentions toward Bisexual Individuals: Does Geographic Area Make a Difference?" *Journal of Bisexuality* 15, no. 4 (2015): 532–53.

175. Lyndon Johnson, "The War on Poverty," *Annals of America* 18 (1964): 212–16.

176. Carl M. Brauer, "Kennedy, Johnson, and the War on Poverty," *Journal of American History* 69, no. 1 (1982): 98–119; David Zarefsky, *President Johnson's War on Poverty: Rhetoric and History* (Tuscaloosa: University of Alabama Press, 2005).

177. Robert E. Hall, *Quantifying the Lasting Harm to the US Economy from the Financial Crisis* (Cambridge, MA: National Bureau of Economic Research, 2014); David Zarefsky, *President Johnson's War on Poverty: Rhetoric and History* (Tuscaloosa: University of Alabama Press, 2005).

178. Maggie Gallagher and Linda Waite, *The Case for Marriage* (New York: Random House, 2000); Walter R. Gove, Michael Hughes, and Carolyn Briggs Style, "Does Marriage Have Positive Effects on the Psychological Well-Being of the Individual?" *Journal of Health and Social Behavior* 24, no. 2 (1983): 122–31; David R. Johnson and Jian Wu, "An Empirical Test of Crisis, Social Selection, and Role Explanations of the Relationship between Marital Disruption and Psychological Distress: A Pooled Time-Series Analysis of Four-Wave Panel Data," *Journal of Marriage and Family* 64, no. 1 (2002): 211–24.

179. Ron Haskins, "The War on Poverty: What Went Wrong?" Op-ed, Brookings, November 19, 2013, www.brookings.edu/opinions/the-war-on-poverty-what-went-wrong/.

CHAPTER 2. HAPPY SINGLEHOOD IN OLD AGE

1. Lawrence Millman, "The Old Woman Who Was Kind to Insects," in *A Kayak Full of Ghosts: Eskimo Tales* (Northampton, MA: Interlink Books, 1987).

2. Stephanie S. Spielmann, Geoff MacDonald, Jessica A. Maxwell, Samantha Joel, Diana Peragine, Amy Muise, and Emily A. Impett, "Settling for Less out of Fear of Being Single," *Journal of Personality and Social Psychology* 105, no. 6 (2013): 1049.

3. Stephanie S. Spielmann, Geoff MacDonald, Samantha Joel, and Emily A. Impett, "Longing for Ex-Partners out of Fear of Being Single," *Journal of Personality* 84, no. 6 (2016): 799–808.

4. Peter Walker, "May Appoints Minister to Tackle Loneliness Issues Raised by Jo Cox," *The Guardian,* January 16, 2018, www.theguardian.com/society/2018/jan/16/may-appoints-minister-tackle-loneliness-issues-raised-jo-cox?CMP=share_btn_link.

5. Vern L. Bengtson and Norella M. Putney, "Who Will Care for Tomorrow's Elderly? Consequences of Population Aging East and West," in *Aging in East and West: Families, States, and the Elderly,* ed. Vern L. Bengtson, Kyong-Dong Kim, George Myers, and Ki-Soo Eun (New York: Springer, 2000): 263–85; Adam Ka-Lok Cheung and Wei-Jun Jean Yeung, "Temporal-Spatial Patterns of One-Person Households in China, 1982–2005," *Demographic Research* S15, no. 44 (2015): 1209–38; Antonio Golini and A. Silverstrini, "Family Change, Fathers, and Children in Western Europe: A Demographic and Psychosocial Perspective," in *The Family on the Threshold of the 21st Century: Trends and Implications,* ed. Solly Dreman (New York: Psychology Press, 2013), 201.

6. Sofia, "Just One Single," *Blogspot,* September 16, 2008, http://justonesingle.blogspot.com.

7. Marja Aartsen and Marja Jylhä, "Onset of Loneliness in Older Adults: Results of a 28 Year Prospective Study," *European Journal of Ageing* 8, no. 1 (2011): 31–38; Margaret Gatz and Steven H. Zarit, "A Good Old Age: Paradox or Possibility," *Handbook of Theories of Aging* (1999): 396–416; Paul Halmos, *Solitude and Privacy: A Study of Social Isolation, Its Causes and Therapy* (New York: Routledge, 2013); Felix Post, "Mental Breakdown in Old Age," *British Medical Journal* 1, no. 4704 (1951): 436; G. Clare Wenger, "Morale in Old Age: A Review of the Evidence," *International Journal of Geriatric Psychiatry* 7, no. 10 (1992): 699–708.

8. Margaret Gatz and Steven H. Zarit, "A Good Old Age: Paradox or Possibility," *Handbook of Theories of Aging* (1999): 396–416.

9. Daniel Perlman and L. Anne Peplau, "Toward a Social Psychology of Loneliness," *Personal Relationships* 3 (1981): 31–56.

10. Tineke Fokkema, Jenny De Jong Gierveld, and Pearl A. Dykstra, "Cross-national Differences in Older Adult Loneliness," *Journal of Psychology* 146, no. 1–2 (2012): 201–28.

11. G. Clare Wenger, Richard Davies, Said Shahtahmasebi, and Anne Scott, "Social Isolation and Loneliness in Old Age: Review and Model Refinement," *Ageing & Society* 16, no. 3 (1996): 333–58.

12. Marja Jylhä, "Old Age and Loneliness: Cross-sectional and Longitudinal Analyses in the Tampere Longitudinal Study on Aging," *Canadian Journal on Aging / La revue canadienne du vieillissement* 23, no. 2 (2004): 157–68.

13. Marja Aartsen and Marja Jylhä, "Onset of Loneliness in Older Adults: Results of a 28 Year Prospective Study," *European Journal of Ageing* 8, no. 1 (2011): 31–38; Lena Dahlberg and Kevin J. McKee, "Correlates of Social and Emotional Loneliness in Older People: Evidence from an English Community Study," *Aging & Mental Health* 18, no. 4 (2014): 504–14; Christopher J. Einolf and Deborah Philbrick, "Generous or Greedy Marriage? A Longitudinal Study of Volunteering and Charitable Giving," *Journal of Marriage and Family* 76, no. 3 (2014): 573–86; Naomi Gerstel and Natalia Sarkisian, "Marriage: The Good, the Bad, and the Greedy," *Contexts* 5, no. 4 (2006): 16–21.

14. D. W. K. Kay, Pamela Beamish, and Martin Roth, "Old Age Mental Disorders in Newcastle upon Tyne," *British Journal of Psychiatry* 110, no. 468 (1964): 668–82; M. Powell Lawton and Renee H. Lawrence, "Assessing Health," *Annual Review of Gerontology and Geriatrics* 14, no. 1 (1994): 23–56; Kerry A. Sargent-Cox, Kaarin J. Anstey, and Mary A. Luszcz, "Patterns of Longitudinal Change in Older Adults' Self-Rated Health: The Effect of the Point of Reference," *Health Psychology* 29, no. 2 (2010): 143.

15. Steven Stack, "Marriage, Family and Loneliness: A Cross-national Study," *Sociological Perspectives* 41, no. 2 (1998): 415–32.

16. Helena Znaniecki Lopata, "Loneliness: Forms and Components," *Social Problems* 17, no. 2 (1969): 248–62; Matthijs Kalmijn and Marjolein Broese van Groenou, "Differential Effects of Divorce on Social Integration," *Journal of Social and Personal Relationships* 22, no. 4 (2005): 455–76.

17. Bella DePaulo, *Marriage vs. Single Life: How Science and the Media Got It So Wrong* (Charleston, SC: DoubleDoor Books, 2015).

18. Christina M. Gibson-Davis, Kathryn Edin, and Sara McLanahan, "High Hopes but Even Higher Expectations: The Retreat from Marriage among Low-Income Couples," *Journal of Marriage and Family* 67, no. 5 (2005): 1301–12; Maureen R. Waller and Sara S. McLanahan, "'His' and 'Her' Marriage Expectations: Determinants and Consequences," *Journal of Marriage and Family* 67, no. 1 (2005): 53–67.

19. Alois Stutzer and Bruno S. Frey, "Does Marriage Make People Happy, or Do Happy People Get Married?" *Journal of Socio-economics* 35, no. 2 (2006): 326–47.

20. Paul R. Amato, "Research on Divorce: Continuing Trends and New Developments," *Journal of Marriage and Family* 72, no. 3 (2010): 650–66; Betsey Stevenson and Justin Wolfers, *Marriage and Divorce: Changes and Their Driving Forces* (Cambridge, MA: National Bureau of Economic Research, 2007).

21. Rose McDermott, James H. Fowler, and Nicholas A. Christakis, "Breaking Up Is Hard to Do, Unless Everyone Else Is Doing It Too: Social Network Effects on Divorce in a Longitudinal Sample," *Social Forces* 92, no. 2 (2013): 491–519.

22. Renee Stepler, *Led by Baby Boomers, Divorce Rates Climb for America's 50+ Population* (Washington, DC: Pew Research Center, 2017).

23. Dan, response to "Aging Alone Doesn't Have to Mean Lonely," *Senior Planet*, January 25, 2017, https://seniorplanet.org/aging-alone-doesnt-have-to-mean-lonely/#comment-190333.

24. R. S. Weiss, *Loneliness: The Experience of Emotional and Social Isolation* (Cambridge, MA: MIT Press, 1973).

25. Nancy E. Newall, Judith G. Chipperfield, Rodney A. Clifton, Raymond P. Perry, Audrey U. Swift, and Joelle C. Ruthig, "Causal Beliefs, Social Participation, and Loneliness among Older Adults: A Longitudinal Study," *Journal of Social and Personal Relationships* 26, no. 2–3 (2009): 273–90; Thomas Scharf, Chris Phillipson, and Allison E. Smith, "Social Exclusion of Older People in Deprived Urban Communities of England," *European Journal of Ageing* 2, no. 2 (2005): 76–87.

26. Jonathan Drennan, Margaret Treacy, Michelle Butler, Anne Byrne, Gerard Fealy, Kate Frazer, and Kate Irving, "The Experience of Social and Emotional Loneliness among Older People in Ireland," *Ageing & Society* 28, no. 8 (2008): 1113–32; Pearl A. Dykstra, and Tineke Fokkema, "Social and Emotional Loneliness among Divorced and Married Men and Women: Comparing the Deficit and Cognitive Perspectives," *Basic and Applied Social Psychology* 29, no. 1 (2007): 1–12.

27. Marja Aartsen and Marja Jylhä, "Onset of Loneliness in Older Adults: Results of a 28 Year Prospective Study," *European Journal of Ageing* 8, no. 1 (2011): 31–38; Lena Dahlberg and Kevin J. McKee, "Correlates of Social and Emotional Loneliness in Older People: Evidence from an English Community Study," *Aging & Mental Health* 18, no. 4 (2014): 504–14.

28. Christopher J. Einolf and Deborah Philbrick, "Generous or Greedy Marriage? A Longitudinal Study of Volunteering and Charitable Giving," *Journal of Marriage and Family* 76, no. 3 (2014): 573–86; Naomi Gerstel and Natalia Sarkisian, "Marriage: The Good, the Bad, and the Greedy," *Contexts* 5, no. 4 (2006): 16–21.

29. Naomi Gerstel and Natalia Sarkisian, "Marriage: The Good, the Bad, and the Greedy," *Contexts* 5, no. 4 (2006): 16–21.

30. Ed Diener and Martin E. P. Seligman, "Very Happy People," *Psychological Science* 13, no. 1 (2002): 81–84.

31. Naomi Gerstel, "Divorce and Stigma," *Social Problems* 34, no. 2 (1987): 172–86.

32. Helmuth Cremer and Pierre Pestieau, "Myopia, Redistribution and Pensions," *European Economic Review* 55, no. 2 (2011): 165–75.

33. Bella DePaulo, *Marriage vs. Single Life: How Science and the Media Got It So Wrong* (Charleston, SC: DoubleDoor Books, 2015); Alois Stutzer and Bruno S. Frey, "Does Marriage Make People Happy, or Do Happy People Get Married?" *Journal of Socio-economics* 35, no. 2 (2006): 326–47.

34. Eric Klinenberg, *Heat Wave: A Social Autopsy of Disaster in Chicago* (Chicago: University of Chicago Press, 2003).

35. Eric Klinenberg, *Going Solo: The Extraordinary Rise and Surprising Appeal of Living Alone* (New York: Penguin, 2012).

36. David Haber, "Life Review: Implementation, Theory, Research, and Therapy," *International Journal of Aging and Human Development* 63, no. 2 (2006): 153–71.

37. Tova Band-Winterstein and Carmit Manchik-Rimon, "The Experience of Being an Old Never-Married Single: A Life Course Perspective," *International Journal of Aging and Human Development* 78, no. 4 (2014): 379–401.

38. C. Schact and D. Knox, "Singlehood, Hanging out, Hooking up, and Cohabitation," in *Choices in Relationships: An Introduction to Marriage and Family,* ed. C. Schact and D. Knox (Belmont, CA: Wadsworth, 2010), 132–72.

39. Robert L. Rubinstein, "Never Married Elderly as a Social Type: Reevaluating Some Images," *Gerontologist* 27, no. 1 (1987): 108–13.

40. Anonymous, *Women-Ish, Blogspot,* August 25, 2008, http://women-ish.blogspot.com; Sofia, "Just One Single," *Blogspot,* September 16, 2008, http://justonesingle.blogspot.com.

41. Ronnie, "Isolation, Loneliness and Solitude in Old Age," *Time Goes By,* December 12, 2012, www.timegoesby.net/weblog/2012/12/isolation-loneliness-and-solitude-in-old-age.html.

42. Pirkko Routasalo and Kaisu H. Pitkala, "Loneliness among Older People," *Reviews in Clinical Gerontology* 13, no. 4 (2003): 303–11.

43. Tova Band-Winterstein and Carmit Manchik-Rimon, "The Experience of Being an Old Never-Married Single: A Life Course Perspective," *International Journal of Aging and Human Development* 78, no. 4 (2014): 379–401.

44. John T. Cacioppo and William Patrick, *Loneliness: Human Nature and the Need for Social Connection* (New York: W. W. Norton, 2008).

45. Marty Beckerman, "Is Loneliness Good for You?" *Esquire,* September 29, 2010, www.esquire.com/lifestyle/sex/a8599/single-and-happy/.

46. Diane, "The Brutal Truth of Dating," *Single Shot Seattle,* July 12, 2016, https://singleshotseattle.wordpress.com.

47. Sofia, "Just One Single," *Blogspot,* August 17, 2009, http://justonesingle.blogspot.com.

48. Clive Seale, "Dying Alone," *Sociology of Health & Illness* 17, no. 3 (1995).

49. Kim Parker and D'Vera Cohn, *Growing Old in America: Expectations vs. Reality* (Washington, DC: Pew Research Center, 2009), 376–92.

50. Jenny Gierveld, Pearl A. Dykstra, and Niels Schenk, "Living Arrangements, Intergenerational Support Types and Older Adult Loneliness in Eastern and Western Europe," *Demographic Research* 27, no. 2 (2012): 167.

51. Alberto Palloni, *Living Arrangements of Older Persons* (New York: UN Population Bulletin, 2001).

52. Linda Abbit, "Urban Cohousing the Babayaga Way," *Senior Planet,* March 6, 2016, https://seniorplanet.org/senior-housing-alternatives-urban-cohousing-the-babayaga-way/.

53. Jane Gross, "Older Women Team Up to Face Future Together," *New York Times,* February 27, 2004, www.nytimes.com/2004/02/27/us/older-women-team-up-to-face-future-together.html.

54. Jon Pynoos, "Housing for Older Adults: A Personal Journey in Environmental Gerontology," in *Environments in an Aging Society: Autobiographical Perspectives in Environmental Gerontology,* ed. Habib Chaudhury and Frank Oswald (New York: Springer, 2018), 147–64; Mariano Sánchez, José M. García, Pilar Díaz, and Mónica Duaigües, "Much More Than Accommodation in Exchange for Company: Dimensions of Solidarity in an Intergenerational Homeshare Program in Spain," *Journal of Intergenerational Relationships* 9, no. 4 (2011): 374–88.

55. Beth Pinsker, "Your Money: Creative Caregiving Solutions for the 'Sandwich Generation,'" *Reuters,* May 31, 2017, www.reuters.com/article/us-money-retirement-sandwichgen-idUSKBN18R2TT.

56. Yagana Shah, "'Airbnb for Seniors' Helps Link Travelers with Like-Minded Hosts," *Huffington Post,* June 1, 2016, www.huffingtonpost.com/entry/airbnb-for-seniors-helps-link-travelers-with-like-minded-hosts_us_57487aa1e4b0dacf7ad4c130.

57. Stephen M. Golant, "Political and Organizational Barriers to Satisfying Low-Income US Seniors' Need for Affordable Rental Housing with Supportive Services," *Journal of Aging & Social Policy* 15, no. 4 (2003): 21–48.

58. California Department of Aging, "Programs & Services," State of California, 2017, www.aging.ca.gov/Programs/.

59. Shannon, response to Jane Gross, "Single, Childless, and Downright Terrified," *New York Times,* July 29, 2008, https://newoldage.blogs.nytimes.com/2008/07/29/single-childless-and-downright-terrified/#comment-2065.

60. Steven R. Asher and Jeffrey G. Parker, "Significance of Peer Relationship Problems in Childhood," in *Social Competence in Developmental Perspective,* ed. Barry Schneider, Grazia Attili, Jacqueline Nadel, and Roger Weissberg (Dordrecht, Netherlands: Kluwer Academic Publishers, 1989), 5–23; Ana M. Martínez Alemán, "College Women's Female Friendships: A Longitudinal View," *Journal of Higher Education* 81, no. 5 (2010): 553–82.

61. Jenna Mahay and Alisa C. Lewin, "Age and the Desire to Marry," *Journal of Family Issues* 28, no. 5 (2007): 706–23.

62. Stephen Katz, *Cultural Aging: Life Course, Lifestyle, and Senior Worlds* (Peterborough, Ontario: Broadview Press, 2005).

63. Bella M. DePaulo, *Singlism: What It Is, Why It Matters, and How to Stop It* (Charleston, SC: DoubleDoor Books, 2011); Neta Yodovich and Kinneret Lahad, "'I Don't Think This Woman Had Anyone in Her Life': Loneliness and Singlehood in Six Feet Under," *European Journal of Women's Studies,* April 8, 2017, doi.org/10.1177/1350506817702411.

64. Todd D. Nelson, *Ageism: Stereotyping and Prejudice against Older Persons* (Cambridge, MA: MIT Press, 2004).

65. Jaber F. Gubrium, "Being Single in Old Age," *International Journal of Aging and Human Development* 6, no. 1 (1975): 29–41.

66. Robert L. Rubinstein, "Never Married Elderly as a Social Type: Reevaluating Some Images," *Gerontologist* 27, no. 1 (1987): 108–13.

67. Tetyana Pudrovska, Scott Schieman, and Deborah Carr, "Strains of Singlehood in Later Life: Do Race and Gender Matter?" *Journals of Gerontology: Series B* 61, no. 6 (2006): S315–S22.

68. Martin E. P. Seligman and Mihaly Csikszentmihalyi, *Positive Psychology: An Introduction* (Washington, DC: American Psychological Association, 2000), 1.

69. Shelly L. Gable and Jonathan Haidt, "What (and Why) Is Positive Psychology?" *Review of General Psychology* 9, no. 2 (2005): 103.

70. John W. Rowe and Robert L Kahn, "Successful Aging," *The Gerontologist* 37, no. 4 (1997): 433–40.

71. Colin A. Depp and Dilip V. Jeste, "Definitions and Predictors of Successful Aging: A Comprehensive Review of Larger Quantitative Studies," *American Journal of Geriatric Psychiatry* 14, no. 1 (2006): 6–20; William J. Strawbridge, Margaret I. Wallhagen, and Richard D. Cohen, "Successful Aging and

Well-Being Self-Rated Compared with Rowe and Kahn," *The Gerontologist* 42, no. 6 (2002): 727–33.

72. Jerrold M. Pollak, "Correlates of Death Anxiety: A Review of Empirical Studies," omega—*Journal of Death and Dying* 10, no. 2 (1980): 97–121.

73. J.M. Tomás, P. Sancho, M. Gutiérrez, and L. Galiana, "Predicting Life Satisfaction in the Oldest-Old: A Moderator Effects Study," *Social Indicators Research* 117, no. 2 (2014): 601–13.

74. David Haber, *Health Promotion and Aging: Practical Applications for Health Professionals* (New York: Springer, 2013).

75. Willard W. Hartup, and Nan Stevens, "Friendships and Adaptation in the Life Course," *Psychological Bulletin* 121, no. 3 (1997): 355.

76. Lorraine M. Bettini and M. Laurie Norton, "The Pragmatics of Intergenerational Friendships," *Communication Reports* 4, no. 2 (1991): 64–72.

77. Rebecca G. Adams, "People Would Talk: Normative Barriers to Cross-sex Friendships for Elderly Women," *The Gerontologist* 25, no. 6 (1985): 605–11.

78. Harry Weger, "Cross-sex Friendships," in *The International Encyclopedia of Interpersonal Communication,* ed. Charles R. Berger (Hoboken, NJ: John Wiley, 2015).

79. Barbara, response to "Aging Alone Doesn't Have to Mean Lonely," *Senior Planet,* February 25, 2017, "https://seniorplanet.org/aging-alone-doesnt-have-to-mean-lonely/#comment-193356.

80. Kendra, "Her Children Would Have Hated Her ... Said Oprah Winfrey," *Happily Never Married,* May 12, 2013, http://happilynevermarried.com /page/2/.

81. David Haber, *Health Promotion and Aging: Practical Applications for Health Professionals* (New York: Springer, 2013).

82. Walker Thornton, "Aging Alone Doesn't Have to Mean Lonely," November 8, 2013, https://seniorplanet.org/aging-alone-doesnt-have-to-mean-lonely.

83. Barbara Barbosa Neves, Fausto Amaro, and Jaime Fonseca, "Coming of (Old) Age in the Digital Age: ICT Usage and Non-usage among Older Adults," *Sociological Research Online* 18, no. 2 (2013): 6.

84. Sabina Lissitsa and Svetlana Chachashvili-Bolotin, "Life Satisfaction in the Internet Age—Changes in the Past Decade," *Computers in Human Behavior* 54 (2016): 197–206.

85. Colleen Leahy Johnson and Donald J. Catalano, "Childless Elderly and Their Family Supports," *The Gerontologist* 21, no. 6 (1981): 610–18.

86. Wendy J. Casper, Dennis J. Marquardt, Katherine J. Roberto, and Carla Buss, "The Hidden Family Lives of Single Adults without Dependent Chil-

dren," in *The Oxford Handbook of Work and Family,* ed. Tammy D. Allen and Lillian T. Eby (Oxford: Oxford University Press, 2016), 182.

87. Susan De Vos, "Kinship Ties and Solitary Living among Unmarried Elderly Women in Chile and Mexico," *Research on Aging* 22, no. 3 (2000): 262–89.

88. Nieli Langer and Marie Ribarich, "Aunts, Uncles—Nieces, Nephews: Kinship Relations over the Lifespan," *Educational Gerontology* 33, no. 1 (2007): 75–83.

89. Anonymous, "Fall Hopelessly in Love with Yourself," October 7, 2016, *Medium,* https://medium.com/@ahechoes.

90. Ronald H. Aday, Gayle C. Kehoe, and Lori A. Farney, "Impact of Senior Center Friendships on Aging Women Who Live Alone," *Journal of Women & Aging* 18, no. 1 (2006): 57–73.

91. Diane Weis Farone, Tanya R. Fitzpatrick, and Thanh V. Tran, "Use of Senior Centers as a Moderator of Stress-Related Distress among Latino Elders," *Journal of Gerontological Social Work* 46, no. 1 (2005): 65–83.

92. Marcia S. Marx, Jiska Cohen-Mansfield, Natalie G. Regier, Maha Dakheel-Ali, Ashok Srihari, and Khin Thein, "The Impact of Different Dog-Related Stimuli on Engagement of Persons with Dementia," *American Journal of Alzheimer's Disease & Other Dementias* 25, no. 1 (2010): 37–45.

93. E. Paul Cherniack and Ariella R. Cherniack, "The Benefit of Pets and Animal-Assisted Therapy to the Health of Older Individuals," *Current Gerontology and Geriatrics Research* (2014), http://dx.doi.org/10.1155/2014/623203.

94. P. L. Bernstein, E. Friedmann, and A. Malaspina, "Animal-Assisted Therapy Enhances Resident Social Interaction and Initiation in Long-Term Care Facilities," *Anthrozoös* 13, no. 4 (2000): 213–24; Katharine M. Fick, "The Influence of an Animal on Social Interactions of Nursing Home Residents in a Group Setting," *American Journal of Occupational Therapy* 47, no. 6 (1993): 529–34.

95. Stephanie S. Spielmann, Geoff MacDonald, Jessica A. Maxwell, Samantha Joel, Diana Peragine, Amy Muise, and Emily A. Impett, "Settling for Less out of Fear of Being Single," *Journal of Personality and Social Psychology* 105, no. 6 (2013): 1049.

CHAPTER 3. DEFYING SOCIAL PRESSURE

1. Arland Thornton and Deborah Freedman, "Changing Attitudes toward Marriage and Single Life," *Family Planning Perspectives* 14, no. 6 (1981): 297–303;

James Q. Wilson, *The Marriage Problem: How Our Culture Has Weakened Families* (New York: Harper Collins, 2002).

2. Eriko Maeda and Michael L. Hecht, "Identity Search: Interpersonal Relationships and Relational Identities of Always-Single Japanese Women over Time," *Western Journal of Communication* 76, no. 1 (2012): 44–64; Anne-Rigt Poortman and Aart C. Liefbroer, "Singles' Relational Attitudes in a Time of Individualization," *Social Science Research* 39, no. 6 (2010): 938–49; Elizabeth A. Sharp and Lawrence Ganong, "'I'm a Loser, I'm Not Married, Let's Just All Look at Me': Ever-Single Women's Perceptions of Their Social Environment," *Journal of Family Issues* 32, no. 7 (2011): 956–80.

3. Brenda Major and Laurie T. O'Brien, "The Social Psychology of Stigma," *Annual Review of Psychology* 56, no. 1 (2005): 393–421.

4. Paul Jay Fink, *Stigma and Mental Illness* (Washington, DC: American Psychiatric Press, 1992).

5. Jennifer Crocker and Brenda Major, "Social Stigma and Self-Esteem: The Self-Protective Properties of Stigma," *Psychological Review* 96, no. 4 (1989): 608–30.

6. Bruce G. Link, Elmer L. Struening, Sheree Neese-Todd, Sara Asmussen, and Jo C. Phelan, "Stigma as a Barrier to Recovery: The Consequences of Stigma for the Self-Esteem of People with Mental Illnesses," *Psychiatric Services* 52, no. 12 (2001): 1621–26.

7. Brenda Major and Laurie T. O'Brien, "The Social Psychology of Stigma," *Annual Review of Psychology* 56, no. 1 (2005): 393–421.

8. Tara Vishwanath, "Job Search, Stigma Effect, and Escape Rate from Unemployment," *Journal of Labor Economics* 7, no. 4 (1989): 487–502.

9. Bella M. DePaulo and Wendy L. Morris, "The Unrecognized Stereotyping and Discrimination against Singles," *Current Directions in Psychological Science* 15, no. 5 (2006): 251–54.

10. Janine Hertel, Astrid Schütz, Bella M. DePaulo, Wendy L. Morris, and Tanja S. Stucke, "She's Single, So What? How Are Singles Perceived Compared with People Who Are Married?" *Zeitschrift für Familienforschung / Journal of Family Research* 19, no. 2 (2007): 139–58; Peter J. Stein, "Singlehood: An Alternative to Marriage," *Family Coordinator* 24, no. 4 (1975): 489–503.

11. Bella M. DePaulo, *Singlism: What It Is, Why It Matters, and How to Stop It* (Charleston, SC: DoubleDoor Books, 2011).

12. Bella M. DePaulo and Wendy L. Morris, "The Unrecognized Stereotyping and Discrimination against Singles," *Current Directions in Psychological Science* 15, no. 5 (2006): 251–54.

13. Tobias Greitemeyer, "Stereotypes of Singles: Are Singles What We Think?" *European Journal of Social Psychology* 39, no. 3 (2009): 368–83.

14. Jennifer Crocker and Brenda Major, "Social Stigma and Self-Esteem: The Self-Protective Properties of Stigma," *Psychological Review* 96, no. 4 (1989): 608; Paul Jay Fink, *Stigma and Mental Illness* (Washington, DC: American Psychiatric Press, 1992); Brenda Major and Laurie T. O'Brien, "The Social Psychology of Stigma," *Annual Review of Psychology* 56, no. 1 (2005): 393–421.

15. Paul C. Luken, "Social Identity in Later Life: A Situational Approach to Understanding Old Age Stigma," *International Journal of Aging and Human Development* 25, no. 3 (1987): 177–93.

16. A. Kay Clifton, Diane McGrath, and Bonnie Wick, "Stereotypes of Woman: A Single Category?" *Sex Roles* 2, no. 2 (1976): 135–48; Alice H. Eagly and Valerie J. Steffen, "Gender Stereotypes Stem from the Distribution of Women and Men into Social Roles," *Journal of Personality and Social Psychology* 46, no. 4 (1984): 735.

17. Dena Saadat Hassouneh-Phillips, "'Marriage Is Half of Faith and the Rest Is Fear of Allah': Marriage and Spousal Abuse among American Muslims," *Violence against Women* 7, no. 8 (2001): 927–46.

18. Calvin E. Zongker, "Self-Concept Differences between Single and Married School-Age Mothers," *Journal of Youth and Adolescence* 9, no. 2 (1980): 175–84.

19. Matt Volz, "Fired Pregnant Teacher Settles with Montana Catholic School," *Boston Globe,* March 15, 2016, www.bostonglobe.com/news/nation/2016/03/15/fired-pregnant-teacher-settles-with-montana-catholic-school/Shlqa NHnaXXWO2HVUcDxiM/story.html.

20. Daniel Kalish, "Teacher Fired for Being Unmarried and Pregnant," HKM Employment Attorneys, February 21, 2014, https://hkm.com/employment-blog/teacher-fired-unmarried-pregnant/.

21. Ashitha Nagesh, "Unmarried Teacher Sacked Because She Was 'Living in Sin' with Her Boyfriend," *Metro,* December 4, 2017, http://metro.co.uk/2017/12/04/teacher-lost-her-job-after-parents-complained-about-her-living-in-sin-7130641/.

22. Bruce Thain, "Jewish Teacher Sacked from Orthodox Nursery for 'Living in Sin' with Boyfriend Wins Case for Religious and Sexual Discrimination," *Independent,* December 4, 2017, www.independent.co.uk/news/uk/home-news/jewish-teacher-zelda-de-groen-orthodox-gan-menachem-nursery-hendon-north-london-wedlock-employment-a8090471.html.

23. Amanda Terkel, "Sen. Jim DeMint: Gays and Unmarried, Pregnant Women Should Not Teach Public School," *Huffington Post,* October 2, 2010, www.huffingtonpost.com/2010/10/02/demint-gays-unmarried-pregnant-women-teachers_n_748131.html.

24. Sarah Labovitch-Dar, "They Did Not Get Accepted," *Ha'Aretz,* June 28, 2001, www.haaretz.co.il/misc/1.713241.

25. Anonymous, response to Bella DePaulo, "Is It Bad to Notice Discrimination?" *Psychology Today,* on June 3, 2008, www.psychologytoday.com/blog/living-single/200805/is-it-bad-notice-discrimination.

26. Kate Antonovics and Robert Town, "Are All the Good Men Married? Uncovering the Sources of the Marital Wage Premium," *American Economic Review* 94, no. 2 (2004): 317–21.

27. Bella M. DePaulo, *Singled Out: How Singles Are Stereotyped, Stigmatized, and Ignored, and Still Live Happily Ever After* (New York: St. Martin's Griffin, 2007).

28. Ibid.; Kinneret Lahad, *A Table for One: A Critical Reading of Singlehood, Gender and Time* (Manchester, UK: University of Manchester, 2017); Wendy L. Morris, Stacey Sinclair, and Bella M. DePaulo, "No Shelter for Singles: The Perceived Legitimacy of Marital Status Discrimination," *Group Processes & Intergroup Relations* 10, no. 4 (2007): 457–70.

29. Bella M. DePaulo, *Singled Out: How Singles Are Stereotyped, Stigmatized, and Ignored, and Still Live Happily Ever After* (New York: St. Martin's Griffin, 2007); Jianguo Liu, Thomas Dietz, Stephen R. Carpenter, Carl Folke, Marina Alberti, Charles L. Redman, Stephen H. Schneider, Elinor Ostrom, Alice N. Pell, and Jane Lubchenco, "Coupled Human and Natural Systems," *AMBIO: A Journal of the Human Environment* 36, no. 8 (2007): 639–49.

30. Bella M. DePaulo and Wendy L. Morris, "Target Article: Singles in Society and in Science," *Psychological Inquiry* 16, no. 2–3 (2005): 57–83; Wendy L. Morris and Brittany K. Osburn, "Do You Take This Marriage? Perceived Choice over Marital Status Affects the Stereotypes of Single and Married People," in *Singlehood from Individual and Social Perspectives,* ed. Katarzyna Adamczyk (Krakow, Poland: Libron, 2016), 145–62.

31. Karen Gritter, *Community of Single People Group* (blog), Facebook, November 1, 2017, www.facebook.com/groups/CommunityofSinglePeople/permalink/1924789547839689/.

32. Lisa Arnold and Christina Campbell, "The High Price of Being Single in America," *The Atlantic,* January 14, 2013.

33. Bella M. DePaulo, *Singled Out: How Singles Are Stereotyped, Stigmatized, and Ignored, and Still Live Happily Ever After* (New York: St. Martin's Griffin, 2007).

34. Vickie M. Mays and Susan D. Cochran, "Mental Health Correlates of Perceived Discrimination among Lesbian, Gay, and Bisexual Adults in the United States," *American Journal of Public Health* 91, no. 11 (2001): 1869–76.

35. Ann R. Fischer and Christina M. Shaw, "African Americans' Mental Health and Perceptions of Racist Discrimination: The Moderating Effects of Racial Socialization Experiences and Self-Esteem," *Journal of Counseling Psychology* 46, no. 3 (1999): 395.

36. Samuel Noh, Morton Beiser, Violet Kaspar, Feng Hou, and Joanna Rummens, "Perceived Racial Discrimination, Depression, and Coping: A Study of Southeast Asian Refugees in Canada," *Journal of Health and Social Behavior* 40, no. 3 (1999): 193–207.

37. Elizabeth A. Pascoe and Laura Smart Richman, "Perceived Discrimination and Health: A Meta-analytic Review," *Psychological Bulletin* 135, no. 4 (2009): 531.

38. Haslyn E. R. Hunte and David R. Williams, "The Association between Perceived Discrimination and Obesity in a Population-Based Multiracial and Multiethnic Adult Sample," *American Journal of Public Health* 99, no. 7 (2009): 1285–92; Nancy Krieger and Stephen Sidney, "Racial Discrimination and Blood Pressure: The Cardia Study of Young Black and White Adults," *American Journal of Public Health* 86, no. 10 (1996): 1370–78.

39. Luisa N. Borrell, Ana V. Diez Roux, David R. Jacobs, Steven Shea, Sharon A. Jackson, Sandi Shrager, and Roger S. Blumenthal, "Perceived Racial /Ethnic Discrimination, Smoking and Alcohol Consumption in the Multiethnic Study of Atherosclerosis (MESA)," *Preventive Medicine* 51, no. 3 (2010): 307–12; Frederick X. Gibbons, Meg Gerrard, Michael J. Cleveland, Thomas A. Wills, and Gene Brody, "Perceived Discrimination and Substance Use in African American Parents and Their Children: A Panel Study," *Journal of Personality and Social Psychology* 86, no. 4 (2004): 517–29.

40. Eliza K. Pavalko, Krysia N. Mossakowski, and Vanessa J. Hamilton, "Does Perceived Discrimination Affect Health? Longitudinal Relationships between Work Discrimination and Women's Physical and Emotional Health," *Journal of Health and Social Behavior* 44, no. 1 (2003): 18–33.

41. Lyn Parker, Irma Riyani, and Brooke Nolan, "The Stigmatisation of Widows and Divorcees (Janda) in Indonesia, and the Possibilities for Agency," *Indonesia and the Malay World* 44, no. 128 (2016): 27–46.

42. Samuel Noh and Violet Kaspar, "Perceived Discrimination and Depression: Moderating Effects of Coping, Acculturation, and Ethnic Support," *American Journal of Public Health* 93, no. 2 (2003): 232–38.

43. Bella M. DePaulo and Wendy L. Morris, "The Unrecognized Stereotyping and Discrimination against Singles," *Current Directions in Psychological Science* 15, no. 5 (2006): 251–54.

44. Eric Klinenberg, *Going Solo: The Extraordinary Rise and Surprising Appeal of Living Alone* (New York: Penguin, 2012); Bella M. DePaulo, *Singled Out: How Singles Are Stereotyped, Stigmatized, and Ignored, and Still Live Happily Ever After* (New York: St. Martin's Griffin, 2007).

45. Bella DePaulo, *How We Live Now: Redefining Home and Family in the 21st Century* (Hillsboro, OR: Atria Books, 2015); Kinneret Lahad, *A Table for One: A Critical Reading of Singlehood, Gender and Time* (Manchester, UK: University of Manchester, 2017).

46. Pieter A. Gautier, Michael Svarer, and Coen N. Teulings, "Marriage and the City: Search Frictions and Sorting of Singles," *Journal of Urban Economics* 67, no. 2 (2010): 206–18.

47. Wendy L. Morris, "The Effect of Stigma Awareness on the Self-Esteem of Singles," Online Archive of University of Virginia Scholarship, 2005.

48. Lauri, response to Bella DePaulo, "Is It Bad to Notice Discrimination?" *Psychology Today*, on June 16, 2008, www.psychologytoday.com/blog/living-single/200805/is-it-bad-notice-discrimination.

49. Ibid.

50. Roy F. Baumeister, Jennifer D. Campbell, Joachim I. Krueger, and Kathleen D. Vohs, "Does High Self-Esteem Cause Better Performance, Interpersonal Success, Happiness, or Healthier Lifestyles?" *Psychological Science in the Public Interest* 4, no. 1 (2003): 1–44.

51. Gian Vittorio Caprara, Patrizia Steca, Maria Gerbino, Marinella Paciello, and Giovanni Maria Vecchio, "Looking for Adolescents' Well-Being: Self-Efficacy Beliefs as Determinants of Positive Thinking and Happiness," *Epidemiologia e psichiatria sociale* 15, no. 1 (2006): 30–43.

52. Ulrich Schimmack and Ed Diener, "Predictive Validity of Explicit and Implicit Self-Esteem for Subjective Well-Being," *Journal of Research in Personality* 37, no. 2 (2003): 100–106.

53. Aurora Szentagotai and Daniel David, "Self-Acceptance and Happiness," in *The Strength of Self-Acceptance: Theory, Practice and Research,* ed. Michael E. Bernard (New York: Springer, 2013), 121–37.

54. Nadine F. Marks, "Flying Solo at Midlife: Gender, Marital Status, and Psychological Well-Being," *Journal of Marriage and Family* 58, no. 4 (1996): 917–32.

55. Evangelos C. Karademas, "Self-Efficacy, Social Support and Well-Being: The Mediating Role of Optimism," *Personality and Individual Differences* 40, no. 6 (2006): 1281–90.

56. Charles S. Carver, Michael F. Scheier, and Suzanne C. Segerstrom, "Optimism," *Clinical Psychology Review* 30, no. 7 (2010): 879–89.

57. Bella M. DePaulo, *Singled Out: How Singles Are Stereotyped, Stigmatized, and Ignored, and Still Live Happily Ever After* (New York: St. Martin's Griffin, 2007); Monica Kirkpatrick Johnson, "Family Roles and Work Values: Processes of Selection and Change," *Journal of Marriage and Family* 67, no. 2 (2005): 352–69.

58. Sally Macintyre, Anne Ellaway, Geoff Der, Graeme Ford, and Kate Hunt, "Do Housing Tenure and Car Access Predict Health Because They Are Simply Markers of Income or Self Esteem? A Scottish Study," *Journal of Epidemiology and Community Health* 52, no. 10 (1998): 657–64.

59. Richard J. Riding and Stephen Rayner, *Self Perception* (London: Greenwood, 2001).

60. Lois M. Tamir and Toni C. Antonucci, "Self-Perception, Motivation, and Social Support through the Family Life Course," *Journal of Marriage and Family* 43, no. 1 (1981): 151–60.

61. Christopher G. Ellison, "Religious Involvement and Self-Perception among Black Americans," *Social Forces* 71, no. 4 (1993): 1027–55.

62. Najah Mahmoud Manasra, "The Effect of Remaining Unmarried on Self-Perception and Mental Health Status: A Study of Palestinian Single Women" (PhD diss., De Montfort University, 2003).

63. Ed Diener and Marissa Diener, "Cross-cultural Correlates of Life Satisfaction and Self-Esteem," in *Culture and Well-Being: The Collected Works of Ed Diener*, ed. Ed Diener (Dordrecht, Netherlands: Springer, 2009), 71–91.

64. Bianca Fileborn, Rachel Thorpe, Gail Hawkes, Victor Minichiello, and Marian Pitts, "Sex and the (Older) Single Girl: Experiences of Sex and Dating in Later Life," *Journal of Aging Studies* 33 (2015): 67–75; Jennifer A. Moore and H. Lorraine Radtke, "Starting 'Real' Life: Women Negotiating a Successful Midlife Single Identity," *Psychology of Women Quarterly* 39, no. 3 (2015): 305–19.

65. Lauren F. Winner, "Real Sex: The Naked Truth about Chastity," *Theology & Sexuality* 26, no. 1 (2015).

66. Christena Cleveland, "Singled Out: How Churches Can Embrace Unmarried Adults," *Christena Cleveland* (blog), December 2, 2013, www.christenacleveland.com/blogarchive/2013/12/singled-out.

67. Bella M. DePaulo, *Singled Out: How Singles Are Stereotyped, Stigmatized, and Ignored, and Still Live Happily Ever After* (New York: St. Martin's Griffin, 2007); Kinneret Lahad, "'Am I Asking for Too Much?' The Selective Single Woman as a New Social Problem," *Women's Studies International Forum* 40, no. 5 (2013): 23–32.

68. Jenny Gierveld, Pearl A. Dykstra, and Niels Schenk, "Living Arrangements, Intergenerational Support Types and Older Adult Loneliness in Eastern and Western Europe," *Demographic Research* 27, no. 2 (2012): 167.

69. WeLive, "We Live: Love Your Life," 2017, www.welive.com/.

70. Lisette Kuyper and Tineke Fokkema, "Loneliness among Older Lesbian, Gay, and Bisexual Adults: The Role of Minority Stress," *Archives of Sexual Behavior* 39, no. 5 (2010): 1171–80.

71. Hyun-Jun Kim and Karen I. Fredriksen-Goldsen, "Living Arrangement and Loneliness among Lesbian, Gay, and Bisexual Older Adults," *The Gerontologist* 56, no. 3 (2016): 548–58.

72. Jesus Ramirez-Valles, Jessica Dirkes, and Hope A. Barrett, "Gayby Boomers' Social Support: Exploring the Connection between Health and Emotional and Instrumental Support in Older Gay Men," *Journal of Gerontological Social Work* 57, no. 2–4 (2014): 218–34.

73. Elyakim Kislev, "Deciphering the 'Ethnic Penalty' of Immigrants in Western Europe: A Cross-classified Multilevel Analysis," *Social Indicators Research* (2016); Elyakim Kislev, "The Effect of Education Policies on Higher-Education Attainment of Immigrants in Western Europe: A Cross-classified Multilevel Analysis," *Journal of European Social Policy* 26, no. 2 (2016): 183–99.

74. Jennifer O'Connell, "Being on Your Own on Valentine's Day: Four Singletons Speak," *Irish Times,* February 11, 2017, www.irishtimes.com/life-and-style/people/being-on-your-own-on-valentine-s-day-four-singletons-speak-1.2964287.

75. Rachel, "A Call for Single Action," *Rachel's Musings,* September 16, 2013, www.rabe.org/a-call-for-single-action/.

76. Bella M. DePaulo, *Singled Out: How Singles Are Stereotyped, Stigmatized, and Ignored, and Still Live Happily Ever After* (New York: St. Martin's Griffin, 2007); Bella DePaulo, *Marriage vs. Single Life: How Science and the Media Got It So Wrong* (Charleston, SC: DoubleDoor Books, 2015); Bella DePaulo, "Single in a Society Preoccupied with Couples," in *Handbook of Solitude: Psychological Perspectives on Social Isolation, Social Withdrawal, and Being Alone,* ed. Robert J. Coplan and Julie C. Bowker (New York: John Wiley & Sons, 2014), 302–16.

77. Alice Poma and Tommaso Gravante, "'This Struggle Bound Us': An Analysis of the Emotional Dimension of Protest Based on the Study of Four

Grassroots Resistances in Spain and Mexico," *Qualitative Sociology Review* 12, no. 1 (2016).

78. Anonymous, "When Singlutionary Is "Sick of Being Single!" *Singlutionary,* October 9, 2011, http://singlutionary.blogspot.com.

79. Wendy L. Morris and Brittany K. Osburn, "Do You Take This Marriage? Perceived Choice over Marital Status Affects the Stereotypes of Single and Married People," *Singlehood from Individual and Social Perspectives* (2016): 145–62; Gal Slonim, Nurit Gur-Yaish, and Ruth Katz, "By Choice or by Circumstance?: Stereotypes of and Feelings about Single People," *Studia Psychologica* 57, no. 1 (2015): 35–48.

80. Wendy L. Morris and Brittany K. Osburn, "Do You Take This Marriage? Perceived Choice over Marital Status Affects the Stereotypes of Single and Married People," *Singlehood from Individual and Social Perspectives* (2016): 145–62; Gal Slonim, Nurit Gur-Yaish, and Ruth Katz, "By Choice or by Circumstance?: Stereotypes of and Feelings about Single People," *Studia Psychologica* 57, no. 1 (2015): 35–48.

81. Gal Slonim, Nurit Gur-Yaish, and Ruth Katz, "By Choice or by Circumstance?: Stereotypes of and Feelings about Single People," *Studia Psychologica* 57, no. 1 (2015): 35–48.

82. Ad Bergsma, "Do Self-Help Books Help?" *Journal of Happiness Studies* 9, no. 3 (2008): 341–60.

83. Linda Bolier, Merel Haverman, Gerben J. Westerhof, Heleen Riper, Filip Smit, and Ernst Bohlmeijer, "Positive Psychology Interventions: A Meta-analysis of Randomized Controlled Studies," *BMC Public Health* 13, no. 1 (2013): 119.

CHAPTER 4. SLEEPING ALONE, BOWLING TOGETHER

1. D'Vera Cohn, Jeffrey S. Passel, Wendy Wang, and Gretchen Livingston, *Barely Half of U.S. Adults Are Married—a Record Low* (Washington, DC: Pew Research Center, 2011).

2. Heather A. Turner and R. Jay Turner, "Gender, Social Status, and Emotional Reliance," *Journal of Health and Social Behavior* 40, no. 4 (1999): 360–73.

3. Donald A. West, Robert Kellner, and Maggi Moore-West, "The Effects of Loneliness: A Review of the Literature," *Comprehensive Psychiatry* 27, no. 4 (1986): 351–63.

4. Megan Bruneau, "I'm 30, Single, and Happy; and Truthfully, That Scares Me," *Medium* (blog), November 6, 2016, https://medium.com/@meganbruneau.

5. Froma Walsh, "The Concept of Family Resilience: Crisis and Challenge," *Family Process* 35, no. 3 (1996): 261–81.

6. Jung-Hwa Ha and Deborah Carr, "The Effect of Parent-Child Geographic Proximity on Widowed Parents' Psychological Adjustment and Social Integration," *Research on Aging* 27, no. 5 (2005): 578–610.

7. Sarah, "The First Confession," *Confessions of a Single Thirty-Something* (blog), October 10, 2011, http://confessions-sarah.blogspot.com.

8. Bella M. DePaulo, *Singled Out: How Singles Are Stereotyped, Stigmatized, and Ignored, and Still Live Happily Ever After* (New York: St. Martin's Griffin, 2007).

9. Christina Victor, Sasha Scambler, John Bond, and Ann Bowling, "Being Alone in Later Life: Loneliness, Social Isolation and Living Alone," *Reviews in Clinical Gerontology* 10, no. 4 (2000): 407–17; Froma Walsh, "The Concept of Family Resilience: Crisis and Challenge," *Family Process* 35, no. 3 (1996): 261–81.

10. Sarah, "The First Confession," *Confessions of a Single Thirty-Something* (blog), October 10, 2011, http://confessions-sarah.blogspot.com.

11. Wendy L. Morris, Stacey Sinclair, and Bella M DePaulo, "No Shelter for Singles: The Perceived Legitimacy of Marital Status Discrimination," *Group Processes & Intergroup Relations* 10, no. 4 (2007): 457–70.

12. Judith Anne McKenzie, "Disabled People in Rural South Africa Talk about Sexuality," *Culture, Health & Sexuality* 15, no. 3 (2013): 372–86; Nattavudh Powdthavee, "What Happens to People before and after Disability? Focusing Effects, Lead Effects, and Adaptation in Different Areas of Life," *Social Science & Medicine* 69, no. 12 (2009): 1834–44; Perry Singleton, "Insult to Injury Disability, Earnings, and Divorce," *Journal of Human Resources* 47, no. 4 (2012): 972–90.

13. Jennie E. Brand, "The Far-Reaching Impact of Job Loss and Unemployment," *Annual Review of Sociology* 41 (2015): 359–75.

14. Kerwin Kofi Charles and Melvin Stephens Jr., "Job Displacement, Disability, and Divorce," *Journal of Labor Economics* 22, no. 2 (2004): 489–522.

15. Naomi Gerstel and Natalia Sarkisian, "Marriage: The Good, the Bad, and the Greedy," *Contexts* 5, no. 4 (2006): 16–21.

16. Bella M. DePaulo, *Singled Out: How Singles Are Stereotyped, Stigmatized, and Ignored, and Still Live Happily Ever After* (New York: St. Martin's Griffin, 2007).

17. Bella M. DePaulo, *Singlism: What It Is, Why It Matters, and How to Stop It* (Charleston, SC: DoubleDoor Books, 2011).

18. Bella M. DePaulo and Wendy L. Morris, "The Unrecognized Stereotyping and Discrimination against Singles," *Current Directions in Psychological Science* 15, no. 5 (2006): 251–54.

19. Eleanore Wells, "How Many Ways to Be Single? (A Guest Post)," *Eleanore Wells* (blog), June 5, 2012, http://eleanorewells.com/.

20. Barry Wellman, "The Development of Social Network Analysis: A Study in the Sociology of Science," *Contemporary Sociology: A Journal of Reviews* 37, no. 3 (2008): 221–22; Barry Wellman, "The Network Is Personal: Introduction to a Special Issue of Social Networks," *Social Networks* 29, no. 3 (2007): 349–56.

21. Rhonda McEwen and Barry Wellman, "Relationships, Community, and Networked Individuals," in *The Immersive Internet: Reflections on the Entangling of the Virtual with Society, Politics and the Economy,* ed. R. Teigland and D. Power (London: Palgrave Macmillan, 2013), 168–79.

22. Elisa Bellotti, "What Are Friends For? Elective Communities of Single People," *Social Networks* 30, no. 4 (2008): 318–29.

23. Ambrose Leung, Cheryl Kier, Tak Fung, Linda Fung, and Robert Sproule, "Searching for Happiness: The Importance of Social Capital," in *The Exploration of Happiness: Present and Future Perspectives,* ed. A. Delle Fave (Dordrecht, Netherlands: Springer, 2013), 247–67.

24. Benjamin Cornwell, Edward O. Laumann, and L. Philip Schumm, "The Social Connectedness of Older Adults: A National Profile," *American Sociological Review* 73, no. 2 (2008): 185–203; Jennifer A. Moore and H. Lorraine Radtke, "Starting 'Real' Life: Women Negotiating a Successful Midlife Single Identity," *Psychology of Women Quarterly* 39, no. 3 (2015): 305–19.

25. Hunni H., "A Happier Hunni, Part 1," *Thirty-One, Single and Living at Home* (blog), October 27, 2012, http://thirtysingleand.blogspot.com.

26. Bella DePaulo, "Who Is Your Family If You Are Single with No Kids? Part 2," *Living Single* (blog), *Psychology Today,* August 21, 2011, www.psychologytoday.com/us/blog/living-single/201108/who-is-your-family-if-you-are-single-no-kids-part-2.

27. Kelly Musick and Larry Bumpass, "Reexamining the Case for Marriage: Union Formation and Changes in Well-Being," *Journal of Marriage and Family* 74, no. 1 (2012): 1–18.

28. Paul R. Amato, Alan Booth, David R. Johnson, and Stacy J. Rogers, *Alone Together: How Marriage in America Is Changing* (Cambridge, MA: Harvard University Press, 2007).

29. Eric Klinenberg, *Going Solo: The Extraordinary Rise and Surprising Appeal of Living Alone* (New York: Penguin, 2012).

30. Shahla Ostovar, Negah Allahyar, Hassan Aminpoor, Fatemeh Moafian, Mariani Binti Md Nor, and Mark D. Griffiths, "Internet Addiction and Its

Psychosocial Risks (Depression, Anxiety, Stress and Loneliness) among Iranian Adolescents and Young Adults: A Structural Equation Model in a Cross-sectional Study," *International Journal of Mental Health and Addiction* 14, no. 3 (2016): 257–67.

31. Nicole B. Ellison, Charles Steinfield, and Cliff Lampe, "The Benefits of Facebook 'Friends': Social Capital and College Students' Use of Online Social Network Sites," *Journal of Computer-Mediated Communication* 12, no. 4 (2007): 1143–68; Nicole B. Ellison, Jessica Vitak, Rebecca Gray, and Cliff Lampe, "Cultivating Social Resources on Social Network Sites: Facebook Relationship Maintenance Behaviors and Their Role in Social Capital Processes," *Journal of Computer-Mediated Communication* 19, no. 4 (2014): 855–70.

32. R.J. Shillair, R.V. Rikard, S.R. Cotten, and H.Y. Tsai, "Not So Lonely Surfers: Loneliness, Social Support, Internet Use and Life Satisfaction in Older Adults," in *iConference 2015 Proceedings* (Newport Beach, CA: iSchools, 2015).

33. Rachel Grieve, Michaelle Indian, Kate Witteveen, G. Anne Tolan, and Jessica Marrington, "Face-to-Face or Facebook: Can Social Connectedness Be Derived Online?" *Computers in Human Behavior* 29, no. 3 (2013): 604–9.

34. Kyung-Tag Lee, Mi-Jin Noh, and Dong-Mo Koo, "Lonely People Are No Longer Lonely on Social Networking Sites: The Mediating Role of Self-Disclosure and Social Support," *Cyberpsychology, Behavior, and Social Networking* 16, no. 6 (2013): 413–18.

35. Ari Engelberg, "Religious Zionist Singles: Caught between 'Family Values' and 'Young Adulthood,'" *Journal for the Scientific Study of Religion* 55, no. 2 (2016): 349–64.

36. Michael Woolcock, "Social Capital and Economic Development: Toward a Theoretical Synthesis and Policy Framework," *Theory and Society* 27, no. 2 (1998): 151–208.

37. Orsolya Lelkes, "Knowing What Is Good for You: Empirical Analysis of Personal Preferences and the 'Objective Good,'" *Journal of Socio-Economics* 35, no. 2 (2006): 285–307; Ambrose Leung, Cheryl Kier, Tak Fung, Linda Fung, and Robert Sproule, "Searching for Happiness: The Importance of Social Capital," *Journal of Happiness Studies* 12, no. 3 (2011); Robert D. Putnam, *Bowling Alone: The Collapse and Revival of American Community* (New York: Simon and Schuster, 2001); Nattavudh Powdthavee, "Putting a Price Tag on Friends, Relatives, and Neighbours: Using Surveys of Life Satisfaction to Value Social Relationships," *Journal of Socio-Economics* 37, no. 4 (2008): 1459–80.

38. John F. Helliwell and Christopher P. Barrington-Leigh, "How Much Is Social Capital Worth?" in *The Social Cure*, ed. J. Jetten, C. Haslam and

S. A. Haslam (London: Psychology Press, 2010), 55–71; Rainer Winkelmann, "Unemployment, Social Capital, and Subjective Well-Being," *Journal of Happiness Studies* 10, no. 4 (2009): 421–30.

39. John F. Helliwell, "How's Life? Combining Individual and National Variables to Explain Subjective Well-Being," *Economic Modelling* 20, no. 2 (2003): 331–60; Florian Pichler, "Subjective Quality of Life of Young Europeans: Feeling Happy but Who Knows Why?" *Social Indicators Research* 75, no. 3 (2006): 419–44.

40. Erin York Cornwell and Linda J. Waite, "Social Disconnectedness, Perceived Isolation, and Health among Older Adults," *Journal of Health and Social Behavior* 50, no. 1 (2009): 31–48.

41. John F. Helliwell, Christopher P. Barrington-Leigh, Anthony Harris, and Haifang Huang, "International Evidence on the Social Context of Well-Being," in *International Differences in Well-Being,* ed. Ed Diener, John F. Helliwell, and Daniel Kahneman (Oxford: Oxford University Press, 2010).

42. Bernd Hayo and Wolfgang Seifert, "Subjective Economic Well-Being in Eastern Europe," *Journal of Economic Psychology* 24, no. 3 (2003): 329–48.

43. John F. Helliwell and Robert D. Putnam, "The Social Context of Well-Being," *Philosophical Transactions of the Royal Society* (London), series B (August 31, 2004): 1435–46.

44. Dani Rodrik, "Where Did All the Growth Go? External Shocks, Social Conflict, and Growth Collapses," *Journal of Economic Growth* 4, no. 4 (1999): 385–412; Paul J. Zak and Stephen Knack, "Trust and Growth," *Economic Journal* 111, no. 470 (2001): 295–321.

45. Anna, "Living Alone in Your Thirties," *Not Your Stereotypical Thirtysomething Woman* (blog), May 30, 2011, http://livingaloneinyourthirties.blogspot.co.il/.

46. Naomi Gerstel and Natalia Sarkisian, "Marriage: The Good, the Bad, and the Greedy," *Contexts* 5, no. 4 (2006): 16–21.

47. Rose McDermott, James H. Fowler, and Nicholas A. Christakis, "Breaking Up Is Hard to Do, Unless Everyone Else Is Doing It Too: Social Network Effects on Divorce in a Longitudinal Sample," *Social Forces* 92, no. 2 (2013): 491–519.

48. Bella DePaulo, *How We Live Now: Redefining Home and Family in the 21st Century* (Hillsboro, OR: Atria Books, 2015).

49. Jacqui Louis, "'Single and …' #6 Parenting," *Medium* (blog), May 22, 2016, https://medium.com/@jacqui_84.

50. Alois Stutzer and Bruno S. Frey, "Does Marriage Make People Happy, or Do Happy People Get Married?" *Journal of Socio-Economics* 35, no. 2 (2006): 326–47.

51. Richard E. Lucas, Andrew E. Clark, Yannis Georgellis, and Ed Diener, "Reexamining Adaptation and the Set Point Model of Happiness: Reactions to Changes in Marital Status," *Journal of Personality and Social Psychology* 84, no. 3 (2003): 527.

52. S. Burt, M. Donnellan, M.N. Humbad, B.M. Hicks, M. McGue, and W.G. Iacono, "Does Marriage Inhibit Antisocial Behavior?: An Examination of Selection vs. Causation Via a Longitudinal Twin Design," *Archives of General Psychiatry* 67, no. 12 (2010): 1309–15; Arne Mastekaasa, "Marriage and Psychological Well-Being: Some Evidence on Selection into Marriage," *Journal of Marriage and Family* 54, no. 4 (1992): 901–11; Alois Stutzer and Bruno S. Frey, "Does Marriage Make People Happy, or Do Happy People Get Married?" *Journal of Socio-Economics* 35, no. 2 (2006): 326–47.

53. To identify social interactions, two subjective measures were estimated. The first is a social-activities-frequency self-assessment ranging on a scale from 1 (Much less than most) to 5 (Much more than most). The second is a social-meetings-frequency self-assessment ranging on a scale from 1 (Never) to 7 (Every day). The first question is phrased in the survey as follows: "Compared to other people of your age, how often would you say you take part in social activities?" The second question is phrased as follows: "How often do you meet socially with friends, relatives, or work colleagues?"

54. Keith N. Hampton, Lauren F. Sessions, and Eun Ja Her, "Core Networks, Social Isolation, and New Media: How Internet and Mobile Phone Use Is Related to Network Size and Diversity," *Information, Communication & Society* 14, no. 1 (2011): 130–55.

55. Phyllis Solomon, "Peer Support/Peer Provided Services Underlying Processes, Benefits, and Critical Ingredients," *Psychiatric Rehabilitation Journal* 27, no. 4 (2004): 392.

56. Bella DePaulo, *How We Live Now: Redefining Home and Family in the 21st Century* (Hillsboro, OR: Atria Books, 2015); Bella DePaulo, "Single in a Society Preoccupied with Couples," in *Handbook of Solitude: Psychological Perspectives on Social Isolation, Social Withdrawal, and Being Alone*, ed. Robert J. Coplan and Julie C. Bowker (New York: John Wiley, 2014), 302–16; Eric Klinenberg, *Going Solo: The Extraordinary Rise and Surprising Appeal of Living Alone* (New York: Penguin, 2012).

57. Clever Elsie, "Single, Not Alone for the Holidays," *Singletude* (blog), January 2, 2010, http://singletude.blogspot.com.

58. Paul R. Amato, Alan Booth, David R. Johnson, and Stacy J. Rogers, *Alone Together: How Marriage in America Is Changing* (Cambridge, MA: Harvard University Press, 2007).

59. Barry Wellman, "The Development of Social Network Analysis: A Study in the Sociology of Science," *Contemporary Sociology: A Journal of Reviews* 37, no. 3 (2008): 221–22; Barry Wellman, "The Network Is Personal: Introduction to a Special Issue of Social Networks," *Social Networks* 29, no. 3 (2007): 349–56.

60. Peter J. Stein, "Singlehood: An Alternative to Marriage," *Family Coordinator* 24, no. 4 (1975): 489–503; Jan E. Stets, "Cohabiting and Marital Aggression: The Role of Social Isolation," *Journal of Marriage and Family* 53, no. 3 (1991): 669–80.

61. Naomi Gerstel and Natalia Sarkisian, "Marriage: The Good, the Bad, and the Greedy," *Contexts* 5, no. 4 (2006): 16–21.

62. Bella DePaulo, *How We Live Now: Redefining Home and Family in the 21st Century* (Hillsboro, Oregon: Atria Books, 2015); Bella DePaulo, "Single in a Society Preoccupied with Couples," in *Handbook of Solitude: Psychological Perspectives on Social Isolation, Social Withdrawal, and Being Alone,* ed. Robert J. Coplan and Julie C. Bowker (New York: John Wiley, 2014), 302–16.

63. E. Kay Trimberger, *The New Single Woman* (Boston: Beacon Press, 2006).

64. Pamela Anne Quiroz, "From Finding the Perfect Love Online to Satellite Dating and 'Loving-the-One-You're-Near': A Look at Grindr, Skout, Plenty of Fish, Meet Moi, Zoosk and Assisted Serendipity," *Humanity & Society* 37, no. 2 (2013): 181.

65. Lucy Rahim, "The 12 Non-dating Apps Single People Need This Valentine's Day," *The Telegraph,* February 14, 2017.

66. Dana L. Alden, Jan-Benedict E.M. Steenkamp, and Rajeev Batra, "Brand Positioning through Advertising in Asia, North America, and Europe: The Role of Global Consumer Culture," *Journal of Marketing* (1999): 75–87; Stuart Ewen, *Captains of Consciousness: Advertising and the Social Roots of the Consumer Culture* (New York: Basic Books, 2008); Christopher Donald Yee, "Re-urbanizing Downtown Los Angeles: Micro Housing Densifying the City's Core" (Master of Architecture thesis, University of Washington, 2013).

67. Bella DePaulo, "Single in a Society Preoccupied with Couples," in *Handbook of Solitude: Psychological Perspectives on Social Isolation, Social Withdrawal, and Being Alone,* ed. Robert J. Coplan and Julie C. Bowker (New York: John Wiley, 2014), 302–16; Gal Slonim, Nurit Gur-Yaish, and Ruth Katz, "By Choice or by Circumstance?: Stereotypes of and Feelings about Single People," *Studia Psychologica* 57, no. 1 (2015): 35–48.

CHAPTER 5. SINGLING IN A
POSTMATERIALIST WORLD

1. Abigail Pesta, "Why I Married Myself: These Women Dedicated Their Lives to Self-Love," *Cosmopolitan,* December 2016.

2. *Sex and the City,* "A Woman's Right to Shoes," season 4, episode 9, aired August 17, 2003.

3. Ronald Inglehart, "The Silent Revolution in Europe: Intergenerational Change in Post-industrial Societies," *American Political Science Review* 65, no. 4 (1971): 991–1017; Dirk J. Van de Kaa, "Postmodern Fertility Preferences: From Changing Value Orientation to New Behavior," *Population and Development Review* 27 (2001): 290–331.

4. Abigail Pesta, "Why I Married Myself: These Women Dedicated Their Lives to Self-Love," *Cosmopolitan,* December 2016.

5. Self Marriage Ceremonies, www.selfmarriageceremonies.com.

6. Ronald Inglehart, *The Silent Revolution: Changing Values and Political Styles among Western Publics* (Princeton, NJ: Princeton University Press, 1977).

7. Rhonda McEwen and Barry Wellman, "Relationships, Community, and Networked Individuals," in *The Immersive Internet: Reflections on the Entangling of the Virtual with Society, Politics and the Economy,* ed. R. Teigland and D. Power (London: Palgrave Macmillan, 2013), 168–79; Anne-Rigt Poortman and Aart C. Liefbroer, "Singles' Relational Attitudes in a Time of Individualization," *Social Science Research* 39, no. 6 (2010): 938–49.

8. David Levine, *Family Formation in an Age of Nascent Capitalism [England],* Studies in Social Discontinuity (New York: Academic Press, 1977).

9. Raymond M. Duch and Michaell A. Taylor, "Postmaterialism and the Economic Condition," *American Journal of Political Science* 37, no. 3 (1993): 747–79; Ronald Inglehart, "The Silent Revolution in Europe: Intergenerational Change in Post-industrial Societies," *American Political Science Review* 65, no. 4 (1971): 991–1017; Ronald Inglehart and Paul R. Abramson, "Measuring Postmaterialism," *American Political Science Review* 93, no. 3 (1999): 665–77.

10. Eric Klinenberg, *Going Solo: The Extraordinary Rise and Surprising Appeal of Living Alone* (New York: Penguin, 2012).

11. Joseph G. Altonji and Rebecca M. Blank, "Race and Gender in the Labor Market," in *Handbook of Labor Economics,* ed. Orley Ashenfelter and David Card (Amsterdam: Elsevier, 1999), 3143–259; Susan R. Orden and Norman M. Bradburn, "Dimensions of Marriage Happiness," *American Journal of Sociology* 73, no. 6 (1968): 715–31; Moshe Semyonov, Rebeca Raijman, and Anat Yom-Tov, "Labor Market Competition, Perceived Threat, and Endorsement of Eco-

nomic Discrimination against Foreign Workers in Israel," *Social Problems* 49, no. 3 (2002): 416–31.

12. Andrew J. Cherlin, "The Deinstitutionalization of American Marriage," *Journal of Marriage and Family* 66, no. 4 (2004): 848–61.

13. Abraham Harold Maslow, Robert Frager, James Fadiman, Cynthia McReynolds, and Ruth Cox, *Motivation and Personality* (New York: Harper & Row, 1970); Abraham Maslow, *Motivation and Personality* (New York: Harper & Brothers, 1954).

14. Verta Taylor and Nancy Whittier, "Analytical Approaches to Social Movement Culture: The Culture of the Women's Movement," *Social Movements and Culture* 4 (1995): 163–87.

15. Rachel F. Moran, "How Second-Wave Feminism Forgot the Single Woman," *Hofstra Law Review* 33, no. 1 (2004): 223–98.

16. Judith Evans, *Feminist Theory Today: An Introduction to Second-Wave Feminism* (New York: Sage, 1995); Imelda Whelehan, *Modern Feminist Thought: From the Second Wave to Post-Feminism* (New York: NYU Press, 1995).

17. Melissa, "Being Happy about Being Single," *Single Gal in the City* (blog), July 13, 2009, http://melissa-singlegalinthecity.blogspot.com.

18. Stephen Castles, Hein de Haas, and Mark J. Miller, *The Age of Migration: International Population Movements in the Modern World* (New York: Guilford Press, 2013).

19. Eliza Griswold, "Why Afghan Women Risk Death to Write Poetry," *New York Times,* April 29, 2012, www.nytimes.com/2012/04/29/magazine/why-afghan-women-risk-death-to-write-poetry.html.

20. Rosalind Chait Barnett and Janet Shibley Hyde, "Women, Men, Work, and Family," *American Psychologist* 56, no. 10 (2001): 781–96.

21. Hans-Peter Blossfeld and Alessandra De Rose, "Educational Expansion and Changes in Entry into Marriage and Motherhood: The Experience of Italian Women," *Genus* 48, no. 3–4 (1992): 73–91; Agnes R. Quisumbing and Kelly Hallman, *Marriage in Transition: Evidence on Age, Education, and Assets from Six Developing Countries* (New York: Population Council, 2005), 200–269.

22. Hans-Peter Blossfeld and Johannes Huinink, "Human Capital Investments or Norms of Role Transition? How Women's Schooling and Career Affect the Process of Family Formation," *American Journal of Sociology* 97, no. 1 (1991): 143–68.

23. Anonymous, "My Uterus Is Hiding," *Shoes, Booze and Losers: A Primer for the Thirty-Something Spinster,* October 24, 2008, http://elusivbutterfli.blogspot .com.

24. Rosalind Chait Barnett and Janet Shibley Hyde, "Women, Men, Work, and Family," *American Psychologist* 56, no. 10 (2001): 781–96.

25. Orna Donath, "Regretting Motherhood: A Sociopolitical Analysis," *Signs* 40, no. 2 (2015): 343–67.

26. Sarah Fischer, *The Mother Bliss Lie: Regretting Motherhood* (Munich: Ludwig Verlag, 2016); Anke C. Zimmermann and Richard A. Easterlin, "Happily Ever After? Cohabitation, Marriage, Divorce, and Happiness in Germany," *Population and Development Review* 32, no. 3 (2006): 511–28.

27. Jan Delhey, "From Materialist to Post-materialist Happiness? National Affluence and Determinants of Life Satisfaction in Cross-national Perspective," *Social Indicators Research* 97, no. 1 (2010): 65–84; Richard Florida, *The Rise of the Creative Class—Revisited: Revised and Expanded* (New York: Basic Books, 2014).

28. Anonymous, "The Introverted Singlutionary," *Singlutionary*, August 3, 2010, http://singlutionary.blogspot.com.

29. Gal Slonim, Nurit Gur-Yaish, and Ruth Katz, "By Choice or by Circumstance?: Stereotypes of and Feelings about Single People," *Studia Psychologica* 57, no. 1 (2015): 35–48.

30. Tim Teeman, "Why Singles Should Say 'I Don't' to the Self-Marriage Movement," *Daily Beast*, December 30, 2014, www.thedailybeast.com/articles/2014/12/30/why-singles-should-say-i-don-t-to-the-self-marriage-movement.html.

31. Bella M. DePaulo and Wendy L. Morris, "The Unrecognized Stereotyping and Discrimination against Singles," *Current Directions in Psychological Science* 15, no. 5 (2006): 251–54.

32. Hilke Brockmann, Jan Delhey, Christian Welzel, and Hao Yuan, "The China Puzzle: Falling Happiness in a Rising Economy," *Journal of Happiness Studies* 10, no. 4 (2009): 387–405.

33. Richard A. Easterlin, "Lost in Transition: Life Satisfaction on the Road to Capitalism," *Journal of Economic Behavior & Organization* 71, no. 2 (2009): 130–45.

34. Bella M. DePaulo and Wendy L. Morris, "The Unrecognized Stereotyping and Discrimination against Singles," *Current Directions in Psychological Science* 15, no. 5 (2006): 251–54; Peter J. Stein, "Singlehood: An Alternative to Marriage," *Family Coordinator* 24, no. 4 (1975): 489–503.

35. Jill Reynolds and Margaret Wetherell, "The Discursive Climate of Singleness: The Consequences for Women's Negotiation of a Single Identity," *Feminism & Psychology* 13, no. 4 (2003): 489–510.

36. Anne-Rigt Poortman and Aart C. Liefbroer, "Singles' Relational Attitudes in a Time of Individualization," *Social Science Research* 39, no. 6 (2010): 938–49.

37. Wendy L. Morris and Brittany K. Osburn, "Do You Take This Marriage? Perceived Choice over Marital Status Affects the Stereotypes of Single and Married People," in *Singlehood from Individual and Social Perspectives*, ed. K. Adamczyk (Krakow, Poland: Libron, 2016): 145–62; Gal Slonim, Nurit Gur-Yaish, and Ruth Katz, "By Choice or by Circumstance?: Stereotypes of and Feelings about Single People," *Studia Psychologica* 57, no. 1 (2015): 35–48.

38. S. Burt, M. Donnellan, M.N. Humbad, B.M. Hicks, M. McGue, and W.G. Iacono, "Does Marriage Inhibit Antisocial Behavior?: An Examination of Selection vs. Causation via a Longitudinal Twin Design," *Archives of General Psychiatry* 67, no. 12 (2010): 1309–15; M. Garrison, and E.S. Scott, *Marriage at the Crossroads: Law, Policy, and the Brave New World of Twenty-First-Century Families* (Cambridge: Cambridge University Press, 2012); Heather L. Koball, Emily Moiduddin, Jamila Henderson, Brian Goesling, and Melanie Besculides, "What Do We Know about the Link between Marriage and Health?" *Journal of Family Issues* 31, no. 8 (2010): 1019–40.

39. Norval Glenn, "Is the Current Concern about American Marriage Warranted?" *Virginia Journal of Social Policy & Law* 9 (2001): 5–47.

40. Matthew E. Dupre and Sarah O. Meadows, "Disaggregating the Effects of Marital Trajectories on Health," *Journal of Family Issues* 28, no. 5 (2007): 623–52; Walter R. Gove, Michael Hughes, and Carolyn Briggs Style, "Does Marriage Have Positive Effects on the Psychological Well-Being of the Individual?" *Journal of Health and Social Behavior* 24, no. 2 (1983): 122–31; Mary Elizabeth Hughes and Linda J. Waite, "Marital Biography and Health at Mid-Life," *Journal of health and Social Behavior* 50, no. 3 (2009): 344–58; David R. Johnson and Jian Wu, "An Empirical Test of Crisis, Social Selection, and Role Explanations of the Relationship between Marital Disruption and Psychological Distress: A Pooled Time-Series Analysis of Four-Wave Panel Data," *Journal of Marriage and Family* 64, no. 1 (2002): 211–24; John McCreery, *Japanese Consumer Behaviour: From Worker Bees to Wary Shoppers* (New York: Routledge, 2014); David A. Sbarra and Paul J. Nietert, "Divorce and Death: Forty Years of the Charleston Heart Study," *Psychological Science* 20, no. 1 (2009): 107–13; Terrance J. Wade and David J. Pevalin, "Marital Transitions and Mental Health," *Journal of Health and Social Behavior* 45, no. 2 (2004): 155–70; Chris Power, Bryan Rodgers, and Steven Hope, "Heavy Alcohol Consumption and Marital Status:

Disentangling the Relationship in a National Study of Young Adults," *Addiction* 94, no. 10 (1999): 1477–87.

41. Rosalind Barnett, Karen C. Gareis, Jacquelyn Boone James, and Jennifer Steele, "Planning Ahead: College Seniors' Concerns about Career-Marriage Conflict," *Journal of Vocational Behavior* 62, no. 2 (2003): 305–19; Wilmar B. Schaufeli, Toon W. Taris, and Willem Van Rhenen, "Workaholism, Burnout, and Work Engagement: Three of a Kind or Three Different Kinds of Employee Well-Being?" *Applied Psychology* 57, no. 2 (2008): 173–203.

42. Sasha Cagen, "Be Grateful for Being Single," *SashaCagen.com*, November 24, 2010, http://sashacagen.com/blog.

43. James Friel, "Letter To: Viewpoint: Why Are Couples So Mean to Single People?" *BBC Magazine*, November 7, 2012.

44. Jill Reynolds, *The Single Woman: A Discursive Investigation* (London: Routledge, 2013); Anne-Rigt Poortman and Aart C. Liefbroer, "Singles' Relational Attitudes in a Time of Individualization," *Social Science Research* 39, no. 6 (2010): 938–49.

45. Heron Saline, "Stories," *Self Marriage Ceremonies*, n.d., www.selfmarriage ceremonies.com/stories.

46. Abraham Harold Maslow, Robert Frager, James Fadiman, Cynthia McReynolds, and Ruth Cox, *Motivation and Personality* (New York: Harper & Row, 1970); Abraham Maslow, *Toward a New Psychology of Being* (New York: Van Nostrand Reinhold, 1968).

47. Bella DePaulo, *How We Live Now: Redefining Home and Family in the 21st Century* (Hillsboro, OR: Atria Books, 2015); Kath Weston, *Families We Choose: Lesbians, Gays, Kinship* (New York: Columbia University Press, 2013).

48. Bella DePaulo, *How We Live Now: Redefining Home and Family in the 21st Century* (Hillsboro, OR: Atria Books, 2015).

49. Rein B. Jobse and Sako Musterd, "Changes in the Residential Function of the Big Cities," in *The Randstad: A Research and Policy Laboratory*, ed. Frans M. Dieleman and Sako Musterd (Dordrecht: Springer, 1992), 39–64.

50. Pieter A. Gautier, Michael Svarer, and Coen N. Teulings, "Marriage and the City: Search Frictions and Sorting of Singles," *Journal of Urban Economics* 67, no. 2 (2010): 206–18.

51. A. Sicilia Camacho, C. Aguila Soto, D. González-Cutre, and J.A. Moreno-Murcia, "Postmodern Values and Motivation towards Leisure and Exercise in Sports Centre Users," *RICYDE: Revista Internacional de Ciencias del Deporte* 7, no. 25 (2011): 320–35.

52. Ramón Llopis-Goig, "Sports Participation and Cultural Trends: Running as a Reflection of Individualisation and Post-materialism Processes in Spanish Society," *European Journal for Sport and Society* 11, no. 2 (2014): 151–69.

53. Andrew J. Cherlin, "The Deinstitutionalization of American Marriage," *Journal of Marriage and Family* 66, no. 4 (2004): 848–61.

54. Norval Glenn, "Is the Current Concern about American Marriage Warranted?" *Virginia Journal of Social Policy & Law* 9 (2001): 5–47.

55. Tim Teeman, "Why Singles Should Say 'I Don't' to the Self-Marriage Movement," *Daily Beast*, December 30, 2014, www.thedailybeast.com/articles /2014/12/30/why-singles-should-say-i-don-t-to-the-self-marriage-movement .html.

56. Bella DePaulo, "The Urgent Need for a Singles Studies Discipline," *Signs: Journal of Women in Culture and Society* 42, no. 4 (2017): 1015–19; Bella DePaulo, Rachel F. Moran, and E. Kay Trimberger, "Make Room for Singles in Teaching and Research," *Chronicle of Higher Education* 54, no. 5 (2007): 44.

57. Wendy Wang and Kim C. Parker, *Record Share of Americans Have Never Married: As Values, Economics and Gender Patterns Change* (Washington, DC: Pew Research Center, 2014).

CHAPTER 6. WORK HARD, (BUT) PLAY HARD

1. Richard F. Thomas, *Virgil: Georgics* (Cambridge: Cambridge University Press, 1988).

2. C. G. Jung, *Mysterium Coniunctionis: An Inquiry into the Separation and Synthesis of Psychic Opposites in Alchemy* (New York: Routledge, 1963).

3. Douglas T. Hall, "The Protean Career: A Quarter-Century Journey," *Journal of Vocational Behavior* 65, no. 1 (2004): 1–13.

4. Amy Wrzesniewski, Clark McCauley, Paul Rozin, and Barry Schwartz, "Jobs, Careers, and Callings: People's Relations to Their Work," *Journal of Research in Personality* 31, no. 1 (1997): 21–33.

5. Raymond A. Noe, John R. Hollenbeck, Barry Gerhart, and Patrick M. Wright, *Human Resource Management: Gaining a Competitive Advantage*, 10th ed. (New York: McGraw-Hill, 2015); Beverly J. Silver, *Forces of Labor: Workers' Movements and Globalization since 1870* (Cambridge: Cambridge University Press, 2003).

6. Prudence L. Carter, *Keepin' It Real: School Success beyond Black and White* (Oxford: Oxford University Press, 2005).

7. Stephanie Armour, "Generation Y: They've Arrived at Work with a New Attitude," *USA Today,* November 6, 2005.

8. Hua Jiang and Rita Linjuan Men, "Creating an Engaged Workforce: The Impact of Authentic Leadership, Transparent Organizational Communication, and Work-Life Enrichment," *Communication Research* 44, no. 2 (2017): 225–43.

9. Daniel M. Haybron, "Happiness, the Self and Human Flourishing," *Utilitas* 20, no. 1 (2008): 21–49.

10. Alan Gewirth, *Self-Fulfillment* (Princeton, NJ: Princeton University Press, 1998); Sheryl Zika and Kerry Chamberlain, "On the Relation between Meaning in Life and Psychological Well-Being," *British Journal of Psychology* 83, no. 1 (1992): 133–45.

11. Robert Ehrlich, "New Rules: Searching for Self-Fulfillment in a World Turned Upside Down," *Telos,* no. 50 (1981): 218–28.

12. Viktor E. Frankl, *The Will to Meaning: Foundations and Applications of Logotherapy* (New York: Penguin, 2014); Eva S. Moskowitz, *In Therapy We Trust: America's Obsession with Self-Fulfillment* (Baltimore, MD: JHU Press, 2001).

13. Saziye Gazioglu and Aysit Tansel, "Job Satisfaction in Britain: Individual and Job-Related Factors," *Applied Economics* 38, no. 10 (2006): 1163–71.

14. Monica Kirkpatrick Johnson, "Family Roles and Work Values: Processes of Selection and Change," *Journal of Marriage and Family* 67, no. 2 (2005): 352–69.

15. Ruth Wein, "The 'Always Singles': Moving from a 'Problem' Perception," *Psychotherapy in Australia* 9, no. 2 (2003): 60–65.

16. Jessica E. Donn, "Adult Development and Well-Being of Mid-Life Never Married Singles" (PhD diss., Miami University, 2005).

17. Ilene Philipson, *Married to the Job: Why We Live to Work and What We Can Do about It* (New York: Simon and Schuster, 2003).

18. Anonymous, "Ten Things Not to Tell Your 30-Something Single Women Friends," *Thirty-Two and Single* (blog), January 7, 2014, http://thirtytwoandsingle.blogspot.com.

19. E. Jeffrey Hill, Alan J. Hawkins, Maria Ferris, and Michelle Weitzman, "Finding an Extra Day a Week: The Positive Influence of Perceived Job Flexibility on Work and Family Life Balance," *Family Relations* 50, no. 1 (2001): 49–58.

20. Mark Tausig and Rudy Fenwick, "Unbinding Time: Alternate Work Schedules and Work-Life Balance," *Journal of Family and Economic Issues* 22, no. 2 (2001): 101–19.

21. Kiran Sahu and Priya Gupta, "Burnout among Married and Unmarried Women Teachers," *Indian Journal of Health and Wellbeing* 4, no. 2 (2013): 286;

Türker Tuğsal, "The Effects of Socio-Demographic Factors and Work-Life Balance on Employees' Emotional Exhaustion," *Journal of Human Sciences* 14, no. 1 (2017): 653–65.

22. Christina Maslach, Wilmar B. Schaufeli, and Michael P. Leiter, "Job Burnout," *Annual Review of Psychology* 52, no. 1 (2001): 397–422.

23. Kim Engler, Katherine Frohlich, Francine Descarries, and Mylène Fernet, "Single, Childless Working Women's Construction of Wellbeing: On Balance, Being Dynamic and Tensions between Them," *Work* 40, no. 2 (2011): 173–86.

24. Jeffrey H. Greenhaus and Nicholas J. Beutell, "Sources of Conflict between Work and Family Roles," *Academy of Management Review* 10, no. 1 (1985): 76–88; Jean M. Twenge and Laura A. King, "A Good Life Is a Personal Life: Relationship Fulfillment and Work Fulfillment in Judgments of Life Quality," *Journal of Research in Personality* 39, no. 3 (2005): 336–53; Jean M. Twenge, W. Keith Campbell, and Craig A. Foster, "Parenthood and Marital Satisfaction: A Meta-analytic Review," *Journal of Marriage and Family* 65, no. 3 (2003): 574–83.

25. Bella M. DePaulo, *Singled Out: How Singles Are Stereotyped, Stigmatized, and Ignored, and Still Live Happily Ever After* (New York: St. Martin's Griffin, 2007).

26. Jeanne Brett Herman and Karen Kuczynski Gyllstrom, "Working Men and Women: Inter- and Intra-Role Conflict," *Psychology of Women Quarterly* 1, no. 4 (1977): 319–33.

27. Wendy J. Casper and Bella DePaulo, "A New Layer to Inclusion: Creating Singles-Friendly Work Environments," in *Work and Quality of Life: Ethical Practices in Organizations*, ed. Nora P. Reilly, M. Joseph Sirgy, and C. Allen Gorman (Dordrecht: Springer, 2012), 217–34.

28. Elizabeth A. Hamilton, Judith R. Gordon, and Karen S. Whelan-Berry, "Understanding the Work-Life Conflict of Never-Married Women without Children," *Women in Management Review* 21, no. 5 (2006): 393–415.

29. Jessica Keeney, Elizabeth M. Boyd, Ruchi Sinha, Alyssa F. Westring, and Ann Marie Ryan, "From 'Work-Family' to 'Work-Life': Broadening Our Conceptualization and Measurement," *Journal of Vocational Behavior* 82, no. 3 (2013): 221–37.

30. Naomi Gerstel and Natalia Sarkisian, "Marriage: The Good, the Bad, and the Greedy," *Contexts* 5, no. 4 (2006): 16–21.

31. Martha R. Crowther, Michael W. Parker, W. Andrew Achenbaum, Walter L. Larimore, and Harold G. Koenig, "Rowe and Kahn's Model of Successful Aging Revisited Positive Spirituality—the Forgotten Factor," *The Gerontologist* 42, no. 5 (2002): 613–20; Dawood Ghaderi, "The Survey of

Relationship between Religious Orientation and Happiness among the Elderly Man and Woman in Tehran," *Iranian Journal of Ageing 5*, no. 4 (2011): 64–71; Jeff Levin, "Religion and Happiness among Israeli Jews: Findings from the ISSP Religion III Survey," *Journal of Happiness Studies 15*, no. 3 (2014): 593–611; Sombat Tapanya, Richard Nicki, and Ousa Jarusawad, "Worry and Intrinsic/Extrinsic Religious Orientation among Buddhist (Thai) and Christian (Canadian) Elderly Persons," *International Journal of Aging and Human Development 44*, no. 1 (1997): 73–83.

32. Mirella Di Benedetto and Michael Swadling, "Burnout in Australian Psychologists: Correlations with Work-Setting, Mindfulness and Self-Care Behaviours," *Psychology, Health & Medicine 19*, no. 6 (2014): 705–15; Ute R. Hülsheger, Hugo J. E. M. Alberts, Alina Feinholdt, and Jonas W. B. Lang, "Benefits of Mindfulness at Work: The Role of Mindfulness in Emotion Regulation, Emotional Exhaustion, and Job Satisfaction," *Journal of Applied Psychology 98*, no. 2 (2013): 310.

33. Abolfazl Rahimi, Monireh Anoosheh, Fazlollah Ahmadi, and Mahshid Foroughan, "Exploring Spirituality in Iranian Healthy Elderly People: A Qualitative Content Analysis," *Iranian Journal of Nursing and Midwifery Research 18*, no. 2 (2013): 163–70.

34. Daryoush Ghasemian, Atefeh Zebarjadi Kuzehkanan, and Ramezan Hassanzadeh, "Effectiveness of MBCT on Decreased Anxiety and Depression among Divorced Women Living in Tehran, Iran," *Journal of Novel Applied Sciences 3*, no. 3 (2014): 256–59; John D. Teasdale, Zindel V. Segal, J. Mark G. Williams, Valerie A. Ridgeway, Judith M. Soulsby, and Mark A. Lau, "Prevention of Relapse/Recurrence in Major Depression by Mindfulness-Based Cognitive Therapy," *Journal of Consulting and Clinical Psychology 68*, no. 4 (2000): 615–23.

35. Yoo Sun Moon and Do Hoon Kim, "Association between Religiosity/Spirituality and Quality of Life or Depression among Living-Alone Elderly in a South Korean City," *Asia-Pacific Psychiatry 5*, no. 4 (2013): 293–300.

36. P. Udhayakumar and P. Ilango, "Spirituality, Stress and Wellbeing among the Elderly Practicing Spirituality," *Samaja Karyada Hejjegalu 2*, no. 10 (2012): 37–42.

37. Christena Cleveland, "Singled Out: How Churches Can Embrace Unmarried Adults," *Christena Cleveland* (blog), December 2, 2013, www.christenacleveland.com/blogarchive/2013/12/singled-out.

38. Gill Seyfang, "Growing Cohesive Communities One Favour at a Time: Social Exclusion, Active Citizenship and Time Banks," *International Journal of Urban and Regional Research 27*, no. 3 (2003): 699–706.

39. Anna, "Only the Lonely?" *Not Your Stereotypical Thirtysomething Woman* (blog), September 2, 2012, http://livingaloneinyourthirties.blogspot.com/2012/09/.

40. Shelley Budgeon and Sasha Roseneil, "Editors' Introduction: Beyond the Conventional Family," *Current Sociology* 52, no. 2 (2004): 127–34.

41. Debra A. Major and Lisa M. Germano, "The Changing Nature of Work and Its Impact on the Work-Home Interface," in *Work-Life Balance: A Psychological Perspective,* ed. Fiona Jones, Ronald J. Burke, and Mina Westman (New York: Taylor & Francis, 2006).

42. Frederick Cornwallis Conybeare, *Philostratus: The Life of Apollonius of Tyana* (Cambridge, MA: Harvard University Press, 1912).

CHAPTER 7. THE FUTURE OF HAPPY SINGLEHOOD

1. Michael Goddard, "Historicizing Edai Siabo: A Contemporary Argument about the Pre-colonial Past among the Motu-Koita of Papua New Guinea," *Oceania* 81, no. 3 (2011): 280–96.

2. Helen V. Milner, *Resisting Protectionism: Global Industries and the Politics of International Trade* (Princeton, NJ: Princeton University Press, 1988).

3. Xuanning Fu and Tim B. Heaton, "A Cross-national Analysis of Family and Household Structure," *International Journal of Sociology of the Family* 25, no. 2 (1995): 1–32.

4. Susan R. Orden and Norman M. Bradburn, "Dimensions of Marriage Happiness," *American Journal of Sociology* 73, no. 6 (1968): 715–31.

5. Christopher J. Einolf and Deborah Philbrick, "Generous or Greedy Marriage? A Longitudinal Study of Volunteering and Charitable Giving," *Journal of Marriage and Family* 76, no. 3 (2014): 573–86; Naomi Gerstel and Natalia Sarkisian, "Marriage: The Good, the Bad, and the Greedy," *Contexts* 5, no. 4 (2006): 16–21.

6. Rhonda McEwen and Barry Wellman, "Relationships, Community, and Networked Individuals," in *The Immersive Internet: Reflections on the Entangling of the Virtual with Society, Politics and the Economy,* ed. R. Teigland and D. Power (London: Palgrave Macmillan, 2013), pp. 168–79; Barry Wellman, "Networked Individualism: How the Personalized Internet, Ubiquitous Connectivity, and the Turn to Social Networks Can Affect Learning Analytics," in *Proceedings of the Second International Conference on Learning Analytics and Knowledge* (New York: ACM, 2012), 1.

7. Shelley Budgeon, "Friendship and Formations of Sociality in Late Modernity: The Challenge of 'Post-traditional Intimacy,'" *Sociological Research Online* 11, no. 3 (2006): 1–11.

8. William James, *The Varieties of Religious Experience* (Cambridge, MA: Harvard University Press, 1985); Carl Gustav Jung, *The Archetypes and the Collective Unconscious,* trans. R. F. C. Hull (London: Routledge, 1959).

9. Hiromi Taniguchi, "Interpersonal Mattering in Friendship as a Predictor of Happiness in Japan: The Case of Tokyoites," *Journal of Happiness Studies* 16, no. 6 (2015): 1475–91.

10. Julia Hahmann, "Friendship Repertoires and Care Arrangement," *International Journal of Aging and Human Development* 84, no. 2 (2017): 180–206.

11. Masako Ishii-Kuntz, "Social Interaction and Psychological Well-Being: Comparison across Stages of Adulthood," *International Journal of Aging and Human Development* 30, no. 1 (1990): 15–36.

12. Bella DePaulo, *How We Live Now: Redefining Home and Family in the 21st Century* (Hillsboro, OR: Atria Books, 2015).

13. Joanne Kersh, Laura Corona, and Gary Siperstein, "Social Well-Being and Friendship of People with Intellectual Disability," in *The Oxford Handbook of Positive Psychology and Disability* (Oxford: Oxford University, 2013), pp. 60–81.

14. Lynne M. Casper and Philip N. Cohen, "How Does Posslq Measure Up? Historical Estimates of Cohabitation," *Demography* 37, no. 2 (2000): 237–45.

15. Natascha Gruver, "Civil Friendship: A Proposal for Legal Bonds Based on Friendship and Care," in *Conceptualizing Friendship in Time and Place,* ed. Carla Risseeuw and Marlein van Raalte (Leiden, Netherlands: Brill, 2017), 285–302.

16. Paul R. Brewer, "Public Opinion about Gay Rights and Gay Marriage," *International Journal of Public Opinion Research* 26, no. 3 (2014): 279–82; Ben Clements and Clive D. Field, "Public Opinion toward Homosexuality and Gay Rights in Great Britain," *Public Opinion Quarterly* 78, no. 2 (2014): 523–47.

17. Carla Risseeuw and Marlein van Raalte, *Conceptualizing Friendship in Time and Place* (Leiden, Netherlands: Brill, 2017).

18. *Times of India,* "Friendship Day 2017: Everything You Want to Know about Friendship Day," updated August 4, 2017, https://timesofindia.indiatimes.com/life-style/events/when-is-friendship-day-2017-everything-you-wanted-to-know-about-it/articleshow/59877813.cms.

19. United Nations General Assembly, Sixty-fifth session, Agenda item 15, "Culture of Peace," April 27, 2011.

20. Mark Zuckerberg, "Celebrating Friends Day at Facebook HQ," Facebook, February 4, 2016, www.facebook.com/zuck/videos/vb.4/10102634961507811.

21. See, for example, Cara McGoogan, "'Happy Friends Day': Why Has Facebook Made Up This Weird Holiday?" February 2, 2017, *The Telegraph,*

www.telegraph.co.uk/technology/2017/02/02/happy-friends-day-has-facebook-made-weird-holiday/.

22. Michelle Ruiz, "Why You Should Celebrate Your Friendiversary," *Cosmopolitan,* February 6, 2014.

23. Robert E. Lane, "The Road Not Taken: Friendship, Consumerism, and Happiness," *Critical Review* 8, no. 4 (1994): 521–54.

24. Tanya Finchum and Joseph A. Weber, "Applying Continuity Theory to Older Adult Friendships," *Journal of Aging and Identity* 5, no. 3 (2000): 159–68.

25. Yohanan Eshel, Ruth Sharabany, and Udi Friedman, "Friends, Lovers and Spouses: Intimacy in Young Adults," *British Journal of Social Psychology* 37, no. 1 (1998): 41–57.

26. Mary E. Procidano and Kenneth Heller, "Measures of Perceived Social Support from Friends and from Family: Three Validation Studies," *American Journal of Community Psychology* 11, no. 1 (1983): 1–24.

27. Jean M. Twenge, Ryne A. Sherman, and Brooke E. Wells, "Changes in American Adults' Sexual Behavior and Attitudes, 1972–2012," *Archives of Sexual Behavior* 44, no. 8 (2015): 2273–85.

28. Marla E. Eisenberg, Diann M. Ackard, Michael D. Resnick, and Dianne Neumark-Sztainer, "Casual Sex and Psychological Health among Young Adults: Is Having 'Friends with Benefits' Emotionally Damaging?" *Perspectives on Sexual and Reproductive Health* 41, no. 4 (2009): 231–37.

29. Jacqueline Woerner and Antonia Abbey, "Positive Feelings after Casual Sex: The Role of Gender and Traditional Gender-Role Beliefs," *Journal of Sex Research* 54, no. 6 (2017): 717–27.

30. Andreas Henriksson, *Organising Intimacy: Exploring Heterosexual Singledoms at Swedish Singles Activities* (Karlstad, Sweden: Karlstad University, 2014).

31. Eric Klinenberg, *Going Solo: The Extraordinary Rise and Surprising Appeal of Living Alone* (New York: Penguin, 2012).

32. Bella DePaulo, "Creating a Community of Single People," *Single at Heart* (blog), PsychCentral, last updated July 10, 2015.

33. Karsten Strauss, "The 12 Best Cities for Singles," *Forbes,* February 3, 2016, www.forbes.com/sites/karstenstrauss/2016/02/03/the-12-best-cities-for-singles /#2315f7a01949.

34. Richie Bernardo, "2016's Best & Worst Cities for Singles," WalletHub, December 5, 2016, https://wallethub.com/edu/best-worst-cities-for-singles/9015/.

35. William B. Davidson and Patrick R. Cotter, "The Relationship between Sense of Community and Subjective Well-Being: A First Look," *Journal of Community Psychology* 19, no. 3 (1991): 246–53.

36. Seymour B. Sarason, *The Psychological Sense of Community: Prospects for a Community Psychology* (San Francisco, CA: Jossey-Bass, 1974).

37. Neharika Vohra and John Adair, "Life Satisfaction of Indian Immigrants in Canada," *Psychology and Developing Societies* 12, no. 2 (2000): 109–38.

38. Dawn Darlaston-Jones, "Psychological Sense of Community and Its Relevance to Well-Being and Everyday Life in Australia," *Australian Community Psychologist* 19, no. 2 (2007): 6–25.

39. Maria Isabel Hombrados-Mendieta, Luis Gomez-Jacinto, Juan Manuel Dominguez-Fuentes, and Patricia Garcia-Leiva, "Sense of Community and Satisfaction with Life among Immigrants and the Native Population," *Journal of Community Psychology* 41, no. 5 (2013): 601–14.

40. Irene Bloemraad, *Becoming a Citizen: Incorporating Immigrants and Refugees in the United States and Canada* (Berkeley, CA: University of California Press, 2006); R. D. Julian, A. S. Franklin, and B. S. Felmingham, *Home from Home: Refugees in Tasmania* (Canberra: Australian Government Publishing Services, 1997).

41. Lia Karsten, "Family Gentrifiers: Challenging the City as a Place Simultaneously to Build a Career and to Raise Children," *Urban Studies* 40, no. 12 (2003): 2573–84.

42. NYU Furman Center, *Compact Units: Demand and Challenges* (New York: New York University, 2014).

43. Claude S. Fischer, *To Dwell among Friends: Personal Networks in Town and City* (Chicago: University of Chicago Press, 1982).

44. Peteke Feijten and Maarten Van Ham, "Residential Mobility and Migration of the Divorced and Separated," *Demographic Research* 17 (2008): 623–53.

45. Caitlin McGee, Laura Wynne, and Steffen Lehmann, "Housing Innovation for Compact, Resilient Cities," in *Growing Compact: Urban Form, Density and Sustainability*, ed. Joo Hwa P. Bay and Steffen Lehmann (New York: Routledge, 2017).

46. Christopher Donald Yee, "Re-urbanizing Downtown Los Angeles: Micro Housing—Densifying the City's Core" (Master's thesis, University of Washington, 2013).

47. Emily Badger, "The Rise of Singles Will Change How We Live in Cities," *Washington Post,* April 21, 2015.

48. Andrea Sharam, Lyndall Elaine Bryant, and Thomas Alves, "Identifying the Financial Barriers to Deliberative, Affordable Apartment Development in Australia," *International Journal of Housing Markets and Analysis* 8, no. 4 (2015): 471–83.

49. Louise Crabtree, "Self-Organised Housing in Australia: Housing Diversity in an Age of Market Heat," *International Journal of Housing Policy*, 18, no. 1 (2016): 1–20.

50. Kiran Sidhu, "Why I'll Be Spending My Golden Years with My Golden Girls," *The Guardian*, August 26, 2017.

51. Sheila M. Peace and Caroline Holland, *Inclusive Housing in an Ageing Society: Innovative Approaches* (Bristol, UK: Policy Press, 2001).

52. Zeynep Toker, "New Housing for New Households: Comparing Cohousing and New Urbanist Developments with Women in Mind," *Journal of Architectural and Planning Research* 27, no. 4 (2010): 325–39.

53. Anne P. Glass, "Lessons Learned from a New Elder Cohousing Community," *Journal of Housing for the Elderly* 27, no. 4 (2013): 348–68.

54. Guy Nerdi, "Living in Communal Communities Has Become a Social and Real Estate Trend," *Globes*, February 2, 2018, www.globes.co.il/news/article.aspx?did=1001224953.

55. Maryann Wulff and Michele Lobo, "The New Gentrifiers: The Role of Households and Migration in Reshaping Melbourne's Core and Inner Suburbs," *Urban Policy and Research* 27, no. 3 (2009): 315–31.

56. Bernadette Hanlon, "Beyond Sprawl: Social Sustainability and Reinvestment in the Baltimore Suburbs," in *The New American Suburb: Poverty, Race, and the Economic Crisis*, ed. Katrin B. Anacker (New York: Routledge, 2015), pp. 133–52.

57. Maria L. Ruiu, "Differences between Cohousing and Gated Communities: A Literature Review," *Sociological Inquiry* 84, no. 2 (2014): 316–35.

58. Mike Davis, *Ecology of Fear: Los Angeles and the Imagination of Disaster* (New York: Henry Holt, 1998).

59. Guy Nerdi, "Living in Communal Communities Has Become a Social and Real Estate Trend," *Globes*, February 2, 2018, www.globes.co.il/news/article.aspx?did=1001224953.

60. Richard L. Florida, *The Flight of the Creative Class* (New York: Harper Business, 2005); Ann Markusen, "Urban Development and the Politics of a Creative Class: Evidence from a Study of Artists," *Environment and Planning A* 38, no. 10 (2006): 1921–40; Allen John Scott, "Beyond the Creative City: Cognitive-Cultural Capitalism and the New Urbanism," *Regional Studies* 48, no. 4 (2014): 565–78.

61. James Murdoch III, Carl Grodach, and Nicole Foster, "The Importance of Neighborhood Context in Arts-Led Development: Community Anchor or Creative Class Magnet?" *Journal of Planning Education and Research*

36, no. 1 (2016): 32–48; Gavin Shatkin, "Reinterpreting the Meaning of the 'Singapore Model': State Capitalism and Urban Planning," *International Journal of Urban and Regional Research* 38, no. 1 (2014): 116–37.

62. Ronald D. Michman, Edward M Mazze, and Alan James Greco, *Lifestyle Marketing: Reaching the New American Consumer* (Westport, CT: Greenwood, 2003).

63. Naveen Donthu and David I. Gilliland, "The Single Consumer," *Journal of Advertising Research* 42, no. 6 (2002): 77–84.

64. Bureau of Labor Statistics, "Consumer Expenditures in 2014," in *Consumer Expenditure Survey* (Washington, DC: US Bureau of Labor Statistics, 2016); Eric Klinenberg, *Going Solo: The Extraordinary Rise and Surprising Appeal of Living Alone* (New York: Penguin, 2012).

65. Olfa Bouhlel, Mohamed Nabil Mzoughi, and Safa Chaieb, "Singles: An Expanding Market," *Business Management Dynamics* 1, no. 3 (2011): 22–32.

66. Martin Klepek and Kateřina Matušínská, "Factors Influencing Marketing Communication Perception by Singles in Czech Republic," Working Paper in Interdisciplinary Economics and Business Research, no. 25, Silesian University in Opava, School of Business Administration in Karvina, December 2015, www.iivopf.cz/images/Working_papers/WPIEBRS_25_Klepek_Matusinska.pdf.

67. Eric Klinenberg, *Going Solo: The Extraordinary Rise and Surprising Appeal of Living Alone* (New York: Penguin, 2012).

68. Marie Buckley, Cathal Cowan, and Mary McCarthy, "The Convenience Food Market in Great Britain: Convenience Food Lifestyle (CFL) Segments," *Appetite* 49, no. 3 (2007): 600–617.

69. Sinead Furey, Heather McIlveen, Christopher Strugnell, and Gillian Armstrong, "Cooking Skills: A Diminishing Art?" *Nutrition & Food Science* 30, no. 5 (2000).

70. Isabel Ryan, Cathal Cowan, Mary McCarthy, and Catherine O'Sullivan, "Food-Related Lifestyle Segments in Ireland with a Convenience Orientation," *Journal of International Food & Agribusiness Marketing* 14, no. 4 (2004): 29–47.

71. Marie Marquis, "Exploring Convenience Orientation as a Food Motivation for College Students Living in Residence Halls," *International Journal of Consumer Studies* 29, no. 1 (2005): 55–63.

72. Stavri Chrysostomou, Sofia N. Andreou, and Alexandros Polycarpou, "Developing a Food Basket for Fulfilling Physical and Non-physical Needs in Cyprus: Is It Affordable?" *European Journal of Public Health* 27, no. 3 (2017): 553–58.

73. Erica Wilson and Donna E. Little, "The Solo Female Travel Experience: Exploring the 'Geography of Women's Fear,'" *Current Issues in Tourism* 11, no. 2 (2008): 167–86.

74. Erica Wilson and Donna E. Little, "A 'Relative Escape'? The Impact of Constraints on Women Who Travel Solo," *Tourism Review International* 9, no. 2 (2005): 155–75.

75. Christian Laesser, Pietro Beritelli, and Thomas Bieger, "Solo Travel: Explorative Insights from a Mature Market (Switzerland)," *Journal of Vacation Marketing* 15, no. 3 (2009): 217–27.

76. Freya Stark, *Baghdad Sketches* (Evanston, IL: Northwestern University Press, 1992).

77. Bella DePaulo, *How We Live Now: Redefining Home and Family in the 21st Century* (Hillsboro, OR: Atria Books, 2015).

78. Bella DePaulo, *Singled Out: How Singles Are Stereotyped, Stigmatized, and Ignored, and Still Live Happily Ever After* (New York: St. Martin's Griffin, 2007).

79. E.J. Schultz, "As Single Becomes New Norm, How to Market without Stigma," AdAge, October 11, 2010, http://adage.com/article/news/advertising-market-singles-stigma/146376/.

80. Michelle Markelz, "Why You Must Market to Single People This Valentine's Day," American Marketing Association, 2017, www.ama.org/publications/MarketingNews/Pages/how-to-market-to-single-people.aspx.

81. Lawrence H. Wortzel, "Young Adults: Single People and Single Person Households," *ACR North American Advances* 4, no. 1 (1977): 324–29.

82. Bella DePaulo, *How We Live Now: Redefining Home and Family in the 21st Century* (Hillsboro, OR: Atria Books, 2015).

83. Zygmunt Bauman, *Liquid Love: On the Frailty of Human Bonds* (Cambridge, UK: Polity Press, 2003).

84. Mitchell Hobbs, Stephen Owen, and Livia Gerber, "Liquid Love? Dating Apps, Sex, Relationships and the Digital Transformation of Intimacy," *Journal of Sociology* 53, no. 2 (2017): 271–84.

85. Valerie Francisco, "'The Internet Is Magic': Technology, Intimacy and Transnational Families," *Critical Sociology* 41, no. 1 (2015): 173–90.

86. Manolo Farci, Luca Rossi, Giovanni Boccia Artieri, and Fabio Giglietto, "Networked Intimacy: Intimacy and Friendship among Italian Facebook Users," *Information, Communication & Society* 20, no. 5 (2017): 784–801.

87. Clément Chastagnol, Céline Clavel, Matthieu Courgeon, and Laurence Devillers, "Designing an Emotion Detection System for a Socially Intelligent Human-Robot Interaction," in *Natural Interaction with Robots,*

Knowbots and Smartphones, ed. J. Mariani, S. Rosset, M. Garnier-Rizet, and L. Devillers (New York: Springer, 2014), pp. 199–211; Kerstin Dautenhahn, "Socially Intelligent Robots: Dimensions of Human-Robot Interaction," *Philosophical Transactions of the Royal Society of London B: Biological Sciences* 362, no. 1480 (2007): 679–704.

88. Sarah M. Rabbitt, Alan E. Kazdin, and Brian Scassellati, "Integrating Socially Assistive Robotics into Mental Healthcare Interventions: Applications and Recommendations for Expanded Use," *Clinical Psychology Review* 35 (2015): 35–46.

89. Mark Hay, "Why Robots Are the Future of Elder Care," *GOOD,* June 24, 2015; United States Patent: [Shinichi] Oonaka, "Child-Care Robot and a Method of Controlling the Robot," February 19, 2013, https://patents.google .com/patent/US8376803B2/en; Fumihide Tanaka and Takeshi Kimura, "Care-Receiving Robot as a Tool of Teachers in Child Education," *Interaction Studies* 11, no. 2 (2010): 263.

90. Interestingly, the rise of robot companionship, whether friendly, romantic, sexual, or otherwise, was preceded by the popularity of dolls. Research shows two reasons why dolls became popular in past centuries. First, they filled the need for intersubjective relations. Second, "ownership" of the dolls allows users to combine pleasure and control in a low-risk fashion. In fact, the use of manufactured dolls for sexual purposes can be traced back to early-twentieth-century Europe, where men turned to dolls for comfort. Although the focus here is mainly men with dolls, women are also recorded as forming emotional ties with dolls and mannequins. Today, however, robots are perceived, and function, more positively and constructively. See Anthony Ferguson, *The Sex Doll: A History* (Jefferson, NC: McFarland, 2010); Heidi J. Nast, "Into the Arms of Dolls: Japan's Declining Fertility Rates, the 1990s Financial Crisis and the (Maternal) Comforts of the Posthuman," *Social & Cultural Geography* 18, no. 6 (2017): 758–85; and Alexander F. Robertson, *Life Like Dolls: The Collector Doll Phenomenon and the Lives of the Women Who Love Them* (London: Routledge, 2004).

91. Benjamin Haas, "Chinese Man 'Marries' Robot He Built Himself," *The Guardian,* April 4, 2017.

92. Ronan O'Connell, "World's First Artificially Intelligent Sex Dolls," *News.com.au,* October 14, 2017, www.news.com.au/lifestyle/relationships/sex /worlds-first-artificially-intelligent-sex-dolls/news-story/755a409e8b16685b56 2eb7987953824c; Rupert Wingfield-Hayes, "Meeting the Pioneers of Japan's Coming Robot Revolution," *BBC News,* September 17, 2015, www.bbc.com /news/world-asia-pacific-34272425.

93. Jennifer Robertson, "Robo Sapiens Japanicus: Humanoid Robots and the Posthuman Family," *Critical Asian Studies* 39, no. 3 (2007): 369–98.

94. Innovation 25 Strategy Council, *Innovation 25 Interim Report* (Tokyo: Government of Japan, 2007).

95. Jennifer Robertson, "Human Rights vs. Robot Rights: Forecasts from Japan," *Critical Asian Studies* 46, no. 4 (2014): 571–98.

96. Rupert Wingfield-Hayes, "Meeting the Pioneers of Japan's Coming Robot Revolution," *BBC News*, September 17, 2015, www.bbc.com/news/world-asia-pacific-34272425.

97. Jen Mills, "Sex Robot Breaks on First Public Outing after Being Groped by Mob," *Metro*, October 15, 2017, http://metro.co.uk/2017/10/15/sex-robot-breaks-on-first-public-outing-after-being-groped-by-mob-7001144/.

98. David Levy, *Love and Sex with Robots: The Evolution of Human-Robot Relationships* (New York: HarperCollins, 2007).

99. Adrian David Cheok, David Levy, Kasun Karunanayaka, and Yukihiro Morisawa, "Love and Sex with Robots," in *Handbook of Digital Games and Entertainment Technologies,* ed. Ryohei Nakatsu, Matthias Rauterberg, and Paolo Ciancarini (Singapore: Springer, 2017), pp. 833–58.

100. Gianmarco Veruggio, Fiorella Operto, and George Bekey, "Roboethics: Social and Ethical Implications," in *Springer Handbook of Robotics,* ed. Bruno Siciliano and Oussama Khatib (Heidelberg: Springer, 2016), pp. 2135–60.

101. Elizabeth Broadbent, "Interactions with Robots: The Truths We Reveal about Ourselves," *Annual Review of Psychology* 68 (2017): 627–52.

102. Jennifer Robertson, "Robo Sapiens Japanicus: Humanoid Robots and the Posthuman Family," *Critical Asian Studies* 39, no. 3 (2007): 369–98.

103. Francesco Ferrari, Maria Paola Paladino, and Jolanda Jetten, "Blurring Human-Machine Distinctions: Anthropomorphic Appearance in Social Robots as a Threat to Human Distinctiveness," *International Journal of Social Robotics* 8, no. 2 (2016): 287–302.

104. David Levy, *Love and Sex with Robots: The Evolution of Human-Robot Relationships* (New York: HarperCollins, 2007).

105. Mark Goldfeder and Yosef Razin, "Robotic Marriage and the Law," *Journal of Law and Social Deviance* 10 (2015): 137–76.

106. Maartje Margaretha Allegonda de Graaf, "Living with Robots: Investigating the User Acceptance of Social Robots in Domestic Environments" (PhD diss., Universiteit Twente, 2015), p. 574.

107. Maartje Margaretha Allegonda de Graaf, Somaya Ben Allouch, and Jan A. G. M. Van Dijk, "Long-Term Acceptance of Social Robots in Domestic

Environments: Insights from a User's Perspective" (paper presented to the AAAI 2016 Spring Symposium on "Enabling Computing Research in Socially Intelligent Human-Robot Interaction: A Community-Driven Modular Research Platform, Palo Alto, CA, March 21, 2016).

108. Ray Kurzweil, "The Singularity Is Near," in *Ethics and Emerging Technologies,* ed. Ronald L. Sandler (London: Palgrave Macmillan, 2016), p. 393.

109. Grace A. Martin, "For the Love of Robots: Posthumanism in Latin American Science Fiction between 1960–1999" (PhD diss., University of Kentucky, 2015).

110. Chris Mack, "The Multiple Lives of Moore's Law," *IEEE Spectrum* 52, no. 4 (2015): 31–37.

111. Christopher L. Magee and Tessaleno C. Devezas, "How Many Singularities Are Near and How Will They Disrupt Human History?" *Technological Forecasting and Social Change* 78, no. 8 (2011): 1365–78.

CONCLUSION

1. H. Chun and I. Lee, "Why Do Married Men Earn More: Productivity or Marriage Selection?" *Economic Inquiry* 39, no. 2 (2001): 307–19; Willy Pedersen and Morten Blekesaune, "Sexual Satisfaction in Young Adulthood Cohabitation, Committed Dating or Unattached Life?" *Acta Sociologica* 46, no. 3 (2003): 179–93; Steven Stack and J. Ross Eshleman, "Marital Status and Happiness: A 17-Nation Study," *Journal of Marriage and the Family,* 60, no. 2 (1998): 527–36.

2. Deborah Carr and Kristen W. Springer, "Advances in Families and Health Research in the 21st Century," *Journal of Marriage and Family* 72, no. 3 (2010): 743–61.

3. John F. Helliwell, Richard Layard, and Jeffrey Sachs, *World Happiness Report 2015* (New York: Sustainable Development Solutions Network, 2015); Adam Okulicz-Kozaryn, Zahir Irani, and Zahir Irani, "Happiness Research for Public Policy and Administration," *Transforming Government: People, Process and Policy* 10, no. 2 (2016); Gus O'Donnell, Angus Deaton, Martine Durand, David Halpern, and Richard Layard, *Wellbeing and Policy* (London: Legatum Institute, 2014); Joseph E. Stiglitz, Amartya Sen, and Jean-Paul Fitoussi, *Report by the Commission on the Measurement of Economic Performance and Social Progress* (Paris: Commission on the Measurement of Economic Performance and Social Progress, 2010).

4. John F. Helliwell and Haifang Huang, "How's Your Government? International Evidence Linking Good Government and Well-Being," *British Jour-*

nal of Political Science 38, no. 4 (2008): 595–619; John F. Helliwell, Haifang Huang, Shawn Grover, and Shun Wang, "Good Governance and National Well-Being: What Are the Linkages?" (OECD Working Papers on Public Governance, No. 25, OECD Publishing), http://dx.doi.org/10.1787/5jxv9f651hvj-en.

5. Bella DePaulo, "Single in a Society Preoccupied with Couples," in *Handbook of Solitude: Psychological Perspectives on Social Isolation, Social Withdrawal, and Being Alone,* ed. Robert J. Coplan and Julie C. Bowker (New York: John Wiley, 2014), 302–16.

6. Simon Abbott, "Race Studies in Britain," *Social Science Information* 10, no. 1 (1971): 91–101; Jayne E. Stake, "Pedagogy and Student Change in the Women's and Gender Studies Classroom," *Gender and Education* 18, no. 2 (2006): 199–212.

7. Eurostat, *Marriage and Divorce Statistics* (Luxembourg: European Commission, 2017); Wendy Wang and Kim C. Parker, *Record Share of Americans Have Never Married: As Values, Economics and Gender Patterns Change* (Washington, DC: Pew Research Center, 2014).

8. Linda Abbit, "Urban Cohousing the Babayaga Way," *Senior Planet,* March 6, 2016, https://seniorplanet.org/senior-housing-alternatives-urban-cohousing-the-babayaga-way/.

9. Jane Gross, "Older Women Team Up to Face Future Together," *New York Times,* February 27, 2004, www.nytimes.com/2004/02/27/us/older-women-team-up-to-face-future-together.html.

10. Yagana Shah, "'Airbnb for Seniors' Helps Link Travelers with Like-Minded Hosts," *Huffington Post,* June 1, 2016, www.huffingtonpost.com/entry/airbnb-for-seniors-helps-link-travelers-with-like-minded-hosts_us_57487aa1e4b0dacf7ad4c130.

11. Jenny Gierveld, Pearl A. Dykstra, and Niels Schenk, "Living Arrangements, Intergenerational Support Types and Older Adult Loneliness in Eastern and Western Europe," *Demographic Research* 27, no. 2 (2012): 167.

12. Bella DePaulo, Rachel F. Moran, and E. Kay Trimberger, "Make Room for Singles in Teaching and Research," *Chronicle of Higher Education* 54, no. 5 (2007): 44.

13. Bella DePaulo, "The Urgent Need for a Singles Studies Discipline," *Signs: Journal of Women in Culture and Society* 42, no. 4 (2017): 1015–19.

INDEX